On Wisconsin!

The Road to the Roses

Dennis Chaptman

Taylor Publishing Company
Dallas, Texas

To Marge, Ann, Tim, and Kate
For the weekends we lost, and the love we kept

Copyright © 1994 by Dennis Chaptman

Published by Taylor Publishing Company
1550 West Mockingbird Lane
Dallas, Texas 75235

Library of Congress Cataloging-in-Publication Data

Chaptman, Dennis.
    On Wisconsin : the road to the roses / by Dennis Chaptman.
      p.   cm.
    ISBN 0-87833-866-7
    1. University of Wisconsin—Madison—Football—History.
  I. Title
  GV958.U587C43   1994
  796.323'64'0977583—dc20   94-21568
                                                                     CIP

Printed in the United States of America

10   9   8   7   6   5   4   3   2   1

This book is printed on acid-free recycled paper.

Contents

Acknowledgments

What timing.

I stepped into the Badgers beat at *The Milwaukee Journal* two days after the University of Wisconsin was beaten 51–3 by the University of Miami in a nationally televised fiasco in 1989.

Former Badgers Coach Don Morton turned to me at his Monday press conference and noted my transition from news side to sports: "Every now and then, someone from sports goes into the real world. It's not often that you find someone that goes from the real world into sports."

It was one of the most feeble college programs in the nation, and in the next ten games it would sink even further. In less than three months, Morton would be sent packing for the real world. I stayed in sports. Friends, neighbors, and relatives gave me sidelong looks about my choice of a new job. They likened my decision to volunteering for a root canal.

Many times, it seemed that way.

Today, the same people are beating a path to my door wanting to know every detail about the Badgers and telling me what a great job I have. All of us have been part of an uplifting cultural experience as the UW has risen so quickly to national prominence.

That's why watching Coach Barry Alvarez pick through the wreckage and build a college football power out of a bunch of overachievers—football's odds and ends—has been so fascinating.

And that's why reliving the Badgers' march to Pasadena has been such a treat. Along the way, many people have helped make it a rewarding experience. Knowingly or unknowingly, so many people have helped get this project off the ground.

First among them is Chuck Salituro, former *Milwaukee Journal* sports editor, now with ESPN. Chuck opened the door to sports reporting and helped guide me along the way. I will always be grateful for his support and encouragement during a time of upheaval on my beat.

Also, thanks are due to *Journal* Editor Mary Jo Meisner for giving me the green light on this project and to everyone on the sports desk for simply putting up with me for the last five years.

Steve Malchow, John Estes, Julie Kluge, and Barb Wyatt in the UW Sports Information Office also are owed a debt of thanks for their patience and aid over the course of this remarkable transition.

And Alvarez and his staff have been accommodating over the years as they endured both good times and bad. To their credit, they have been accessible, instructive, and fair throughout the sometimes strained rebuilding process. The same can be said of UW Athletic Director Pat Richter and the professional management staff he has put in place at Camp Randall Stadium.

At Taylor Publishing, Michael Emmerich and Lynn Brooks. Plus, copy editor Marcia Stern.

And, for their support on a personal level, several folks deserve a mention and heartfelt thanks. At the head of that list, of course, is my family who endured many weekends of my absence with grace and understanding. My wife, Marge, also a journalist, has been of constant help either as copy editor, conscience, time manager, or fiercely loyal friend. Thanks, too, to my parents, Gene and Jean Chaptman, for their love, their encouragement on this project, and for imparting a sense of fairness that's lasted a lifetime. Others include Peg Giesfeldt, Bill Brohaugh, and Chuck Carlson for advice and help along the way. They know what they did.

Finally, my thoughts drift to Frank Collins. A true sports fan, he always thought my job was great, even in those dark days of 1989. He died last fall, and I miss him.

How much he would have loved the ending to this story.

Foreword

Dreams kept coming true.

You can't imagine how far away the Rose Bowl seemed for a goofy kid sweating his way through a redshirt season as a defensive lineman at the University of Wisconsin-Whitewater.

When no one recruited me coming out of high school, I wasn't too surprised. I hadn't had a winning season during my career at Brookfield East and as I headed to Whitewater, I only wanted to continue playing the game I loved.

But dreams were my family's stock-in-trade. My mother and father came from the old country to make a better life through hard work and dedication. Thankfully, their persistence wore off on me. I wear it like a badge, with more than a little pride.

But there was always this dream: to play Division I football. And, coming from Wisconsin, the other dream was more specific: to be a Badger.

When Barry Alvarez took over the Wisconsin program, he added a new vitality to a tradition that had gone to seed over the years. But there was still that home-state devotion, something that ran deep for a kid who grew up next door to Butch Kellogg, a player on the 1963 Rose Bowl team.

When coach Alvarez let me walk on with the Badgers in his first year, it started a chain reaction. Coach Alvarez and I are alike in a number of ways. But it's a work ethic that brings us together and made the team successful in 1993.

This wasn't a team of stars. It was a team of workers, who strived to be better. And we worked to hang together. I remember one day at practice, somebody put down a walk-on after one play and I looked at him and said, "Listen, there's nothing wrong with a walk-on."

Somehow, coach managed to find a group of assistants and players who all felt the same way and were driven by a pursuit of excellence. They made me their co-captain in our Rose Bowl season, and it was an honor I did not take lightly.

With the help of coach Alvarez and the brilliance of offensive line coach Bill Callahan, I grew both as a person and as a player. They allowed me to have a rare thrill. I was able to make my dreams come true, while at the same time fulfilling the dreams of thousands of Wisconsin football fans who have waited so patiently for a winner.

Dennis has written the story of that season, a season of dreams and of rebirth for a football program that has emerged from its spotted past into a bright future. It's a future I'm sure Wisconsin fans will enjoy with the same fervor that they did as we ran off the field at the Rose Bowl on Jan. 1, 1994.

Fresh from that dream season, I'm about to set off on a pro career, another goal that seemed so far off four years ago. But the euphoria of my last season at Wisconsin will never be erased, nor will its lesson: that hope, work, and heart can make dreams come true.

Joe Panos

1

A Night to Howl

In a twelfth-floor hotel suite overlooking the garish lights of an Asian megalopolis, Barry Alvarez had the last laugh.

Five hours after his team had beaten Michigan State 41–20 in the Coca-Cola Bowl at the Tokyo Dome, Alvarez was wrapped comfortably around a Jack Daniels and settling into a cushioned chair in the Miyako Hotel.

This was the reward of Alvarez's constant prodding, molding, and wrestling to transform the Big Ten butt of college football jokes into not only a national power, but a national power on the rise.

A sudden look of amazement breezed across his face, and the University of Wisconsin's head football coach hooted with vigor, savoring each of the words.

"We're going to the damn *Rose Bowl*!"

A deep, rolling belly laugh followed and Alvarez, clad in a heavy, multicolored sweater, shook his head slowly in disbelief, as his laughter wilted. Then he refreshed himself from the highball glass and smacked his lips.

"It's ridiculous. . . ."

Still, Alvarez knew instinctively it wasn't that outrageous. Four years of hard-nosed recruiting across the nation, scrupulous attention to game preparation, and rebuilding a depleted booster base created this moment. There was a logical, carefully mapped progression involved in the Badgers' turnaround. Yet the moment seemed to defy logic.

Assistant coaches wandered in and out of the appetizer-littered suite, grabbing a beer out of an ice-filled sink, slapping each other on the back and shaking their heads, too. The strain of days on the road, first finding top prep players, then convincing them to play for a down-at-the-heel team far from home, and finally coaching them into Big Ten champions was beginning to show its reward. For them, and for a state 6,000 miles away inebriated with the enthusiasm of its first winning football season since 1984, it was an overload—too much, too soon to fully comprehend.

When the game in Tokyo was finished amid tumult and outpouring of emotion from both players and fans, it was obvious that the Badgers' season was
built on sturdier material than sleight-of-hand tricks. If the season had proved
anything, it proved that the Badgers' success was no fluke. As a satisfied UW
Athletic Director Pat Richter proclaimed after Wisconsin's landmark 35–10
victory at Illinois in November: "This is stick to the wall stuff."

Standing outside the Badgers' locker room at Illinois' Memorial Stadium,
Richter seemed to sense for the first time what he had hoped for all along.
The Badgers were entrenched competitors on a national scope. So much, so
soon.

Coaches, fans, and players stepped into the 1993 football season knowing
that the Badgers were a vastly improved team. But this much improved?

No one could have seen it coming. Not the Rose Bowl. Not a 9–1–1 regular
season with the bizarre twists this one had taken. Not this level of national
prominence from a team carpentered together with solid recruits and self-made
overachievers.

When the Big Ten held its annual preseason football meetings in Chicago,
none of the media in attendance picked Wisconsin to win the league's championship. Why would they? Wisconsin was improved, but conventional wisdom held
that a 7–4 season would be the most dramatic sign of improvement the Badgers
could hope for. And, it would be a significant sign of betterment after a pair of
5–6 seasons. Besides, Michigan entered the season ranked number one and
had clear aspirations for a national title. Wisconsin contending for a conference
championship seemed a laughable notion. *Street and Smith's* preseason preview
of the Big Ten, for example, pegged Wisconsin to finish in sixth place in the
conference.

This, however, was not a season of conventional wisdom but of eccentric
twists. It was a season marred by dozens of injuries, and a display of heroism
by Badgers players in a stadium crowd surge following Wisconsin's 13–10 victory
over Michigan. The season featured a near-victory over third-ranked Ohio State
and a surprise loss to hapless Minnesota. It traversed the Midwest, spanned
the Pacific Ocean, and would end up just miles from the Pacific shore as the
Badgers played UCLA in the fabled "Granddaddy of Them All."

Part of the wonderment that filled Alvarez's room was born in the swiftness
of the turnaround. Only four years earlier, a mere moment in the continuum of
college football, Alvarez had taken control of one of the nation's most wayward
football programs as a first-time head coach.

The obstacles he faced in rebuilding were legion, but the barriers came
down methodically and with the help of a new and eager athletic administration
and a chancellor focused on the importance of sports success to the entire
university.

The omniscient "they" were skeptical that it could be done this quickly.

Wisconsin couldn't recruit nationally and be successful, they said. In fact, the Badgers might have a tough time keeping top in-state players at the UW, they asserted. After all, the University of Iowa had routinely swooped into Wisconsin to pull top prep football players away, leaving the UW's image even more scarred.

The litany continued: Wisconsin couldn't draw sellout crowds back to Camp Randall Stadium in an age of declining football attendance, they said. And the Badgers certainly were in for a long haul before the program was again able to field a competitive team, they said.

And a competitive team was all Wisconsin fans sought. The 1970s and 1980s had not been kind to state sports fans. The Green Bay Packers, for all of their gilded tradition, had largely been in retreat. The Packers had not been to the playoffs in years and the last time the Milwaukee Brewers played postseason baseball was in their World Series year in 1982. And the NBA's Milwaukee Bucks also had struggled vainly for years to build a consistent playoff contender.

There was a hunger for winning in Wisconsin, one that could be satisfied with mere mortal accomplishments. The people who followed sports in the Badger State venerated the late Packers Coach Vince Lombardi, but their next hero would not have to rival his god-like stature. They just wanted someone to pull for, someone who would bring an end to the embarrassment.

Those who follow the Badgers are not as myopically fixed on the 11–0 season as are the football zealots of Ann Arbor and Columbus. The expectations of Wisconsin fans, so precipitously lowered during years of mediocrity and failure, were not too exacting. They wanted some entertainment value in exchange for their twenty dollars, and they wanted to harbor the wild hope that someday Wisconsin could beat Michigan or Ohio State. If it wasn't too much to ask, maybe even a bowl game for the first time since the Badgers competed in a series of low-voltage games like the Garden State Bowl, the Independence Bowl, and the Hall of Fame Bowl in the early 1980s.

Even Wisconsin's corps of die-hard fans, represented most prominently by the Mendota Gridiron Club booster organization, had thinned considerably as the debacle of the later 1980s played out. Outside of Madison, the only active chapter was in the populous Milwaukee area and that group was a hairsbreadth from dormancy.

Former Coach Don Morton's act wouldn't be hard to follow. Morton's teams went 3–8 in 1987, 1–10 in 1988, and 2–9 in 1989. Overall, he scraped together only 3 Big Ten victories in as many years and never won a game on the road. Even a modicum of success would make Wisconsin fans forget Morton and his failed option-oriented offense that was jinxed in the Big Ten.

The question that lingered was how long it would take for Wisconsin's next coach to polish the Badgers into a program that could be consistently capable of fulfilling fans' minimalist expectations. If there was hope, Badgers fans were willing to wait.

Alvarez stepped down from the heights of college football success, away from a job as defensive coordinator and assistant head coach to Lou Holtz at Notre Dame, to lead a team that had won only 6 of 33 games in the previous three seasons under the fired Morton.

To be sure, Alvarez had a history of success as an assistant both with Notre Dame and in eight seasons working for Hayden Fry at the University of Iowa. All told, Alvarez had coached in nine bowl games and was on the staff when Notre Dame won the 1988 national championship.

He was considered one of the nation's top catches among assistants looking for head coaching jobs. Madison, however, wasn't draped in the football glory so evident in South Bend or even in Iowa City. Hell, at times in Madison over the last three decades even Northwestern's football prowess was admired.

Since 1963 the Badgers had logged only seven winning seasons and hadn't finished better than fourth in the Big Ten Conference. As Alvarez interviewed for the job in December 1989, he knew that Wisconsin hadn't had a winning season since 1984, hadn't won on the road since 1986, and had a stable of marginal players poorly trained in the fundamentals of football.

The moon seemed closer than Pasadena.

Still, Alvarez angled for the job, politicked for it, believing that Wisconsin's dust-encrusted football tradition could be revived. It wasn't a decision to take the first job that came along; it would have been infinitely better in Alvarez's mind to stay with Holtz at Notre Dame than to take a dead-end job.

Certainly the Big Ten job was thick with opportunity, considering that football's most golden moment in more than 100 years at Wisconsin was a 42–37 loss to the University of Southern California in the 1963 Rose Bowl. But as Morton and some of his predecessors had demonstrated, it also could be an uncompromising quagmire.

Alvarez felt he'd found an ally in Richter, the man hired to bring vigorous leadership to the sleepy, bumbling department. Richter had the savvy and the connections to tap into resources for the program and Alvarez had the moxie to use those resources to turn the oil tanker that was UW football.

Iowa's Fry hit it on the head when he said Alvarez had carved himself out a challenge at Wisconsin best met by "plowing up snakes," ridding the program of its drab history and supplanting it with an electricity generated by winning.

"Barry was aware that Wisconsin was a jewel waiting to be turned around," said Fry, dean of Big Ten football coaches. "Jaw-to-jaw football, those rascals were as strong and physical as anybody we played."

Alvarez, who possesses a keen focus on recruiting, sized up the raw materials at Wisconsin and liked what he saw. Years earlier, he and his wife had attended a conference in Madison and were attracted by its picturesque setting.

The campus of 43,000 students is situated on 900 acres of a narrow isthmus between Lakes Mendota and Monona, separated from the state capitol by a mile-long stretch of State Street. That thoroughfare is the yeasty center of the UW's retail and entertainment district and a powerful magnet for people, especially young people, new to Madison.

At the center of 150-year-old campus is Bascom Hill, a grassy incline lined with elm trees and embodying the soul of college life. At the foot of the hill is the Memorial Union, where the lakeside terrace is a favorite gathering spot. Beyond Bascom Hill to the west is Observatory Hill, with a commanding view of the Lakeshore dorms, where many of the younger football players live, and Lake Mendota.

The university gained national attention as a hotbed of campus radicalism during the antiwar days of the 1960s, which had focused national attention on the city. Madison was known for its liberal attitude dating to the early 1900s, when the Progressive Party was born there under the guidance of Fighting Bob LaFollette.

Even as the decade started to unfold, Madison retained its liberal, hip, party-hearty image and that played well into luring promising young athletes to play for the Badgers. The campus, even in the more conservative 1990s, is often cited nationally for its party culture and anything-goes mentality.

Those attributes, Alvarez knew, gave Wisconsin an undeniable edge in recruiting over dowdier Big Ten campuses such as Purdue University in tired West Lafayette, Indiana, and the University of Illinois in drab Champaign.

"We thought it was special. The key to it is getting good players and we thought there were a number of things you could sell here," said Alvarez. "There are some schools in some communities where you can't sell. You don't go to those places because you can't recruit top players. We always felt we could do that here and we've proven that."

Athletic facilities were also a consideration, and Wisconsin had some of the finest in the nation. Camp Randall Stadium, with 77,745 seats, was the twelfth largest in the nation. Although average attendance sagged to 41,743 in Morton's last season, Alvarez saw potential. Only four years earlier, the Badgers had averaged 74,681 fans.

And Wisconsin recently had erected the $9.5 million McClain Indoor Practice Facility to stay competitive with other Big Ten schools in the recruiting wars. While the building didn't appear to help much during Morton's tenure, Alvarez saw another plus.

The facility was dressed out with one of the nation's premier weight training rooms and a sophisticated training room, one of the few nationally with on-site X-ray gear. More potential, Alvarez knew.

Amid the hype surrounding Alvarez's hiring on December 31, 1989, came a prediction from *USA Today* analyst Danny Sheridan that Wisconsin would go to the Rose Bowl within five years.

Although Alvarez and his credentials gained near-immediate respect in Wisconsin, Sheridan's forecast was laughed off in Wisconsin circles.

Wisconsin's return trip to the Rose Bowl, assured by the Badgers' 41–20 victory over the Spartans in Tokyo, was its first since that storied loss when John Kennedy was president. Alvarez's players, now giddily cruising night spots in Tokyo's Roppongi district without the burden of a curfew, had suffered through Alvarez's first 1–10 season and two disappointing 5–6 years to reach this point.

They had endured the transition to a coaching staff that drove players harder than any were used to being driven, but at the outset of Alvarez's fourth season, signs were increasingly abundant that the turnaround was under way and the long-sought breakthrough was at hand.

There was finally quality depth at every position, largely due to hard-nosed recruiting efforts. The staff's work paid off with one decent class that was hurriedly assembled in the month after Alvarez arrived on campus and three consecutive nationally rated classes.

Players by 1993 began to assume the mannerisms and pace of their coaches and the machine began to lurch forward under its own power, with athletes as extensions of their hard-driven coaches. They had not only bought in to Alvarez's philosophy, they had in many ways taken on the identity of his ambitious staff.

"I think right now, we're real aggressive, real tough, and real persistent, and that's the way our coaching staff coaches," said tailback Terrell Fletcher shortly after the Japan game. "It's not hard to take on their character."

Alvarez demanded constant improvement from players and the rough edges were sanded smoother each year. Although he gladly would have accepted a superstar, Alvarez was no dreamer. He wanted players motivated to get better and not make game-killing mistakes. Competence, he knew, was the framework for a winning program.

"I want you to get a little better than last week. Follow the plan and improve," he said. "If you improve, we'll beat these guys. That's our slogan, that's our motto, that's our credo. And the kids believe in what we've been telling them, because they're successful."

The aching, exhausted feeling of success started to feel comfortable to Wisconsin players whose work helped yank the program out of the depths. New and innovative training methods and a strong dedication to hard work marked the ethic that won Wisconsin more games in 1993–94 than any other in the Badgers' history.

Cory Raymer, the Badgers' starting center, came to the UW from Fond du Lac Goodrich High School where he was a defensive lineman. Throughout his sometimes confusing conversion to offense, Raymer was mindful of Alvarez's work ethic.

"Excellence. That's what we stand for," said Raymer. "And we know that every time we run or every time we lift, it's work to be the best. And after you're done working, it feels pretty good."

As that ethic started to spread among players, the results became increasingly evident to the ticket-buying public. The enormous financial pressures that had weighed on the UW Athletic Department since the late 1980s, pressures brought on by poor planning and bungling in past administrations, started to lift as management became more sophisticated and the football program began its rise.

In 1988, the department's budget deficit stood at $1.4 million, but bloated to $2.1 million when an accounting error turned up in 1989.

Wisconsin is no different from most Division I-A universities: football drives the budgets of all athletic departments and as Alvarez's stock rose, the department's deficit shrank. Finally, in 1994, the deficit disappeared altogether and the long-sought objective of saving for the future began.

It was a dramatic reversal of fortune. In Morton's last season, there were about 19,000 season ticket holders. In 1993, the public's optimism about the program's improvement had sold a record 42,000 season tickets.

Getting rid of Morton became an imperative for then-Chancellor Donna Shalala, who went on to become secretary of Health and Human Services under President Bill Clinton in January 1993. Shalala, a diminutive woman of boundless energy, was Wisconsin's athletic visionary.

For the first time at UW, the university had a leader in Bascom Hall with a clear recognition of the role of athletics and how powerfully college sports affect an institution's public image. Shalala used her power to clean house at the Athletic Department and put Badger football hero Pat Richter, star of the 1963 Rose Bowl, in charge as athletic director. It was a defining moment for Badger athletics.

Now, in December 1993, Richter, the former tight end for the Washington Redskins who hired Alvarez in 1989, was sitting on a sofa in Alvarez's Tokyo suite trading barbs with assistant coaches and reveling in the moment. It was Richter's savvy in personnel and his gut feeling about Alvarez's skills that helped put his university back on the college football map.

And, it was Shalala's persistence in wooing Richter, who left a high-paying job as vice president of personnel for Madison's Oscar Mayer Co., to accept the director's job in December 1989, that straightened out the whole mess.

As they talked with irrepressible, self-congratulatory smiles, the coaches in the suite knew that there had never been a season like this at Wisconsin in its 105-year history. They were the architects of a season that ended at 9–1–1 and had shoved powerful Ohio State out of the Rose Bowl in a tie-breaker.

Some wore cream-colored baseball caps with red brims that were handed out to players and staff on the field after the Tokyo game. The caps bore the Wisconsin "W" with the Rose Bowl emblem, the Big Ten trademark, and the words "Rose Bowl."

Within days, fans literally were fighting over the hats in souvenir stores in Madison. The unexpected demand forced retailers to ration the twenty-five-dollar caps. This hysteria came three weeks before the Badgers headed to Pasadena. Things were bound to get hairier as the Rose Bowl loomed.

After the Badgers' victory in Tokyo, which was final at about 1 a.m. Madison time, an estimated 30,000 fans rushed from bars and apartments into State Street to celebrate.

Thousands marched to Camp Randall Stadium to occupy the field, chanting "Rose Bowl! Rose Bowl!" amid the honking of car horns and screaming of fans who'd had all day to get a head start on the celebration.

"I talked to my wife in Madison and she said the place is up for grabs, and why not?" Alvarez asked, exulting in the moment.

Alvarez turned back to his whiskey and ruminated on the season just past and the landmark bowl game to come. In the short space of four seasons, he'd made himself a college football hero, transforming the image of the UW and lifting the spirits of an entire state.

"We went from no bowl to the Rose Bowl," Alvarez said.

Before the night was out, Alvarez would phone Minneapolis sports columnist Sid Hartman's Sunday morning radio call-in show. "Get Sid's number," Alvarez told Running Backs Coach Jim Hueber, a former Minnesota assistant who traipsed off to his room and returned minutes later.

Alvarez wanted to make sure the people of Minnesota, whose university was the only one to beat the Badgers in 1993, knew Wisconsin was headed for the party in Pasadena.

This was Alvarez's night to howl.

2

Under the Big Top

Whenever people close to Wisconsin football start cracking wise about Don Morton's three-season tenure, the elephant invariably comes up.

During the halftime show of a Badgers game at Camp Randall Stadium in 1988, the pachyderm was part of the festivities on Circus Day. What was not scripted was the way the elephant took up position at midfield and relieved itself before thousands of the Badger faithful. The resulting mess required extra effort to clean up. To many, the elephant's untimely performance was a metaphor for Morton's hexed stay in Madison.

Well before either Morton or the elephant set foot on Camp Randall's worn-out, yellowing, rock-hard artificial turf, however, the football program had begun its inexorable descent to the depths of the Big Ten. That nose dive began April 28, 1986, when Wisconsin's head football coach, Dave McClain, died of a heart attack he sustained in a sauna room at the stadium.

Aside from the personal tragedy inflicted by McClain's death, the event was a shattering blow for Wisconsin football. The chain of events set in motion on that cold Madison morning cascaded uncontrolled throughout the late 1980s, as Wisconsin football tumbled into one of its darkest eras.

McClain, who took over the Wisconsin program in 1978 after coming from Ball State, had built the most solid version of Wisconsin football tradition since the years of Milt Bruhn in the early 1960s. In doing so, he led the Badgers to three postseason bowl games. Though they were minor bowls, they seemed like an embarrassment of riches for the success-starved program.

McClain's coaching returned Wisconsin to the bowl picture for the first time since Bruhn's team made it to the 1963 Rose Bowl. In 1981, McClain parlayed a 7–4 season into a berth in the Garden State Bowl against Tennessee, a game the Volunteers won 28–21.

Still, the bowl berth showed progress and helped generate enthusiasm for the program. The following year, the Badgers returned to postseason competition, defeating Kansas State 14–3 in the Independence Bowl at Shreveport, Louisiana. The game marked the first postseason victory in Wisconsin history.

And in 1984, McClain's most talented team posted a 7–3–1 record. Using a stiff shot of in-state and Chicago-area talent, McClain crafted a Badgers team unlike any since that 1963 Rose Bowl team. A team that would have eleven players drafted by National Football League teams wound up in the Hall of Fame Bowl in Birmingham, Alabama, where the Badgers lost to Kentucky 20–19.

That was a particularly hurtful game, as a fumbled snap on Todd Gregoire's 26-yard game-winning field-goal attempt ended the Badgers' chances late in the game. It was the last time Wisconsin would play in a bowl game until New Year's Day 1994.

Facing the timing problem of having to find a football coach as spring practice was commencing, then-Athletic Director Elroy "Crazylegs" Hirsch decided to appoint McClain assistant Jim Hilles to serve as the Badgers' interim coach until a successor could be found. Any hopes that Hilles may have harbored of keeping the head-coaching job were damaged by his 3–8 showing in 1986.

The events of the coming year set up a knotted and backward hiring process that new Chancellor Donna Shalala would have to unravel years later. Just before Morton was hired on November 28, 1986, by Hirsch, former Chancellor Irving Shain resigned to take an executive post with the Olin Corp. in Stamford, Connecticut.

It was already known that Hirsch, the former Los Angeles Rams running back and Hollywood film star, would be retiring, but he hired Morton because the program needed leadership. That would put Morton at the mercy of a new athletic driector and a new chancellor.

Morton had a solid track record. Hired at age 39, he had been a head coach for eight years and had not suffered through a losing season. As he accepted the Wisconsin job, his record was 70–24. He spent six seasons at North Dakota State University before leaving in 1985 to become head coach at Tulsa. Morton-coached teams won ten or more games in four of those seasons.

Hirsch retired as the department head in 1987, making way for Ade Sponberg, who came to Wisconsin after fourteen years as athletic director at North Dakota State. Sponberg worked with Morton at North Dakota State and the two were close friends, something both Sponberg and Morton would need desperately in coming seasons.

Sponberg inherited a department under fire for its mounting budget deficits. Also a 1989 report by the state Legislative Audit Bureau was critical of management decisions over the years as football crowds dwindled.

Shalala put Sponberg on a tight leash in 1989. Each Monday, he was required to meet with Shalala in her Bascom Hall office to report on Athletic

Department finances and events. No other department head at the university was known to have undergone such intense scrutiny by the chancellor.

To help fix finances, she turned to Al Fish. The gregarious Fish was a state government troubleshooter known for his ability to clean up the affairs of wayward state agencies. He had a reputation as one of government's rising stars. Fish came to the department as its fiscal officer from the state Department of Health and Social Services and provided Shalala with a trusted information pipeline into the Athletic Department.

Further, Fish was well liked in the state capitol, and had connections that could help the department's lobbying efforts with legislators. But first the hemhorraging had to stop, or at least slow down. The department's well-publicized money problems had strained relations with legislators and made it all but impossible to get state money for needed projects until officials could show improvement.

Sen. Gary George, then co-chairman of the legislature's budget-writing Joint Finance Committee, was already firing off letters critical of the department. The Monday after the Badgers lost 51-3 to Miami in their nationally televised 1989 home opener, the Democratic senator fired off an indignant letter to Shalala, ripping the Athletic Department. No effort was made to veil his feelings about what he called "an embarrassing spectacle of defeat."

George said fans, taxpayers, students, and businesses "should not be forced to subsidize and bail out an administration that refuses to make the tough decisions." The rain-soaked loss to third-ranked Miami drew only 38,646 fans, which also irritated George.

"Victories need not be guaranteed, but a program worthy of our tradition should be. Both are missing now. What will you do to correct this situation before it gets worse?" George asked.

He also fired a salvo at the Athletic Board: "I am sure that all the Athletic Board members are dedicated, thoughtful academics and sincere in their desire to help your program. But college sports in the Big Ten are going into the 1990s and big business is too."

For an institution arguing for less legislative oversight, the Athletic Department's lethargy seemed to invite interference in university affairs. And George wasn't the only one taking note of the Badgers' flagging fortunes.

UW Regent Frank Nickolay said he had a hard time unloading a pair of tickets for the UW-Miami game on a friend. His friend joked he would consider accepting the tickets if Nickolay paid his expenses and found him a parking place.

Such was the state of Badgers football as Morton and Sponberg entered an autumn of discontent. It was a season rife with turmoil and offbeat behavior. At one point, Morton opened his television show lying in a coffin, suddenly declaring, "We're not dead yet!"

It was only a matter of time.

Shalala didn't need critics to draw her attention to the deepening problems on Monroe Street. The more Shalala saw, the less she liked what was happening at the stadium. The budget was roiling in $2.1 million worth of red ink while there were few hard-edged suggestions from Sponberg for eliminating the deficit. More disturbing to Shalala was that there was even less action toward righting the ship.

For instance, it was Shalala who spearheaded an unpopular 1989 drive for a ten dollar a semester student fee and campus parking surcharges to help raise $750,000 a year for the department. That money continues to keep the far-healthier UW athletic budget solvent today.

It became apparent to Shalala that Sponberg, fully capable of leading a Division II school such as North Dakota State, was over his head in the sophisticated world of Big Ten finances.

The bubble burst for Sponberg in early November. *The Milwaukee Journal* reported on Friday, November 10, 1989, that Sponberg's job was in jeopardy following months of review. Shalala, who had already greased the skids for Sponberg's departure in an October 23 meeting, was now faced with a wider leadership crisis at Camp Randall. She decided to make an announcement about Sponberg on November 13, though she refused to say what action she was planning.

The press box was an uneasy place November 11, as Wisconsin took the field to stretch just before its game against Indiana. The press accounts had put both Sponberg and Shalala on the spot, and reporters swirled around both seeking more definitive answers.

Sponberg was quietly gracious, trying to avoid direct answers while sitting with his wife, Donna, in his stadium box. Shalala, too, was guarded. It was clear from their evasion that something was in the works. And Sponberg gave no indication that he was off the hook.

To make matters worse, the game was an embarrassment to everyone who bought a ticket or listened to the radio play-by-play. Indiana tailback Anthony Thompson shredded the addled Badgers' defense for an NCAA record 377 rushing yards as the Hoosiers raced to a 45–17 victory.

Finally, Sponberg's Black Monday had arrived. Shalala called a morning news conference in Bascom Hall. A cavernous meeting room was filled with echoes as she ended Sponberg's career at Wisconsin at 10 a.m. on November 13, 1989.

Sponberg stood beside her, looking lonely and embarrassed, but still wearing a Bucky Badgers lapel pin. Nothing was going right for Sponberg, who later that day walked into a partially closed overhead door at the stadium and required six stitches to close a cut on his head.

"Although we have begun to work through the financial crisis that we inherited here two years ago, I think it's fair to say that neither the chancellor nor I are entirely satisfied with our current situation. Both she and members of the Athletic Board believe that the department would benefit from fresh leadership. That's their belief and I respect it," he said.

"I think it's fair to say that the situation I faced after I arrived here was a difficult one. The financial crisis that was developing was far worse than most people realized," Sponberg added. "I feel I've made a contribution toward righting the ship, but it's time for someone else to take up the challenge."

That night a bandaged, but somehow relieved, Sponberg relaxed in the family room of his spacious home in fashionable Arbor Hills. The home was dotted with items bearing Bucky Badger's likeness, from sun-catchers to framed artwork.

Whatever people said about his administrative skills, no one ever challenged Sponberg's integrity or decency. He was a gentleman whose word could be trusted and whose outlook tended to the positive. Cordial to the end, he sat on a sofa, loosened his tie, and sifted through the wreckage of his career. While he questioned the decision, Sponberg refused to show bitterness.

The search for a successor began immediately. Renowned names in Wisconsin sports such as former Green Bay Packer Willie Davis and former Badgers hockey coach and USA Hockey Director Bob Johnson quickly came up. They were the type of names the Athletic Board was looking for. New Board Chairman Roger Formisano, a business professor, said the choice needed to carry the "ooh, ahh factor."

"I want people to say, 'Ooh, ahh. The Wisconsin athletic program is going somewhere now,' when we make the announcement," said Formisano.

From the outset, however, Shalala knew who she wanted: Pat Richter. He had the blend of qualities that almost everyone involved with the process was looking for. In the early 1960s, Richter was one of the UW's most highly decorated athletes, earning three letters each in football, baseball, and basketball. His pass-catching performance in the UW's storied Rose Bowl loss to Southern Cal in 1963 was etched in state sports history.

Richter also had established himself in professional football, playing tight end for the Washington Redskins for eleven years before retiring and going on to earn his law degree at the UW. Eventually, Richter's career took him to Oscar Mayer, the giant Madison-based meat processor, where he was vice president for personnel.

In Richter, Shalala saw a complete package. He was well known and admired among alumni and had a keen business sense and an eye for personnel matters. Here seemed to be the ideal candidate to move the balky Athletic Department into the 1990s.

There needed to be some arm-twisting first, however. At first, Richter said he wasn't interested in the job, but Shalala continued to work him. He was reluctant to give up a lucrative, stable job with a major corporation to plunge into the new endeavor. But the more Shalala talked, the more the 48-year-old Richter listened.

She bumped the salary for the job from $85,000 up to $135,000. And she allowed Richter to take posts on corporate boards, all the while persuading him that he was the man to pull Wisconsin's fortunes out of the mire. On December 12, 1989, Richter interviewed with the search committee for about ninety minutes.

Three days later, Richter accepted the job and the announcement was made at center court in the UW Fieldhouse.

Sponberg's November ouster in some ways made it more complicated to push Morton overboard. No longer was the decision about Morton left to one person; now it was in the hands of a committee reporting to Shalala. The next three weeks played out as an excruciating public ordeal for Morton and those weighing his performance.

At the most crucial time in his career, Morton wasn't doing himself any favors. In mid-October, he admitted to paying nine assistant coaches $14,000 out of his pocket to compensate them for salary cuts previously ordered by the Athletic Board.

Because of a mixup, Morton wrongly believed that the salary cuts, which amounted to two weeks' pay, would not be effective until August 1990. Instead, they took effect on August 1, 1989, and caused panic among his staff.

Feeling responsible, Morton arranged a ninety-day personal loan to cover the cost of the salaries and withholding. He paid his assistants, but while Sponberg was aware of the plan, the Athletic Board was not. After a series of hearings, the board informed the NCAA of the payments along with a laundry list of measures to prevent similar episodes in the future.

The public spotlight that shone on the arduous process of judging Morton's performance was becoming more irritating for the head coach. In a letter delivered to Shalala and members of the review panel on November 19, Morton complained he had not been given a fair shot at defending his program.

"I have said from the outset that I welcome a fair and honest evaluation of my efforts over the past 36 months," he wrote. "What has been difficult to deal with is the rumor mill, the leaks, the interviews with former players and, quite frankly, the cheap shots from the print media."

By the day, Morton became more beleaguered, more exasperated with trying to stem a tide that seemed sure to drive him out of his $113,950-a-year job.

His season finale, on November 25, was of no help to his cause. On a cold, sun-splashed fall day, the Badgers played Michigan State at Camp Randall and it was Morton's last chance to make a statement about his program. But it was the first weekend of deer hunting season and fans had opted for the north woods over Morton's struggling program.

The posted attendance for the game was 29,776, the smallest crowd since 1945 when the Badgers drew 26,810. Some observers were convinced that no-shows may have made the actual attendance closer to 20,000.

The Badgers' performance mirrored the pitiful attendance. The Spartans held Wisconsin to 19 yards rushing on 42 attempts, while Michigan State's offense surged for 296 yards on the ground. When the day was over, the committee members evaluating Morton's effectiveness, many of whom attended the game, had a fresh piece of damning evidence—Wisconsin's 31-3 loss to Michigan State.

With that loss as a backdrop, Morton got his chance to defend his wobbly program two days later. He met with Shalala for fifty minutes at Bascom Hall the morning of November 27 and then prepared for a crucial four-hour presentation to the review panel that night. In a top-floor conference room in the Nuclear Engineering Building, Morton faced the panel. He arrived in a buff-colored trench coat and with assistant Scott Seeliger. They brought a sheaf of notes, overhead projections, and charts designed to magnify what little progress the Badgers had made since Morton took over.

Morton's sales job was viewed icily by the committee, which hammered on his record, recruiting, and lack of outreach to the larger football community. He countered with charts showing grade-point averages and arcane football statistics that just didn't wash.

Morton pointed out that during McClain's first three seasons his record went from 5-4-2 to a pair of 4-7 years. And during that time, average point production fell from 20.3 points to 12.4 points per game.

That was then. This is now.

After his presentation and grilling by the committee, Morton emerged looking ashen and downcast. "I voted for me. They got my vote. I'm very confident," he said unconvincingly. He answered reporters' questions briefly, then got into the elevator and disappeared.

Several minutes later, the elevator returned and Morton stepped out. Mistakenly, he had taken the coat of one of the committee members and he was forced to go back into the meeting room to find his own.

Looking back on the meeting, Morton said the session snuffed out whatever hope he had for staying at Wisconsin. "I went home and told my wife it was over," he said.

The following day was November 28, 1989, a gray Tuesday, exactly three years after Morton had accepted the job at the UW. The committee met that day in Bascom Hall to discuss its findings with Shalala. By this time, Morton didn't have a prayer. His allies, of which there were few, were either powerless to stop the push for his ouster or silent.

Politically, like a cornerback in man coverage, Morton was on an island. He waited for the news at the office of his lawyer, Ed Garvey, the former executive director of the National Football League Players Association.

After the panel's closed-door meeting, Shalala went to her office and phoned Morton at Garvey's Capitol Square office to break the news. Shalala and the Athletic Board had decided to sidestep an outright firing by exercising a reassignment clause in Morton's contract. This clause had slipped past Morton when he signed at Wisconsin because he never had a lawyer review the language. It allowed the UW to reassign Morton to other university duties.

"I said when I arrived at Wisconsin that we would strive for excellence in everything we do as a university. That includes the football program," Shalala said in announcing the decision. "I want to make it clear that no celebration is in order today. We made a tough decision for our university and for the people of Wisconsin. They have high expectations of us and we don't intend to let them down."

Shalala said the decision to oust Morton was not drawn along won-loss lines. She insisted that the review panel and Athletic Board were more concerned with the long-term potential for success under Morton. And those involved in the process said they also weighed poor attendance, Morton's sub-par recruiting performance, and his communication with the public.

"From my point of view, the choice all along was not to decide whether to give the current program one more year. We wanted to either make a commitment to Coach Morton for the full length of his contract or make a change," Shalala said.

The UW extended a generous offer to assistant coaches, many of whom had young families. Although their contracts were set to expire February 14, Shalala agreed to pay their salaries through June 30, or until they found other work.

Just two days after the Morton firing, Shalala mailed letters to all of Wisconsin's high school coaches seeking their aid in finding a new coach. The move was seen as an effort to rebuild bridges in the prep ranks.

Shalala urged coaches to suggest possible successors to Morton and outlined her intentions to rebuild the program under new leadership. She also underscored the importance of their support to the UW's success.

"The Wisconsin football team doesn't belong to the coach or to the chancellor. It belongs to all the people of the state," she wrote. "I ask that you look closely at the changes we make over the next few weeks and months to make our athletic program a source of pride once again."

Sponberg was disheartened for Morton, his friend. "I'm concerned about the message it sends," said Sponberg. "The bottom line is: you've got to win. If winning is that important, the University of Wisconsin has a big job to do."

Morton, caught up in his own bitterness over the previous three weeks, called a news conference in the auditorium of the McClain Indoor Practice Facility. Incensed with Shalala's move, he railed at the process and those involved in making the decision.

It certainly made matters worse for Morton.

In a quavering voice often basted in sarcasm, Morton faced the media with many players draped disconsolately over seats in the rear of the room. Morton had just finished his last team meeting with the Badgers. He railed at what he viewed as the ignorance of the committee and the unfairness of the process.

"As a youngster, I didn't know whether I wanted to be a football coach or join the circus. In the last three weeks, I've had the opportunity to do both," Morton said.

Especially nettlesome to Morton was the fact that his judges were professors, not football professionals. "We have to start dealing with football coaches as real people. We have to give them the same rights and evaluation process as everyone else. If you evaluate an English professor, they are evaluated by other English professors. You don't bring a physics professor in," he argued.

In the rear of the auditorium, Morton acknowledged Sponberg, his longtime friend. The "reassigned" coach called out: "Ade, what do you want me to do? Does your walk need shoveling?"

That night, the Mortons invited assistant coaches and their families to their home for the football equivalent of a wake. The old stories were retold, the spleens vented. Garvey joined the group, drinking a beer and making small talk.

It was clear the university did not want Morton to step aside to become an associate athletic director in charge of facilities, despite the reassignment. The shift was used as a wedge to leverage a contract buyout. Morton had two years remaining on a contract that paid him a base salary of $113,280 a year, plus a car and a country club membership.

Morton and Garvey, though, were digging in. They demanded that the UW not only pay Morton for the wages it owed him under the contract, but for revenues Morton would lose from broadcast revenue.

Melany Newby, associate chancellor for legal affairs, also girded for battle. She contended the university was not obliged to pay Morton for his TV and radio appearances and summer camp revenue, since those monies were not covered in his contract.

During coming days, Garvey's bluster intensified. He threatened to file a claim alleging the state breached its contract with Morton and seek his reinstatement. Morton wanted a $557,000 settlement, but the UW was steadfast in its demands. In fact, the university's first settlement offer came in at $155,000. By December 20, behind-the-scenes negotiations produced an agreement, and Morton accepted a buyout of $329,950.

"We had a good three years at Wisconsin. The football program is in excellent shape, there's good athletes, good players, and some positive things happening," Morton said, again unconvincingly.

Echoing in the background were the words of the upbeat, vibrant Don Morton of 1987.

"I want to be the football coach at Wisconsin until retirement," he said then. "I want this to be my final job."

Today, he's in insurance.

Who's Recruiting Who?

$$3$$

Troubled history be damned.

The job opening at Wisconsin had commanded the interest of dozens of coaches nationally, but only a few had done the behind-the-scenes spade work needed to cultivate an edge with Richter and Shalala.

Alvarez was an intriguing possibility. With his Notre Dame sheen and record of success at Iowa, he was not a Brand X sort of guy. His credentials were distinguished, covered with postseason glory and recruiting success. His experience at both schools indicated to Richter that Alvarez could recruit the bruisers from the Midwest and pry top prospects out of areas known for their speedy athletes in the South and West.

And Alvarez was a campaigner, massaging the politics to suit his ends, working prominent alumni to put in a good word for him at every available opportunity.

"Lots of people called me to say, 'You've got to look at Alvarez,'" said Shalala. "He recruited us in some ways. He really wanted the job."

Shalala stayed out of the hiring process, but watched Richter's progress closely. She had an eager interest in who was applying and who was getting interviewed, but she allowed Richter to conduct the interviews and make the call.

Alvarez's name surfaced early in the process, just more than two weeks before Morton was fired. During a SportsChannel America broadcast of Notre Dame's 59-6 victory over Southern Methodist, analyst Paul Hornung raised the possibility of Alvarez coming to Wisconsin.

That night, at his South Bend home, Alvarez denied having any contact with Wisconsin officials or boosters, indicating that it would be unseemly to crusade for a job still held by another coach. He did not, however, deny his fervent interest in becoming a head coach. But if he did not begin his campaign before Morton was out, he started it soon after.

The Friday after Morton's firing, even Gov. Tommy G. Thompson weighed in with an opinion on Morton's firing. "Don Morton is a nice man, and I like Don Morton, but I support the decision," Thompson said. "If I was coach, where would I want to coach? I think either Notre Dame or the Big Ten. I think that is going to be the magnet, the attraction of coming to Wisconsin."

Once Morton was out, coaches from across the nation had a field day applying for the job and having friends lobby friends for the Wisconsin job.

During the hiring process, Richter joked that he only asked one question in interviews: whether any of the candidates had run the veer. Still, he was serious about finding a coach able to run a pro-style offense that would be more popular among players and more attractive at the gate.

Thirty-six men applied or were nominated for Morton's job. *The Milwaukee Journal* successfully sued the UW, seeking release of the list in 1989, and the list was finally made available in the summer of 1991 after courtroom appeals.

It was a diverse group, ranging from former Notre Dame Coach Gerry Faust to NFL assistants such as Miami's Gary Stevens, Atlanta's Rod Dowhower and Jim Hanifan, and Kansas City Chiefs Assistant John Hadl. Eastern Michigan's Jim Harkema was on the list, as were former Badgers assistants Doug Graber, then defensive coordinator at Tampa Bay of the NFL, and Roger French, at Brigham Young University.

During the week of December 17, Richter began meeting candidates face-to-face. He went on the road to interview Alvarez, Ohio State Offensive Coordinator Jim Colletto, who the following year became head coach at Purdue, and Michigan Defensive Coordinator Lloyd Carr. All were highly respected assistants.

The personnel expert in Richter took over as the process unfolded. Although he weighed the paper credentials of each candidate carefully, he followed his gut. And he followed one overriding principle: that a football coach is a manager.

"Head coaching is not just the X's and O's," Richter said. "And getting things done through other people is the key to any manager's success."

Beyond that, Richter was looking for someone willing to invest not only in the program, but in the athletes. "We'd love to win and be successful, but that should never override a coach's long-term relationship with his players," he said.

Richter traveled to South Bend wondering about Alvarez. Would an assistant coach with no previous head coaching experience be able to take the reigns at a Big Ten school and elevate the program to a respectable level? It was a big job and Richter's first decision as athletic director would color not only his standing at the university, but Shalala's as well.

Richter likes to joke that he wondered not only about Alvarez's coaching style and philosophy, but about the man. He'd seen the resume, heard rave reviews, and had seen pictures of him. He found himself musing about Alvarez's physical stature.

"How tall is this guy? Five-three, six-one? My biggest fear was that I'd come to the door and be face to face with [actor] Danny DeVito," the six-five Richter joked.

Richter was impressed with Alvarez's thorough knowledge of the game, but more important, Alvarez showed an adroitness when it came to handling people. At once, Richter was put at ease with Alvarez and the interview meandered into a good-natured bull session.

"The guy had drive, energy, enthusiasm, and charisma," Richter recalled. "And he truly liked to be with people and people liked him."

In truth, the two were not far removed in upbringing and background. Richter grew up in a middle-class household on Madison's east side, playing whatever sport was in season. Like Alvarez, Richter had been influenced by legendary figures in football. Late in Richter's career with the Redskins he was coached by Vince Lombardi, whose drive and work ethic were inspirations.

Richter came into the job of athletic director carrying a private-sector philosophy. At Oscar Mayer, the job was providing customers with the best product possible whether it be hot dogs or bologna. "This is not any different from selling a product," he said the day he was hired by the UW.

Shalala received a call from Green Bay Packers Head Coach Lindy Infante recommending his wide receivers coach, Buddy Geis, for the job, and Richter arranged an interview with Geis. Also getting an interview was Eastern Michigan's Jim Harkema. And on December 27, Richter flew to Chicago's O'Hare International Airport to interview University of Oklahoma Assistant Jim Donnan.

All the while, Richter was making inquiries about West Virginia Head Coach Don Nehlen and Georgia Tech Head Coach Bobby Ross. Although Ross was not interested, Richter spent time trying to cultivate Nehlen, who had led the Mountaineers to seven bowl games in nine years. The two men had an hourlong conversation the Saturday after Richter finished interviewing the three assistants but failed to reach agreement.

Nehlen was a long shot for the Wisconsin job and Richter knew it. In addition to having a package worth an estimated $250,000 a year, Nehlen had a fully vested endowment of private funds set up seven years earlier that totaled $1 million. Still, Richter wanted to keep avenues of communication open with Nehlen.

Richter sent Mario Russo, administrative assistant for the football program, to the Gator Bowl in Jacksonville, Florida, on December 29, where the Mountaineers were preparing to play Clemson. Russo's instructions were to determine if Nehlen was still interested in talking about the position.

Russo coached under Nehlen from 1972–76 at Bowling Green and the two remained good friends. But, as it turned out, he never made an offer.

While Richter was covering all of his bases as the hiring process entered its final days, so was Alvarez. As the Fighting Irish were preparing to face Colorado in the Orange Bowl, Alvarez interviewed for the head coaching job with Rutgers University. Earlier, he had interviewed at the University of Pittsburgh, which had fired Mike Gottfried, but Pitt instead went with Paul Hackett. But in the days just before the Orange Bowl Alvarez went to Holtz and told him Wisconsin was the only job he wanted. If Richter decided to offer the coaching job to someone else, he told Holtz he would stay at Notre Dame. Shortly after, the call he'd been waiting for finally came.

Following a Notre Dame team meeting on December 30, Alvarez returned to his Miami hotel room. "We were just putting a movie on for our players when I went up to the room and got the call from Pat and he offered me the job," Alvarez said.

Alvarez, not accustomed to having goals slip away, narrowly missed this one. He had hoped to have a head coaching job at age 42. The day Richter called was Alvarez's birthday. He had just turned 43.

Wisconsin was a place where Alvarez could win, he felt. He kept in mind the advice of Johnny Ray, former defensive coordinator for Fighting Irish Coach Ara Parseghian. "He said, 'Anyplace you go, make sure you can win,'" Alvarez said. "I just felt like everything was in place. I knew how tough Camp Randall could be to play in and how rabid the fans were.

"This is the job I wanted. I know the Midwest. I know Chicago," Alvarez said later in Japan, referring to his well-worn recruiting base. "If you know what the hell you're doing, it's [Madison] a sports-minded town, and we've got a great place. Wisconsin people just didn't believe it. We're just convincing them and teaching them how to win."

Alvarez and Richter got along well and Alvarez sensed that the university under Shalala would make a sustained commitment to Badger athletics.

"I was just dumb and naive and I guess I believed them," said Alvarez. "I did a little investigating beforehand and Pat convinced me there was going to be a commitment made to athletics. I think Donna showed that when she hired Pat."

Wisconsin's drive for excellence may be what impressed Alvarez most. "Donna wanted the Athletic Department to be as strong as academics were," he said. "That kind of commitment was important to me, because if you don't have that, you have no chance."

After Notre Dame's victory in the Orange Bowl, Alvarez phoned Richter's room. "How's that?" he asked.

A running joke was born, and from then on after a big win or outstanding accomplishment, the question was put to Richter again: "How's that?"

"Many times over the last couple of years we've met at different occasions on the field. It's not because we need to hug each other particularly. It's just that certain occasions warrant that type of treatment," Richter said after the 1993 season. "People are often wondering what we're whispering out there," he added. "How's that? How's that?"

The night Richter met with Alvarez in Miami, the new head coach presented Richter a small medal that the Fighting Irish give their players and coaches when they participate in a bowl game.

Richter squired Alvarez to Shalala's office before his news conference unveiling, to meet the chancellor and to sign the fourteen-page, single-spaced contract drawn up by the university lawyers around a broad framework agreed to earlier by Alvarez and Richter.

The three chatted in Shalala's first-floor office in Bascom Hall until it was time to present Alvarez with the four-year contract that would pay him $110,000 a year, and give him a car and country club membership.

"I couldn't get him to read the contract," said Shalala. "When he came in with Pat, I said, 'Pat, doesn't he want to get a lawyer and read that stuff?' And he said, 'No, no. He just wants to sign it.' Barry was saying, 'Where do I sign?' and I kept wanting to talk to him about it."

Within twenty-four hours of being named football coach at Wisconsin, Alvarez set off on a frantic mission to erect the recruiting walls he promised. Flown from city to city in a small plane by Madison pilot Perry Armstrong, Alvarez wanted to prove he valued the top prospects in Wisconsin. Since few of those top prospects had committed to any school, the door was open to the new-look Badgers.

Beyond that, he wanted to salvage a passable recruiting class in the four weeks before prospects could start signing national letters of intent.

Alvarez flew to Marinette to meet with defensive back Jeff Messenger and his parents; to Racine to see J.C. Dawkins and running back Brent Moss, high school teammates; and to Portage to see defensive lineman Mike Thompson. Fresh from Notre Dame's victory in the Orange Bowl, Alvarez was an impressive salesman.

Moss, who had turned an icy shoulder to Morton's veer offense, was close to committing to George Perles at Michigan State. Dawkins, a sure-handed receiver who scored a touchdown on 12 of 15 high school receptions, was eyeing Purdue.

Messenger, the state's player of the year in 1989, also was leaning toward Michigan State and Thompson was considering Iowa. Within days of Alvarez's visits, all had committed to Wisconsin.

"I had the belief that we were going to turn this around," Messenger said. "I hoped it was while I was here, but that's hard to do and I'm glad I was part of it."

Indeed, the rewards of Alvarez's first days on the job were long-lasting as all four of those players started when Wisconsin aimed for a Big Ten champion-ship four years later.

To assure a constant flow of good players, Alvarez wanted a staff that could recruit. And he wanted assistants who knew what it took to win in the Big Ten. If you can't recruit, you don't stay in Alvarez's good graces for long. The X's and O's guys are a dime a dozen, but Alvarez wanted coaches who have the skills to recruit at a national level.

Some he knew from the recruiting trail. But his key appointments, an-nounced at his inaugural press conference, were former Iowa assistants Dan McCarney and Bernie Wyatt. Both had driven from Iowa City that day to stand beside Alvarez in the McClain Facility as he launched a new era at Wisconsin. Alvarez named McCarney as his defensive coordinator and Wyatt took over as recruiting coordinator.

Their depth of feeling about Alvarez and his new adventure was apparent from the jobs and security they surrendered in Iowa City.

McCarney grew up in Iowa City, and played on the Hawkeyes' offensive line from 1972 to 1974. After landing free-agent contracts with Atlanta in 1975 and Denver the next year, McCarney returned as an Iowa assistant under former Coach Bob Commings.

Hayden Fry kept him on as Iowa's defensive line coach, and McCarney cranked out at least one all-Big Ten player in his last nine seasons there.

Meanwhile, Wyatt's Iowa roots also ran deep. Another former Iowa player, he served as an assistant to Commings and Fry for sixteen years before heading for Wisconsin.

Here was the core of Alvarez's brain trust. Then Alvarez added recruiting punch with Offensive Line Coach Bill Callahan and Inside Linebackers Coach Kevin Cosgrove, who both worked on Mike White's staff at Illinois in the early 1980s. Both were respected for their success in attracting top recruits.

Alvarez also kept on Scott Seeliger from Morton's staff as tight ends coach. For an offensive coordinator, Alvarez tabbed Northwestern Offensive Coordinator Russ Jacques, whose multiple offense with the Wildcats was well respected.

Working under Head Coach Francis Peay at Northwestern, Jacques' units had set fourteen individual and team records during his three seasons.

Coaching the running backs would be Paul Winters, who came to Wisconsin from the University of Toledo; Dave Anderson, defensive coordinator at Miami of Ohio, was hired to coach outside linebackers. Anderson had played defensive tackle at the UW from 1973–75.

Rounding out the staff was Defensive Backfield Coach Paul Jette, a former defensive coordinator at Texas, Oklahoma State, and Miami of Florida.

The raid on Iowa's staff continued as Alvarez chose John Chadima, a gradu-ate assistant in administration, as his administrative assistant. While at Iowa,

Chadima staked his claim to fame in helping to paint the visitors locker room at Kinnick Stadium a demeaning pink as Fry had ordered. Chadima came to Wisconsin with the nickname "Meatloaf," a moniker earned simply because the guy he followed at Iowa was nicknamed "Pork Chop," and coaches needed to call him something.

None of the assistants had a wealth of talent upon which to draw. But the defensive coaches probably had an easier time. They had players with innate skills and a self-focused work ethic such as defensive lineman Don Davey and cornerback Troy Vincent. Offensive coaches were faced with the chore of shifting players who were recruited to play the veer.

Yes, the tradition was tarnished. When Alvarez arrived at the university, its only Heisman Trophy—won by Alan "The Horse" Ameche in 1953—was on display with other bric-a-brac in a poorly lit corridor in the stadium outside the administration offices. The collection in the trophy case, in a hallway appointed in 1960s rumpus room paneling, resembled a pile of rummage sale items.

There was no clue to passersby that this was the most coveted award in college football, a rich treasure from Wisconsin's football past. To those who didn't recognize it, the statue was just another artifact of a history fractured by defeat.

Alvarez saw to it the Heisman was cared for. After his office complex was remodeled, the trophy was placed outside Alvarez's door, labeled, and enshrined in a display case. Above it was hung a photograph and biography of the late Ameche—whose jersey number 35 is one of only four retired at Wisconsin.

It may have been a tenuous link with what seemed like an antique past, but it was a strand of tradition and a goal worth attaining, and Alvarez wanted to keep it on display.

The same sort of attention to detail won the job for Alvarez and put him on the path to success. Richter's choice had paid off, making both men look like heroes.

Four years later, two months after the Rose Bowl, Richter examined the picture on the program for the presentation of the Coach of the Year Award given by the Atlanta-based Bobby Dodd Foundation. It was Alvarez's. This was no Danny DeVito likeness, but Richter surmised that had more to do with trick photography than with Alvarez.

"It's one of those Doris Day pictures taken through the fog," he joked.

4

Lunch Pail Life

A teenaged Barry Alvarez peered out the front window of his Uncle John's grocery store each night and was reminded of the toll exacted by life in the mills of western Pennsylvania.

Working behind the butcher counter—where he claims he learned more about sawing the block than cutting meat—Alvarez saw the same scene played out every night.

Workers, their faces encrusted with soot and lunch pail in hand, were disgorged from steel-mill buses on a street corner in Burgettstown, Pennsylvania. Often the faces were drawn and weary as they headed home after a grueling day at mills and smelters in Aliquippa, Pittsburgh, and West Mifflin.

Day in, day out, the workers provided and then reinforced a lesson for Alvarez, a stand-out athlete at Burgettstown High School. The lesson: steel-mill life was more than hard work, it was a grind that could suck the life out of sturdy men.

"I didn't want to spend my life doing that," said Alvarez, who grew up in nearby Langeloth, a drab zinc-mining town just ten miles from Pennsylvania's western border with West Virginia. "Sports was a way of life for a lot of kids so you wouldn't end up in the mills."

Alvarez's journey from the Burgettstown Lions midget football team to head coach of the University of Wisconsin's program involved some of the most storied names in college football.

It started with midget football at age nine, on a team sponsored by the local Lions Club. It was a point of pride to nine-year-olds and parents alike. In a town in which sports was a refuge, sports-minded kids flocked to the midget teams.

"It was a big thing for everyone. We had uniforms, cheerleaders, the whole bit," said Alvarez. "We used to design uniforms; we'd watch games and talk about strategies. We used to go to Steelers practices and Pitt games."

Alvarez and his friends used to go to a Burgettstown factory that reconditioned football helmets and shoulder pads and beg for old helmets to use in sandlot games. Even then, football was sinking in as a way of life for Alvarez.

Despite his aversion to working in the mills, Alvarez grew up with a strong blue-collar ethic and a passion for hard work. Much of that ethic was imparted by his parents, Anthony and Elvira.

Anthony was a greenskeeper at a Weirton, West Virginia, country club and Elvira managed the dining room at the same club. He watched and admired their workmanlike efforts and also learned a bit from his maternal grandmother, who lived with the family.

Alvarez said his grandmother was a stern woman who enforced her will on Alvarez and his brother, Woody, with occasional beatings. But she was also one of his strongest advocates, seated unfailingly in the stands for all Alvarez's baseball, football, and basketball games.

In high school, Alvarez worked to achieve a B-minus average and played whatever sport was in season.

When the time came in 1966, Alvarez chose to attend the University of Nebraska on an inside linebacker's football scholarship. His indoctrination into college football came from one of the game's greats, Coach Bob Devaney.

Devaney liked Alvarez's work habits and his sixth sense for the game. "As a player, Barry was a good linebacker. You could tell back then he really understood the game. Linebackers have to know the game because they make all the adjustments," said Devaney, now athletic director at Nebraska.

But Alvarez learned more than schemes and strategies. Devaney's insatiable quest for excellence and the sacrifices it demands were lessons in themselves for Alvarez.

"That was like a death match in those days. At the beginning of spring practice, if you weren't pressing the two-deep [first or second team], you were called in and asked where you'd like to go to school next year," said Alvarez, who wore jersey number 33.

Devaney's concern, however, ran deeper than football. He rode Alvarez to do well in the classroom. "My priorities were not academics, but because of a guy like Devaney, who kept his foot on my neck, I got my degree," Alvarez said.

One thing Alvarez learned from Devaney was an appreciation for the diplomacy and politics that are required of a head coach at the college level. "I was always impressed with the way he could mingle with people in a blue-collar tavern or at a black-tie affair," Alvarez said.

Devaney said Alvarez's background on the football field helped him develop into a top college coach: "Barry is also a people person. His knowledge of the game and love for people are the reasons he's an excellent coach."

During his career with the Cornhuskers, Alvarez earned three varsity letters and played in the Orange and Sugar bowls for Nebraska. After his senior year, Alvarez's play was judged good enough to earn him slots in the Senior Bowl and Blue-Gray Classic all-star games.

Alvarez met wife Cindy, daughter of an Army general, during his football days at Nebraska. They met by accident when Cindy and some of her friends stopped at his house thinking there was a party there. Their first date flopped when Cindy, a physical education major, stood him up after deciding he was too intimidating.

But Alvarez called her again and the two went out the following night. They decided to get married during Alvarez's senior year.

Following his college career, Alvarez was crushed by the refusal of any NFL team to draft him. He finally landed an invitation to the Minnesota Vikings' training camp in the summer of 1969. At the camp, Alvarez was surprised to find his appetite for playing the game had waned.

"You can't turn on and off to play football," he said. "Either you want to play or you don't. I was basically done playing and wasn't mentally ready when the time came."

That epiphany led him back to Lincoln, where he began to work on a master's degree and accepted Devaney's offer to become a graduate assistant coach. He served at the same time as Jim Walden, who later became head coach at Iowa State, and the two often drove to work together.

The meager wages accorded a graduate assistant were barely enough to squeak by on so Alvarez became a police officer, walking a beat in Lincoln from 10 p.m. to 7 a.m. Police Capt. Robert Flansburg recalls that Alvarez had some uncommon skills. "He likes to put on a macho image, but he was able to finesse people by talking to them. He had a way of de-escalating situations without using force," Flansburg said.

Beside breaking up bar brawls, Flansburg recalled Alvarez's most thrilling police action came in a forty-five-minute car chase at speeds of up to 100 miles per hour and in campus antiwar protests.

The grind was intense for Alvarez, who had little sack time during 1970. Returning from walking the beat, Alvarez took classes in the morning, caught a couple hours of sleep, coached, and returned to the beat.

Today, the Alvarezes live in a two-story contemporary Tudor in a newer development in Madison's west-side suburbs. The spacious home, not surprisingly, was designed and decorated with football in mind.

The home's lower level features an L-shaped walk-out room with a pool table, big-screen television, and video games, and is festooned with football memorabilia, including pictures and trinkets from bowl games. The idea for the inviting and airy room, designed for entertaining recruits on official visits, was borrowed from Alvarez's former boss, Notre Dame Coach Lou Holtz.

Alvarez loves to entertain and is known for inviting people over for dinner parties at the drop of a hat. Win or lose, after each home game Alvarez and his wife host a party at their house for staff and friends.

And although that room is a focal point for football, even more important to Alvarez is his first-floor office. It is also well appointed with football mementos and reminders of past glories.

When the Badgers made the traditional pilgrimage to Disneyland during their week of preparations for the Rose Bowl, Alvarez was presented with a sixteen-inch-tall ceramic trophy of Mickey Mouse to commemorate the event.

"That's going in my closing room," Alvarez said afterward. Closing room? "My office. That's where I take recruits to close the deal," he said.

Just another functional, college football home.

High school football provided a rich testing ground for Alvarez as a coach and further honed some of his political skills along the way.

Alvarez's first job outside of the University of Nebraska was as an assistant at Northeast High School in Lincoln, Nebraska. He took the job in 1971 and the following year the team captured a state championship.

But Alvarez was looking for better money and control over a program, something he found when he accepted the head coaching job at Lexington High School in Nebraska from 1974 to 1975. Alvarez made an immediate splash, as Lexington rolled to a 16–4 record in 1974, good enough to get him named the state prep coach of the year.

From there, Alvarez went to Mason City High School in Iowa from 1976 to 1978, where he built a 21–9 record and won the Division 4A state title in 1978. He once shaved his head on television to raise money for the football program.

Throughout his high school coaching career, Cindy Alvarez pushed her husband to broaden his contacts and firm up associations outside of athletics. It was another step in learning to cultivate a political base. And it was a way to escape continual talk about football.

"There's more to life than football," said Cindy Alvarez. "If you can go out to dinner with a millionaire on Friday and you're making $20,000, it builds confidence."

It also helped his confidence to have as tutors some of the most respected names in college football. After his Division 4A state championship at Mason City, Alvarez was invited in 1979 to join Iowa Head Coach Hayden Fry's staff coaching inside linebackers.

Alvarez stayed for eight seasons and six postseason bowl games, as Fry rapidly rebuilt the Hawkeyes' lamentable football tradition. The Hawkeyes had not had a winning season since 1961, and in his third year in Iowa City, Fry had the Hawkeyes bound for the Rose Bowl.

Alvarez said Fry taught him to master the minutiae of running a top-notch program: "From Hayden, I learned systems and organization, from how to set up recruiting to how to hire secretaries."

But after those eight seasons, Alvarez saw there was no chance for upward mobility at Iowa. Fry's defensive coordinator and assistant head coach, Bill Brashier, was a long-time associate who was a defensive coordinator for Fry for six years at North Texas State before coming to Iowa.

A job coaching linebackers at Notre Dame came open before the 1987 season and Alvarez's interest was piqued. So, too was Holtz's, and he brought Alvarez to South Bend.

Only a year later, when defensive coordinator Foge Fazio left Notre Dame, Holtz turned to Alvarez to mold the defense as its new coordinator.

There were immediate, stunning results. In 1987, Notre Dame was ranked forty-first nationally against the rush and improved to tenth in 1988. It was the twenty-first-ranked scoring defense in 1987 and third in 1988.

The year before Alvarez came on board with Holtz, Notre Dame detractors insisted the Fighting Irish had lost their fight on defense. Alvarez took that personally.

"I got tired of people talking about Notre Dame not being physical," Alvarez told the *South Bend Tribune*. "That's embarrassing to me as a coach and it should be embarrassing to them as players. I wanted to make sure that when the season was over, that image was changed."

Holtz and Alvarez became, and remain, close friends. The two phone each other weekly and Alvarez traveled to South Bend during one of the Badgers' bye weeks in 1993 to have dinner at Holtz's house and watch from the sidelines as Notre Dame defeated top-ranked Florida State.

"Lou taught me football philosophy. My thoughts and his coincided in a lot of areas," Alvarez said. "He made me put down my thoughts in writing and analyze schemes."

"He has great people skills in terms of leadership, compassion, and motivation," said Alvarez. "Lou is driven to reach success in all areas of life. His list of achievements underlines how well he has met his own rigorous expectations. As a football coach, the honors and championships his team has won speak volumes. But he makes his real mark in the way he shapes the lives of young people."

And then in 1988, the Fighting Irish copped a national championship as Alvarez's stock continued to rise. By 1989, Alvarez was being mentioned nationally as destined for the head coaching ranks.

Confidence is something Alvarez has not lacked since he came to Wisconsin with a promise to keep the best athletes and build a program worthy of national respect.

Alvarez can swagger even when he's seated behind his massive desk on the second floor in the closed end of horseshoe-shaped Camp Randall Stadium.

He's capable of exuding confidence usually without the added, unflattering edge of arrogance that taints some college coaches.

And that's one of the secrets to his magnetism in a state loaded with unpretentious farmers and blue-collar workers. Confident enough, profane enough in a funny way, Alvarez has an everyman quality. When others are dining on steak at Smoky's steak house in Madison, a place frequented by visiting Big Ten luminaries such as Indiana basketball Coach Bob Knight, Alvarez has been known to order a burger.

Alvarez was holding court one summer evening just before the 1993 season at Fitzgerald's supper club in Middleton (a Madison suburb), discussing football loudly enough to be heard at the next table.

Seated there was an official from Penn State who engaged Alvarez in an animated discussion about Nittany Lions Coach Joe Paterno. The two bantered good-naturedly about football as they finished their dinners and paid their checks. On the way out, the Penn State guy asked Alvarez: "So, what's your position with the university?"

Alvarez smiled slyly at those with him and said, "I'm the head football coach." As Alvarez walked to his car, the man pulled his jaw off the curb and joined his friends.

Although he drives a Cadillac leased for him by the UW, he doesn't stand on ceremony. At the Big Ten's summer football meetings in Chicago in 1992, Cindy convinced him to go to a theater presentation of "Les Misérables." And, for Alvarez, it was. "It went on and on and on. I never thought it was going to end," he said.

Another Alvarez trait, particularly important for a school so long downtrodden, is his refusal to be intimidated. A prime example came after the 1992 season as professional scouts were evaluating the Badgers' 300-pound offensive lineman Chuck Belin.

Throughout Belin's senior year, Alvarez was disappointed with his spotty performance. The coaching staff sometimes questioned his effort, especially in a year in which he was being watched carefully by the NFL.

For the Illinois game, Alvarez even took away his starting job, in hopes the bruiser from Milwaukee Vincent High School would respond.

As the scouts came around to Alvarez's office seeking his opinions on Belin, Alvarez was frank in his answers, sometimes questioning Belin's effort. That surprised some of the scouts, who expected rave reviews from Alvarez.

In turn, some of those scouts spoke anonymously to *The Milwaukee Journal*, wondering why Alvarez was running down a star player.

In his defense, Alvarez said he was simply offering an honest opinion. The anonymous comments by personnel people irritated Alvarez, who had no personal grudge with Belin and who pulled strings to get him exposure in postseason all-star games.

After the episode, Alvarez sent an angry letter to every player personnel director in the NFL, telling them his staff would no longer offer opinions on players but simply make film available and allow the scouts to make up their own minds.

Belin was drafted in the fifth round by the Los Angeles Rams and eventually became a member of their practice squad. And Alvarez had clearly drawn the line with scouts.

Throughout his Wisconsin career, Alvarez has worked diligently to repair the UW's image with boosters and the public. His patience with autograph seekers is well known.

The confidence and the years of schooling by some of the scions of college football paid off in 1993. Alvarez's hard work in retooling the Wisconsin program resulted in national coach of the year honors from the Bobby Dodd Foundation, Kodak, and *College and Pro Football Newsweekly.*

Beyond the national acclaim, though, Alvarez was relieved on a personal level to have finally achieved success.

He recalled sitting in his office after his first 1–10 season at Wisconsin with his left arm numb from the tension in his upper body. The frustration of trying to rebuild that wayward group was fading into memory as the 1993 season played out.

"I don't know if I've ever been involved in a more enjoyable season, looked [so] forward to going to practice or a game," said Alvarez. "That's why we're champions."

When Alvarez's ego gets out of hand, though, he always has his family to pull him back to earth. A favorite pastime in Alvarez's house is for his wife and grown daughters—Dawn and Stacy—to critique in minute detail his mannerisms and what he wears.

Perhaps the quality that draws players to Alvarez more than any other is a tenacious brand of confidence he has imparted so successfully to a group of sometimes underskilled but big-hearted players.

Joe Panos, the once-undersized walk-on who became an all-Big Ten offensive lineman four years after joining Alvarez's ragtag squad in 1990, reveres Alvarez for his ability to convey a winning spirit.

"If you don't believe in yourself, then you might as well not play," said Panos, a co-captain on the 1993 team. "We don't play to tie, we don't play to lose, we don't play to play close. We play to win and we practice to win. That's how we go about our business.

"I don't know how he does it, but he makes us believe in ourselves."

5

One Olive in
the Jar

Bubble gum and football players are the same to Barry Alvarez. He works both with a fury on the practice field. Invariably, they are both chewed out.

There was a certain tension among players at Alvarez's first practice, March 29, 1990. And why not? They were at the epicenter of an upheaval the likes of which they had never encountered in their football lives. Seniors felt like freshmen again, and freshmen didn't know how to respond.

"I was real nervous and naive," said free safety Scott Nelson, a redshirt freshman in Alvarez's first season. "I didn't know if I was going to be on the team, but they didn't push the Morton guys aside. They've never lied to us. Whoever showed that they could play, they'd play."

While players did not know how to gauge the new situation, Alvarez seemed right at home. Clad in a gray sweatshirt and red sweat pants, he patrolled the grass practice field north of Camp Randall Stadium on that overcast but comfortable spring day, getting his first true look at the team he'd inherited.

The scope of the rebuilding project was magnified not only by years of subpar recruiting, but by the fact that the players had been brought to Wisconsin to play option football. Alvarez was faced with unraveling the veer and installing a pro-style, multiple offense that was infinitely better suited to the Big Ten.

An itchy anticipation preceded the day's workout, with Alvarez eager to embark on a new adventure. He roamed the field, blowing large pink bubbles, popping them, and shouting orders to virtually every unit on the team. When Irish-born punter Mike Mullen, a walk-on, let loose with a pitiful 10-foot-high, 20-yard-long punt, Alvarez raced across the field to dress him down. "What the hell kind of kick is that?" he bellowed.

On a punt coverage drill, Alvarez pointedly, and loudly, instructed linebacker Brad Pavlowski on the finer points of his assignment as he pointed to the ground. "You're supposed to be here! Not here! Not here! Not here!"

Along the way, he stopped to correct technique, administering praise for good effort and working with assistants to assure the drills remained focused.

Wide receiver Tony Spaeth understated the case when he said that "they really get after you when you blow it." From the outset, Alvarez's practices were run with an unprecedented urgency and a new vigor. Players were unaccustomed to the brisk pace of Alvarez's practices.

"The intensity was really up and everyone was ready to work at it," said Spaeth. "Everyone's going to be fighting for a job and I expect it will be pretty intense."

After only two hours of Alvarez, Spaeth had no idea how intense things would become.

Months earlier, under Morton, practices were funereal. They had a sluggish and defeated feel, with much of the instruction being conducted on the field. Players stood around while coaches conducted mini-lectures to establish better technique.

To measure the skill of a college football team, watch how many players wind up on the ground after each play in practice. Good players don't finish on the ground. But in Alvarez's first year, piles of players seemed to be everywhere after each play. "That first year it seemed like every guy was on the ground constantly," he said. "That's the mark of a sloppy football team."

Alvarez goosed the pace, and added two video camera angles at practice. That enabled his staff to coach on the run while on the practice field and teach off the tapes later in meetings. Economy was vital to milking every last repetition out of every practice. This team was too far behind to squander practice time, which was becoming increasingly scarce because of tightened NCAA rules designed to unburden time-starved players.

Understand this about a Wisconsin football practice: there is little time or tolerance for laziness, excuses, or apologies. Practice grinds on at breakneck speed, and in this first season that pace became overwhelming for some players.

"Regardless of what happened here in the past, we were going to stay on their butts every snap," Dan McCarney said.

For some players, the change was literally like an alarm clock. At McCarney's first meeting with the defense one player fell asleep. He was awakened when McCarney flew over a row of chairs to regain his attention.

Quarterback Tony Lowery, who returned to the team under Alvarez after leaving for a year because of disagreements with Morton, was stunned by the changes. "Practice was constantly moving. It was real up-tempo. That's a big change," Lowery said.

After practice, Alvarez assessed the team's performance as he showered in the coaches' locker room in the basement of the McClain Indoor Practice Facility. "We had a couple of missed snaps early, but that's going to happen when you're installing a system. Kids knew where they were going for the most part," he said. "The attitude of the defense is great. You can get by on defense with good fundamentals and great enthusiasm."

Although Alvarez put the best face on the first practice for the media's consumption, he would later admit that he had no idea how talent-poor the Badgers were when he took the job. But he was only 120 minutes into the Alvarez era and was confident things would improve.

They couldn't get much worse.

One of the first jobs Alvarez faced was building self-esteem in players who previously refused to wear their varsity letter jackets on campus for fear of being ridiculed by other students. And he needed to instill a winning attitude in a team with pitifully little experience in winning. "They have to learn how to win." If Alvarez said it once, he said it a thousand times.

Before the inaugural drill was over, Alvarez interrupted practice and huddled his players around UW ice hockey Coach Jeff Sauer, whose team was leaving that night for the NCAA hockey championship in Detroit.

Sauer gave a brief talk, and afterward Alvarez outlined his reason for inviting Sauer to practice: "For us to be successful, we have to learn from these people."

Alvarez and his staff deliberately avoided watching film of Wisconsin from the 1989 season. They reasoned that the team's performance in a vastly different scheme and under flagging leadership had no bearing on what they would be asked to do in 1990.

They wanted to start with a clean slate, with every position open to competition. They took on all comers, with no players blackballed for past performance. The Badgers' doghouse, at least for now, was vacant.

Lowery's return was good news for Alvarez. Shortly after Alvarez was hired, Lowery asked Alvarez if he could return to the team. Alvarez gladly agreed, since his team needed an experienced signal caller.

The Columbus, Ohio, native won distinction as the Big Ten freshman of the year during Morton's first season, when he completed 42 of 89 passes for 579 yards and a pair of touchdowns. And during the 1988 season, Lowery showed improvement as he threw for 721 yards in Morton's option offense.

Lowery, however, had philosophical differences with Morton and left the program in 1989. He'd heard enough about the Alvarez era to know that he now wanted back in, to get another chance to prove himself. After a year of playing pickup basketball in the Camp Randall Memorial Sports Center, commonly called the "Shell," Lowery itched to take a snap.

The night of the spring game, the Badgers hit a rough spot for the first time under Alvarez. After a postgame party, defensive lineman Don Davey and

tight end Dave Czech were charged by authorities with damaging property in
an early-morning incident in which a door was kicked in at an apartment near
where Davey lived.

Once inside, the misdemeanor complaint said the six-foot-four-inch, 257-
pound Davey found a mountain bike and rode it through the apartment. Czech
later was alleged to have ridden the bike into a fence before heaving it to the
other side.

Both later paid restitution and apologized for their actions, which were a
source of embarrassment for the program. They wrote letters of apology to all
concerned, including to Donna Shalala.

"We realize that we have embarrassed not only ourselves, but the entire
football team, the coaching staff and the University of Wisconsin with our
juvenile behavior," they wrote.

Davey was a key component of Alvarez's first team because of his attention
to detail, making his short-lived legal problems more of an irritation. He was
one of the few players on the squad whom coaches could use as an example in
teaching technique and attitude.

He was a four-time academic all-American and *Sports Illustrated* used him
as an example of a classroom achiever in a seven-page article in 1988.

As the season opener approached, Alvarez felt he had another problem to
contend with: newspaper reporters. Even though he had worked for high-profile
programs, Alvarez had never been subjected to this much daily scrutiny.

While the coverage of his program had been favorable, Alvarez was not
accustomed to the intense coverage he found in Madison. In addition to the
two Madison papers, a beat reporter for each of the two Milwaukee dailies was
stationed in town. That, plus regular coverage from local radio and television
outlets, made this job different for Alvarez.

"I've never seen this much coverage, not even at Notre Dame," he said.
At South Bend, although the press box was crammed with reporters from
across the nation on game days, there was little daily press coverage of the
Fighting Irish. Most of that came from the South Bend paper and the *Chicago
Tribune*.

And during Alvarez's stay at Iowa, coaches and players were largely shel-
tered from reporters by Head Coach Hayden Fry's Neanderthal press-relations
policies. Under Fry, players and coaches are largely inaccessible and practices
are always closed. Getting interviews and information out of the Iowa program
was a major headache for reporters, and Fry liked it that way.

Although Morton's tolerance of the media declined sharply in his final
weeks at the UW, he had established some of the most open press policies in
the Big Ten. The Badgers' locker room and most practices were open to the
media, and Morton was generally accessible.

Now Alvarez was faced with formulating a media policy along with hand-picked Sports Information Director Steve Malchow, who came to Wisconsin from Iowa. Malchow was hired in the summer after longtime department spokesman Jim Mott retired.

Reporters were immediately suspicious of Malchow, given his Hawkeye roots. That, along with the presence of McCarney and Bernie Wyatt on Alvarez's staff, didn't bode well for the media, the scribes felt.

Alvarez, however, managed to walk a fine line between assistants who wanted practices closed and the reporters' needs.

During the first years, Alvarez needed the media to pump up the program and help put some fannies in the seats by regenerating interest in UW football. But he didn't want media intrusion to disrupt his team, either.

One of his first moves was to close the locker room both after practices and after games. He reasoned that a locker room is a sanctuary for players, a place much like their own homes that must be respected with privacy. The UW asked reporters to request players for interviews and the staff produced them. That move generally was accepted by the media, and the policy exists today.

The sticky question of whether practices would be open, however, troubled Alvarez. In trying to give his team whatever slim advantage he could, he felt that media access to practice could jeopardize game planning. But reporters were willing to abide by the standard of not reporting on exotic plays or certain formations in exchange for access, and Alvarez seemed to accept that.

More important, Alvarez felt that open practices could set up an information pipeline about Wisconsin injuries that could help opponents. Walk into any Big Ten football office and somewhere you'll find a stack of newspapers from every other Big Ten program. Coaches are fond of saying they don't pay attention to what the newspapers write. That's a ruse. They soak up every word of what's written, especially about their opponents.

Knowing that, Alvarez was inclined to close practice. But he wanted to meet with beat reporters first to seek their cooperation.

In his office, he gathered the writers, Malchow, and Community Relations Director Jim Bakken, the former UW and St. Louis Cardinal placekicker.

Then Alvarez laid out his case, pointing out that reporters would love going to bowl games as much as he did. The new coach clearly felt it was the responsibility of reporters to contribute to the team's success. He asked writers to ignore injuries at practice.

This was such a competitive beat, however, that if one reporter refused to join his plan, the whole thing would fall apart. Predictably, Alvarez met considerable resistance from writers who didn't feel it was their job to perform a counterespionage mission for the Badgers.

Not used to this, he quickly angered. "Then I might as well shut the whole thing down, if I can't get cooperation!" he blurted.

But his tone mellowed as reporters laid out their cases. After all, they weren't coming to practice to avoid writing things. The idea was to carry away some news. So Alvarez asked if they would simply black out news of an injury to Lowery.

Knowing this wasn't possible either, the writers took a safer, noncommittal course that helped defuse the situation. They suggested that Alvarez deal with the situation only if it came up.

The likelihood of the starting quarterback getting hurt in practice was minimal anyway. And since it was transparent that Alvarez's only concern was reporting about a practice injury to Lowery, it was worth the gamble to keep the sessions open.

Lowery was never hurt in practice and the issue never came up. Meanwhile, although Alvarez was less than satisfied with the meeting's outcome, he stuck with the tradition of keeping practices open. For now.

But Alvarez went to some lengths to conceal what he could. On the chain link fence surrounding the grass practice field north of the stadium, he had workers hang black vinyl tarps to hide the action to passersby. And, for the first time, a security guard was present at every practice.

Alvarez also had a different theory about using the $9.5 million McClain Indoor Practice Facility than Morton had. Morton leaned heavily toward using the stadium, even in the sleety chill of November. The building was constructed to wow high school prospects, so the UW could keep up with the Joneses of the Big Ten. It seemed oddly counterproductive to use the building to get players on your team, but then refuse to use it for practice.

Realizing that inclement weather was an obstacle to learning and could slow the pace of the team's drills, Alvarez has made extensive use of the building.

Even though the financing of the building was difficult, the structure is impressive. It includes artificial turf with an eighty-yard field and a fabric roof supported by an arching white superstructure. To Alvarez, it provided a teaching environment that enabled players to concentrate on technique, not the elements.

One thing Alvarez learned at Iowa was Fry's attention to nuances. The details, Fry knew, helped instill confidence and a sense of self-worth in players and conveyed to them a sense that the coaching staff sweated even the smallest details.

From then on at Wisconsin, players wore jackets and ties when traveling and making public appearances. It used to be that players' head shot photos were taken in batches, with them clad in jerseys, by photographers from newspapers around the state on media day. No more. Their hair was sometimes unkempt and the UW lacked control over the images.

The UW began distributing packets of photos taken by campus-approved photographers. No longer were the players depicted in their jerseys. Now they wore a standard red jacket, white shirt, and black tie.

And the facilities themselves started to take on a new look. Icons of success were applied liberally around the football complex. Over the door leading from the team's locker room in the basement of the McClain Facility to Camp Randall Stadium were the bold white letters on a red background: "The Road to the Rose Bowl Begins Here."

Along the white walls leading up the ramp from the basement were red Badger paw prints and a huge block "W" with the superimposed image of Bucky Badger painted on the heretofore blank white wall overlooking the indoor practice field.

In the 150-seat auditorium on the center's second floor, a room used for team meetings, the icons were also abundant. The coaching staff's credo, "Trust, belief, commitment, love," was spelled out in foot-tall raised red letters on one wall of the auditorium.

There were other new twists, such as an area for displaying pictures of the players of the week from each game, on offense, defense, special teams, and the scout team. And outside the weight room, a records board was erected to show who held conditioning records in several categories for each position. It quickly became a point of pride for players to be listed among the speediest, strongest, or most agile at their position and the innovation immediately started to show results.

The football offices themselves also were spruced up, with new carpet and a jazzed-up reception area including a nine-foot-tall color mural of a sold-out Camp Randall Stadium, obviously from several years earlier.

On a larger issue, Alvarez began lobbying for a new artificial surface for Camp Randall Stadium. The eight-year-old rug was yellowed, rock hard, and posed a significant injury hazard. Alvarez found agreement among administrators and the $1 million AstroTurf project was headed for the state bureaucracy for final approval. If everything went as expected the new carpet would be installed for the start of his second season.

For Alvarez, the little things mattered and all contributed to an overall impression of the program. Things were changing.

After a year's absence because of Wisconsin's ailing sports budget, the Badgers under Alvarez paid the $60,000 to return to Holy Name Seminary for training camp in August 1990. It's been their summer headquarters ever since.

Wisconsin is one of the few universities to move training camp off campus so players can fully focus on the task at hand. The red-brick seminary with its trademark white spire, located on High Point Road in the town of Middleton, offers panoramic views of Madison's bustling west side.

Players are housed at the facility and moved off the grounds only when the weather forces practice indoors or for scrimmages requiring the use of the stadium. The rooms lack air conditioning, but the basement cafeteria is a popular gathering spot for players who pore over sports sections while devouring vast quantities of food.

The urgency that characterizes Alvarez's coaching style was shown in abundance as he opened his first training camp in mid-August. The months of hype that generated the catchphrase "Barry knows football" were grinding down and the season opener against the University of California loomed.

"Barry knows football" was widely used as the UW tried to capitalize on the anticipation inherent in a first-year coach to sell season tickets. The phrase was published on T-shirts, hats, and other paraphernalia.

It gained such wide credence that four years later, after Barry Davis was named to replace Andy Rein as wrestling coach at Wisconsin, the department mailed out T-shirts to introduce Davis bearing football and wrestling logos and the words "Barry knows Barry."

The measuring of the Badgers had begun. Coaches measure seasons by turning points, real or perceived. Those moments came steadily throughout the two and one-half weeks of drills at the seminary, though to the coaches who worked twenty-hour days to script practices and analyze film, they couldn't come quickly enough.

For Alvarez, a major turning point came during two-a-day practices on August 27. Players that day were subjected to perhaps their most demanding drills, a death march on a day when the temperature hit ninety degrees under an unremitting sun.

"Some were checking their low-hole cards, some deciding whether they wanted to quit or play football," said Alvarez. "But they all came back and we had a hell of a practice. From then on, our morale was sky high."

The heavy-hitting drills reminded him of a three-hour scrimmage that Lou Holtz foisted on the Fighting Irish in 1988, the year Notre Dame won the national championship. After ninety minutes, as players started believing that the scrimmage was coming to a close, Holtz announced it was halftime. No one flinched, no one moaned. And Alvarez knew then that this was going to be a good team.

Another turning point showed how the team was coming together emotionally. Alvarez banks a certain number of scholarships to award to walk-on players who have performed exceptionally well. It is a strong motivational tool, one that has become a badge of accomplishment.

During a team meeting in the seminary's auditorium, Alvarez announced he was awarding that first scholarship to walk-on free safety Mike Barker. Players leaped over chairs to embrace and congratulate Barker, who was moved to tears by the honor. Emotionally, Alvarez saw the promising underpinnings of team unity.

Players noticed other turning points during their stay at the seminary. Nick Polczinski, a 321-pound offensive tackle, noticed that the staff's focus was changing during a drill in which the offense scored a touchdown. Usually, then-Offensive Coordinator Russ Jacques would huddle up the offense for a pep talk. Not this time.

"Coach, how come you didn't say anything?" Polczinski asked afterward. "Because I expect it," said Jacques. "That's what our job is. Let's get excited after we win."

Before and during the season, Alvarez and his assistants worked Wisconsin like politicians. They appeared at every possible alumni golf outing, sports dinner, coaches gathering, and Optimists Club breakfast.

It was an intense period in which Alvarez pushed himself and his program like a vacuum cleaner salesman. The outreach effort sapped virtually all of his spare time, but there were signs that the booster base was growing and that Wisconsin was welcoming him and his staff with open arms.

Between practices and personal appearances, the coaches also were working the campus. During the 1970s and early 1980s Camp Randall Stadium's student section was the bedrock of a fire-breathing crowd atmosphere that made it rough on Badgers' opponents. Alvarez, used to the thick and partisan crowds at Notre Dame and Iowa, knew how a faithful crowd could breathe life into a team and he yearned for the students to return.

He appeared at fraternity houses on Langdon Street and in dormitory meeting rooms, shaking hands with students and urging them to buy student season tickets. In Morton's last year, the UW sold a paltry number of discounted student season tickets and Alvarez knew that had to increase to make the 12,500-seat student section what he called a "hornet's nest."

His efforts paid off, marginally at first, but there were signs that the student population was beginning to notice football again. As his first season began to unfold, 8,000 student tickets were sold, a slight increase. Although it wasn't the quantum leap he'd hoped for, Alvarez saw it as a hopeful start, one that would pay dividends in years to come.

The road to winning appeared all uphill as the Badgers' opener against California loomed. *USA Today*'s Sagarin power ratings ranked the Badgers 106th among the 197 Division I-A programs. Their first opponent, the University of California, came to Wisconsin ranked fifty-fifth.

Alvarez tried to downplay his emotions on the eve of the Cal game. Expectations ran high, but Alvarez was used to big-time expectations at Notre Dame and Iowa. This, however, was his first game as a head coach since he led the Mason City High School team to a state championship in 1978. Although he admitted some nervousness about his first game as a head coach, Alvarez was far from flustered.

It didn't take any pep talks to get players motivated for the game, which was being broadcast on ESPN, the first national television appearance for the

Badgers since they were mauled by Miami 51–3 in the 1989 opener under Morton.

"With the beginning of the Alvarez era, we want to put on a good show," said defensive back Greg Thomas.

Finally, September 9, 1990, came. The rhetoric and hype were over. It was time for football, time to see whether Barry really knew football. The momentous, sun-drenched day had attracted 45,980 fans to Camp Randall Stadium. Although that seemed like a large crowd to those who slogged through Morton's last year, Alvarez was stunned.

When the Badgers' bus pulled up to the stadium before the game, there was virtually no one milling around outside the stadium. Amazed, Alvarez turned to McCarney and pledged that this, too, would be remedied in seasons to come.

The crowd, though, was soon forgotten. From the time Alvarez set foot on Camp Randall's turf that morning, he was thinking football, looking over the play script and deciding what to do if Wisconsin won the coin toss.

The Badgers did win the toss, and elected to kick off. Things went downhill from there. While the Badgers' story ends like a fairy tale, it started like a nightmare.

Predictably, Wisconsin's own mistakes helped give the game to the Golden Bears. Its youth and lack of depth were easily apparent as the Badgers surrendered a 100-yard interception return for a touchdown, and had a field goal blocked and a touchdown nullified on a penalty.

Alvarez's first offensive series went smoothly after linebacker Aaron Norvell recovered a Cal fumble at the Badgers' 42. Lowery led the Badgers to the Golden Bears' 1-yard line, where he handed off to tailback Robert Williams, who dived for a touchdown that would have put Wisconsin ahead.

Officials, however, flagged wide receiver Lionell Crawford for illegal motion and the Badgers settled for a 21-yard field goal.

The Golden Bears scored 3 touchdowns in the first half, including the 100-yard interception return by John Hardy. That play was especially devastating, since the Badgers were threatening at the Cal 8-yard line when Lowery's pass was tipped and picked off.

Looking back on it four years later, Richter said that play showed the difficult assignment Alvarez had in trying to reverse the defeatist mindset that was so ingrained in the program.

"If that interception just before the half hadn't occurred, maybe we would have been OK," said Richter. "But all of a sudden, it was: Here we go again. It's tough work for a coach to change the whole mental attitude because you can't wash out all of those negative things you've had for years."

Although the Badgers outgained Cal and held a possession-time advantage, the mistakes were too much, giving the Golden Bears a 28–12 victory and Alvarez an 0-1 record to start his head coaching career.

Alvarez came into the game with a scripted offense, but the script was discarded almost immediately. Wisconsin's first scripted play was supposed to have been a long pass, but Alvarez decided to go with the second play, an inside run that went for 4 yards. Although Russ Jacques had experience using a script, similar to the approach used by Bill Walsh when he coached the San Francisco 49ers, the script never caught on with Alvarez.

Although Wisconsin often came in with a script, it usually was nothing more than a rule meant for breaking.

In a season overloaded with embarrassing losses, the Badgers would enjoy their only victory the following week as they played a weak Ball State team before a home crowd of 44,698.

Alvarez brought tailback Williams off the bench, and he rushed for a pair of touchdowns and Crawford scored on a reverse in the second quarter to give the Badgers a 21–0 halftime lead. It was the most points the Badgers had scored in a single quarter since 1988.

The defense again proved to be the Badgers' strongest unit, however, as it came within 2:09 of assembling its first shutout since 1983. Those hopes were ruined when Ball State scored on a 67-yard bomb.

But Alvarez's first victory was achieved. After the game, he joked that the triumph was akin to opening a jar of olives. "Get the first one out," he said, "and out they tumble."

The Badgers had another strong chance at victory the following week, as they held an 18–14 lead in the fourth quarter against Temple. The Owls snookered the UW defense on a run-and-pitch play in which quarterback Matt Baker picked up 6 yards before pitching back to Conrad Swanson, who ran 26 more yards for the touchdown.

Temple wound up with a 24–18 victory, as the weakness of Wisconsin's offense was exposed once more. Although the Badgers outgained their opponent for the third straight week under Alvarez, they were stopped on two crucial fourth-and-one situations.

The Big Ten season awaited and the 6-point losing margin to Temple was the best outcome Wisconsin would see until the season finale. The death march was on.

Inside the locker room, some of Wisconsin's newly recruited players were baffled by the attitude of many of the shell-shocked veterans. It became obvious that many, though certainly not all, of Wisconsin's players expected defeat and disaster.

Freshman defensive tackle Carlos Fowler said he was shocked at the attitude of players (many of whom left the team after that first season) before the

Michigan game. In the locker room, Fowler was pumped up about getting his first significant game experience.

"And all the while, these guys were nervous. They were shaking about having to play Michigan. For them, it was, 'Oh my God! We have to play the Wolverines. What'll we do?'" said Fowler, twitching in mock anguish. "They were losers."

The misery deepened with every passing week:

Michigan 41, Wisconsin 3

Iowa 30, Wisconsin, 10

Northwestern 44, Wisconsin 34

Illinois 21, Wisconsin, 3

Minnesota 21, Wisconsin, 3

Indiana, 20, Wisconsin, 7

Ohio State 35, Wisconsin, 10

"I'll never forget those games in the first year where we played our best game and still got beat by 15 points," said Nelson. "You can't find answers. You go out and play your best game the next week and get beat by 10 points. It may not have shown to the fans, but we were doing the things it would take to win."

One of the first chances the Badgers had to make an impression in the Big Ten came in the season finale at Michigan State. The twenty-fourth-ranked Spartans were bowl-bound and were a 29-point pregame favorite. The 1–9 Badgers were desperate to take a shred of respect away from the calamitous season.

Before a crowd of 60,517, the Badgers' defense started slowly but built an onerous pace as the game progressed. Michigan State running back Hyland Hickson rushed for a pair of first-quarter touchdowns, one on a 1-yard plunge and the other a 27-yarder.

Between Hickson's touchdowns, however, the Badgers scored their only touchdown of the day as Troy Vincent intercepted Dan Enos's pass and returned it 71 yards. Although the extra point was blocked, the Badgers saw some hope as the first quarter ended with Michigan State ahead 14–6.

Michigan State would not score for the remainder of the game, as Wisconsin's front seven defused the Spartans' offense. Davey had 16 tackles in the game, including 3 for losses, and linebacker Brendan Lynch came up with 15 tackles and a fumble recovery.

Like so many games in the Badgers' first seasons, this one was lost because Wisconsin could not finish what they started on offense. Wisconsin had four chances to drive for the winning score, but never got closer than the Michigan State 41. For the game, the Badgers had only 69 yards rushing on 31 attempts.

The heartbreaker, though, came when Lowery hit Spaeth between the numbers in the end zone, but the pass was dropped. The Badgers added a 31-yard field goal, but took only despair away from Spartan Stadium.

Following the Michigan State game, Alvarez got together with John Palermo, one of his former assistant coaching colleagues at Notre Dame, who came to watch the game. Palermo, who left South Bend at the same time as Alvarez to become head coach at Austin Peay University in Clarksville, Tennessee, was angling for a job on the Wisconsin staff.

At Austin Peay, Palermo quickly found that the lack of resources took their toll and after an 0–11 season he was eager to return to a major program. It wasn't long before he was Alvarez's assistant head coach and outside linebackers coach.

After the season, two assistants left the program, Scott Seeliger and Dave Anderson. Both had more laid-back coaching styles that clashed with Alvarez's in-your-face aggression. Paul Winters moved over to coach tight ends, and Alvarez hired Brad Childress, a Utah assistant, to coach running backs.

As for Davey, he was selected in the third round of the NFL draft by the Green Bay Packers and still plays at Lambeau Field, only forty-five miles from his hometown of Manitowoc.

Looking back on the wreckage of the 1990 season, Alvarez offered this: "There can be no quick fix. I want to have a consistent program, and there are no shortcuts to get there. People are hungry for a winner and I believe we'll have that at Wisconsin."

6

More Olives Tumble

They all came to Alvarez's office with the same spiel.

After that first season of struggle, transformation, and defeat, a virtual line formed outside Alvarez's office as football players bailed out of a program many felt was too demanding.

In most cases, it was not their fault. Many never should have been offered Division I scholarships and would have been better off at lower-division schools, and that's where some went.

For example, reserve quarterback Jason Gonnion pulled out of the Wisconsin program after holding a clipboard for most of Alvarez's first season and became the starter for UW-La Crosse, which went on to win a national championship in Division III.

Most were not ready to make the year-round commitment that Alvarez knew was required of successful major college players, and they freely admitted as much. One by one, players came to Alvarez's second-floor office to quit.

Between those who had used up their eligibility and those who backed out, Alvarez lost fifty-two players. And only eighteen of those had used up their eligibility.

"He wanted to weed out the program, find the winners, the people who were going to stick with him," said offensive lineman Joe Panos. "It's a credit to the guys who did stick with it, because it wasn't easy."

The defections did not bother Alvarez, except that it sometimes made scrimmaging difficult because there were not always enough players at each position.

"There were a lot of them who were forced to play and they [defectors] weren't Big Ten caliber and they knew it," said Alvarez.

A combination of factors was at work in the departures: for some it was personal relationships, while others cited the time demands and lack of playing time.

"There were a lot of egos," said Scott Nelson. "When you keep screwing up and coach is in your ear all the time, that's hard to take. Some guys, instead of getting jacked up about getting better, take it personally and get down on themselves."

The volume at practice had certainly risen since Alvarez and his staff took over.

"I've never been yelled at like that before," Nelson said. "That's something you have to listen to, and let the personal stuff go. They want to make practice as hard as possible, mentally and physically, so when it comes to game time, it's a piece of cake."

The departures put more pressure on Wisconsin coaches to recruit athletes who had the stamina and outlook to endure the rigors of football on the Big Ten stage.

"We were thin. We were going out with twenty scholarships trying to fill sixty needs," Alvarez said. "Now we've built a foundation for the future. We don't have to depend on a recruiting class to come in and play right away. Our first years were a different story."

In those formative years, recruiting took on a stark urgency. And Alvarez's polished staff of recruiters quickly proved they could leverage their share of top athletes. Along the way they sold hope and smart talk.

Rob Ianello makes his living as a smart-talker.

The twenty-four-year-old came to UW as part of Alvarez's original staff, with the unenviable mission to work the phones night and day to convince the nation's best prep players that the Badgers were on the rise.

Ianello had established a reputation as assistant recruiting coordinator for Alabama Coach Bill Curry in 1988 and 1989. Those in the industry knew the Catholic University graduate as one of the best in the nation in building a rapport with kids over the phone.

His first-ever recruit was the Crimson Tide's Derrick Lassic, who went on to become the 1993 Sugar Bowl MVP. In fact, Ianello was part of a staff that recruited seventeen of twenty-two starters on Alabama's 1993 national championship team. For all of this, and his constant attachment to the telephone, they called him "The Mouth of the South."

Never having seen Madison before, Ianello was impressed with Alvarez and with the attributes of the city and campus and saw the on-campus recruiting coordinator's job as a step up. It also was a mountainous challenge. Even the most basic tools were lacking as Alvarez's staff moved into their offices with high standards and expectations.

"One of the good and bad things here was that everything we did was new to the University of Wisconsin. We came in with an idea of what it took to achieve championship performance. Coach Alvarez set the tone from that. Everything revolved around that, from the way we set up weekends to the phone system to a state-of-the-art fax machine and the commitment from everyone," Ianello said.

Ianello worked closely with Recruiting Coordinator Bernie Wyatt, a recruiting legend on the East Coast. Wyatt's skills and connections along the Eastern seaboard helped provide the raw materials to sustain Iowa's success in the 1980s.

Born in Brooklyn, Wyatt was a high school all-American at Amityville, New York, who played for Iowa and wound up as the Hawkeyes' 1960 MVP. After one year with the Pittsburgh Steelers, he went into high school coaching in Iowa City.

Later, as a sixteen-year assistant coach for the Hawkeyes and their first recruiting coordinator, Wyatt tapped a rich vein of East Coast talent and convinced some top players to trek to Iowa to play football. Wyatt seldom came back empty-handed from the New York area.

He recruited Andre Tippett, who went on to become an all-pro selection for the New England Patriots, and NFL players Ronnie Harmon, Bob Kratch, and Quinn Early.

"The hardest thing to do," said Wyatt, "is to overcome players' reluctance to come because of the distance."

Still, Wyatt did it repeatedly with top athletes. One way was through the cultivation of one of the best junior college programs in the nation at Nassau Community College on Long Island.

And the Nassau connection was vital in Alvarez's rebuilding of the Wisconsin program. Beginning in 1991, the Badgers took many players out of the junior college coached by John Anselmo, one of the top juco coaches in the nation.

Players who came out of Nassau included outside linebacker Dwight Reese, cornerbacks Kenny Gales and Donny Brady, and linebackers Sylas Pratt and Royston Jones.

After the Badgers' hastily assembled class in Alvarez's first month on the job, Wyatt and Ianello set about putting their stamp on Badgers recruiting in 1991. The task, they knew, was formidable. Coming off a 1–10 season, Alvarez knew the Badgers had to sell a good deal of what he called "blue sky."

The staff knew that if a nationally known high school prospect would commit to play at Wisconsin it would be easier for the Badgers to leverage commitments from other top athletes. Those prospects, however, weren't exactly lining up at Alvarez's door.

"Now that Wisconsin's winning, people forget how tough it was for a non-powerhouse to compete," said recruiting analyst Tom Lemming, of Schaumburg, Illinois. "When you're 1–10 after their first year and after the

Morton years when there was no credibility at all, it is impossible unless you've really got some persuasive powers. You have to be aggressive, knowledgeable, and personable."

One thing the Badgers were able to sell was the chance to play early and often. High school stars often aren't willing to redshirt then work as backups for two or even three years before playing. The Michigans and Ohio States of the world often had trouble convincing those athletes to sign after they had a chance to analyze the depth charts.

Wisconsin's meager depth, however, was a strong inducement for players who were inclined to play early and help a struggling program rebuild. Coaches sold the nobility of that undertaking, and many kids responded. Throughout Alvarez's stint at Wisconsin, the staff has aimed high, refusing to be cowed by programs such as Florida State.

"They [Wisconsin] went after every top kid. They didn't care if they were competing with Michigan or Notre Dame or UCLA, they got their guys. Obviously a coach can't get to the Rose Bowl without the talent," said Lemming.

Wisconsin's first big recruiting coup came in January 1991 in the Hazelwood, Missouri, living room of running back Terrell Fletcher. The Badgers, through Assistant Coach Kevin Cosgrove, had waged a relentless campaign to get Fletcher to commit, but he was looking at programs such as Pitt, Colorado, and Iowa.

Fletcher's high school numbers were impressive. As a senior, he rushed for 1,687 yards and 37 touchdowns at Hazelwood East High School and rolled up 4,414 all-purpose yards in his high school career. Videotapes showed he had the ability to make an immediate contribution at a position where the UW lacked depth and proven talent. Fletcher was a priority.

"The first guy who made a big difference for us was Fletcher, because he visited five schools, four of which went to bowl games, and chose Wisconsin," said Ianello. "From a guy who could have gone anywhere in the country, after we just had a 1–10 season, he picks us. He made a statement about himself. And he allowed us to make a statement about Wisconsin football to a lot of other recruits: 'Here's an all-American, player of the year in Missouri. He's coming.'"

Ianello said Cosgrove's hard work got Fletcher to campus, which was the decisive factor in getting him to sign a national letter of intent. "He was a hard sell until he got on the campus, then he wasn't a hard sell anymore," Ianello said.

Along the way, Ianello picked up strategies from Badgers' coaches as he expanded his recruiting repertoire. Alvarez's staff was polished in recruiting affairs and knew all of the tricks and tactics to build trust and rapport.

"Bernie taught me the value of knowing who the guy is who's going to make the decision and Kevin Cosgrove taught me the idea of how important family is and how important it is to get the mom on your side," Ianello said. "The attitude around recruiting here and the intensity is remarkable. You have to develop a pace and that helps us all stay on the same page."

Alvarez also had a major influence on Ianello's approach to recruiting. "The thing Barry ingrained in me was the relationship with the players and how much you care for your players and how well they will play for you if you treat them the right way," he said.

Ianello's brash talk and big ego, though grating on some, seemed effective on recruits. He talked a good game, smug and self-assured, and his manner played well with many of the prep stars he was courting. He was close to their age, spoke their language, and understood the big-shot-athlete mentality.

"He has that cockiness about him that went over well. He's a lot like one of the best I've met, Vinny Cerrato, who left Notre Dame to become a scout with the San Francisco 49ers," Lemming said.

Alvarez's first full-fledged recruiting class was ranked twenty-sixth nationally by Lemming, an assessment that would rise in the coming two years.

After Alvarez's second season at Wisconsin, the recruiters had a bit more to sell and a few more ways to spruce up the university's reputation. One important factor was the direct involvement of Shalala in the recruiting process.

She enthusiastically took on the role of a recruiter, showing up during recruiting weekends to gab with the prospects and their parents. It was a scene most of the athletes had not encountered, since most chief executives do not dirty their hands with football recruiting. Many came away impressed.

More impressive, of course, was the way the Badgers engineered a 5–6 record in 1991, Alvarez's second season. In the bottom-line world of recruiting, records speak volumes.

Wisconsin started its season with three straight victories in a soft nonconference schedule including Western Illinois, Iowa State, and Eastern Michigan. The Badgers then lost six consecutive games in the Big Ten before finishing with a 19–16 victory at Minnesota and a 32–14 victory over Northwestern.

The Minnesota victory was the most meaningful and dramatic in Alvarez's young career at Wisconsin. On Minnesota's last offensive play of the game deep in Wisconsin territory, Golden Gophers quarterback Marquel Fleetwood fired a pass for tight end Patt Evans in the end zone.

But a crushing tackle by Badgers defensive back Melvin Tucker separated Evans from the ball as Wisconsin took possession of the Paul Bunyan Axe, the trophy of college football's longest-running rivalry. The moment was huge for Wisconsin, as it won its first road game since 1986.

Already Alvarez was being viewed as something of a hero, having led the Badgers to their winningest season in seven years. The Badgers had improved their win total by four games, the fourth-largest improvement in the nation over 1990.

All season, Alvarez experimented with quarterbacks. Not impressed with Tony Lowery's season, he inserted Jay Macias, a freshman from Montebello, California. Russ Jacques and Alvarez had disagreed on whether to play Macias or redshirt him. Alvarez won, and Macias played in seven games and started six.

In Macias's debut, he completed 6 of 11 passes for 126 yards and a pair of touchdowns in relief of a struggling Lowery. As the season progressed, both looked rocky as the offense continued to sputter and put the Badgers' defense on the field for up to 85 snaps a game. Inevitably, the offense's failure to control the ball exhausted the defense, leading to costly lapses all season.

At least the look of the Badgers was fresh as they plunged ahead in Alvarez's second season. The new $1 million AstroTurf was installed over the summer and its end zones were bedecked with white letters on a deep red background—Wisconsin written in the north end zone, Badgers written in the south.

There also was a new look for the players. Alvarez scrapped the old helmets, with their plain-looking red block "W." They were replaced by a new design, with a bolder "flying W," a shadowed letter tilted at a rakish angle which is still used today.

Attendance was up an average of 10,000 per game, and the crowd of 75,053 for the Iowa game in 1991 was the largest turnout at Camp Randall Stadium since 1986. For the first time in years, there was reason for hope.

The star of the 1991 season had been cornerback Troy Vincent, who performed up to everyone's expectations. He ended the season as an all-American, having intercepted 2 passes and broken up 13, and averaging 25 yards per kickoff return.

Vincent was pestered by agents throughout the season and was forced to change his unlisted telephone number several times. Finally, he relied on his family to help him iron out a deal with the Miami Dolphins, who made him the seventh player chosen in the first round of the draft.

Like Don Davey the year before, Vincent was one of the few Badgers players who showed a good understanding of what it took to be a winner. Throughout the season, Alvarez kept hammering on what he insisted was a key: teaching players what it took to win and what winning was all about. Defeat, coming as it had with jackhammer redundancy, had worn down his players.

But the five wins, Alvarez felt, was a start. "That was the biggest job we had, was convincing players they could win," he said. "We spent a lot of time on basically feeling good about yourself and believing in themselves."

After that second season, Alvarez accepted Jacques' resignation from his $70,000 a year job, ostensibly to "pursue other career opportunities." Despite having publicly supported Jacques late in the season, the results left him little choice. In those two seasons, Jacques presided over the most troubled offense in the Big Ten. In 1990, the Badgers averaged 269.7 yards a game and its 11.5-point scoring offense was the worst in the nation.

If Jacques was looking for relief in 1991, he found none. Wisconsin's average yardage dropped to 242.2 yards as he struggled with younger players who often played out of position. Alvarez slid Brad Childress into the coordinator's role and things started to change.

Jacques was not the only staffer to hit the bricks after that second season. Paul Winters left as well, and was later named the UW's compliance officer, working out of the university's legal department to ensure that NCAA rules were followed. His departure allowed Alvarez to hire former Minnesota Assistant Jim Hueber to coach running backs.

During and after the 1991 season, Alvarez encountered problems with staff, players, and rules.

Strength Coach Scott Raridon, whom Alvarez brought to Wisconsin from Notre Dame, was fired by the university in December 1991 when it was discovered he was involved in a payroll scam in which his girlfriend was paid for more than 300 hours of salary she did not earn. He was later convicted on criminal charges, fined, and put on probation.

For the most part, Alvarez's players have been well behaved. But certain incidents have focused unwanted attention on the program.

The incident gaining the widest notoriety occurred on Halloween night 1991 when a twenty-year-old Rhinelander man was severely beaten outside of a campus bar. Starting linebackers Gary Casper and Aaron Norvell and former player Sean Wilson were at the scene of the beating.

Casper and Wilson told police they defended themselves after the man jumped them. Norvell fled the scene and was not part of the fight, authorities said.

Although the man was hospitalized for six weeks, no charges were filed after Dane County District Attorney William Foust said witness accounts varied so widely that he could not make a case against anyone involved in the fight.

Alvarez levied one-game suspensions against both Casper and Norvell for breaking team curfew rules in the incident.

Before training camp began in 1992, Fletcher ran into legal problems after a July fight in a campus bar in which he broke a man's jaw. The following January, he entered into a plea bargain on misdemeanor charges that resulted in two years' probation, restitution, and 100 hours of community service.

The NCAA rules infractions Alvarez's program has encountered have been few and minor. And that's no small achievement, considering the NCAA manual is an inch thick and 478 pages long. A 1992 investigation by UW law professor Frank Tuerkheimer spanned several months and turned up several secondary infractions, which the UW reported to the Big Ten.

The probe, begun after the Big Ten received an anonymous complaint in spring 1992, found that eight assistant coaches at various times viewed off-season workouts from a film booth overlooking the practice field in the McClain Facility. Watching such practices is forbidden by NCAA rules.

The coaches were watching voluntary, seven-on-seven drills, in which an offensive backfield and receivers go against linebackers and defensive backs. The investigation found that coaches watched the practice on four occasions for a total of about two hours.

Tuerkheimer, a former U.S. attorney, also found that Bill Callahan answered football-related questions at an academic session involving the offensive line and telephoned a Chicago-area prep linebacker he was recruiting twice in one week, more than the single call allowed by the NCAA.

Although the complaint also stated that players were given gifts of cash or motor scooters for outstanding play, Tuerkheimer said there was no evidence to support those claims.

The assistant coaches involved—and all except Dan McCarney were—received formal reprimands and the program relinquished four practice sessions as part of the UW's effort to address the infractions. Alvarez said the violations occurred because of a misunderstanding of the rules and pledged to educate his staff more thoroughly. "The University of Wisconsin is committed to running a clean program," Alvarez asserted.

If the uproar of those incidents was a distraction, the Badgers' growing success on the recruiting circuit was a source of pride for Alvarez's staff. After that second season, they were able to land some of the nation's top players, including six *Parade* magazine all-Americans, more than Wisconsin had ever recruited in one season. That coup led to Alvarez's class being rated sixteenth best in the nation by Lemming.

Perhaps the most bizarre tale from the 1991–92 recruiting wars came out of Indianapolis, where Purdue and Wisconsin were vying for quarterback Kevin Lyles at Lawrence North High School. He was ranked among the top ten quarterbacks nationally. After making several oral commitments to both schools, then changing his mind, Lyles set up a rare confrontation by inviting recruiters from both schools into his living room for a showdown. Despite the tensions that existed between Boilermakers coaches and the Badgers, the meeting was civil, but spirited.

Lyles's decision went down to the last day, and Wisconsin won out. Today, he's a third-string tight end.

7

Down to the Last Play

I t seemed like only politics stood between the Badgers and a bowl game.

The backstage arm twisting and apple polishing was under way and all
Alvarez's team needed to do was defeat Northwestern on November 21, 1992,
at Dyche Stadium to win a berth in either the Freedom or Independence bowl.

A victory would give the Badgers a 6–5 record, their first winning season
since 1984 and a chance at the postseason play Alvarez treasured.

Richter, Alvarez, and other UW officials met informally with officials from
both bowls at the North Shore Hilton in Skokie, Illinois, and proceeded to
stroke them.

Representatives from both bowls were keenly interested in having Wisconsin play in their games. The Badgers had played in Shreveport's Independence
Bowl in 1982 and officials there knew bowl-hungry Badgers fans would turn out
in force, making Wisconsin a top choice.

Although the Freedom Bowl also recognized that prospect, Executive Director Don Anderson saw another up side to inviting the Badgers to come to
Anaheim. As the season shook out, it became clear that the Pac-10 representative in the game would be the University of Southern California.

The potential seemed huge. Wisconsin's participation in the Freedom Bowl
would set up a rematch between the Badgers and USC thirty years after their
legendary Rose Bowl encounter. Anderson, a Racine native, saw a potential
marketing bonanza.

Alvarez had been working the phones all week, calling bowl representatives
and coaching friends to enhance Wisconsin's standing. He knew the bowl bid

would buy his team extra practice time to season young players and boost the exposure of his rising program.

Quarterback Darrell Bevell, meanwhile, was making alternative arrangements to reschedule his wedding, set for Christmas week, in case Wisconsin wound up in a bowl game.

A bowl berth would be the crowning touch on a season of struggle that started at Husky Stadium at the University of Washington as the Badgers took on the defending national champions.

Schedule-makers from the pre-Alvarez regime were cursed around the football office as the season opener approached. The last thing a program hungry for the postseason needed was to face the nation's top-ranked team on the road.

"I'm not real crazy about going up there," Alvarez said the Monday before the game. "I don't think it's very wise to have a game like this to open your season, particularly in our situation."

Alvarez tried to view the experience as a classroom exercise for a young team trying to learn the winning ways of college football. Certainly the Huskies were in a position to teach some hard lessons.

Things, however, could have been worse. Wisconsin officials in 1987 had scheduled a two-game series with Washington, well before Alvarez arrived in Madison. But one dose of the Huskies seemed to be enough for him.

Officials at both schools worked to renegotiate the contract, and Wisconsin prevailed. At the Badgers' request, Washington dropped its 1994 game at Madison, allowing Wisconsin to sign the University of Cincinnati to play at Camp Randall on November 12.

Husky Stadium, snug on Lake Washington, is a breathtaking but inhospitable environment for visitors. The stadium was packed with 72,800 fans, a larger crowd than any the Huskies had attracted during their run to a national championship the previous season. Expectations were high and Wisconsin seemed to be ripe for the picking. Even though the oddsmakers buried the Badgers as a 33-point underdog, the Badgers' fans were undaunted.

Several thousand, both from Wisconsin and UW alumni from the Pacific Northwest, made their loud presence known from the end-zone seats.

In the weeks leading up to the game, Alvarez asked beat reporters to avoid reporting receiver Lionell Crawford's spot use as an option quarterback. Since that fact had been widely reported in the spring and in preseason coverage, and because Wisconsin was using the option only as a novelty, the writers agreed to cooperate in return for access to practice.

But Brad Childress was expecting big things from Crawford: "People are going to know that they're not only going to face multiple formations, but they'll have to deal with a little option, too. And Lionell is a natural."

Until Alvarez arrived on campus, Crawford was quarterback of Morton's veer offense. Alvarez moved Crawford to wide receiver to make better use of his speed. Now he was the change-up guy in Childress's first-year offense.

There were other changes: Childress added the wishbone in some goal-line situations, something Alvarez called the "Wis-bone."

Washington's offense sputtered through most of the day, despite running up 455 yards to Wisconsin's 218, and the Badgers acquitted themselves well against an opponent that was supposed to annihilate them.

The Badgers dampened Washington's rushing game, as quarterback Billy Joe Hobert was the Huskies' leading rusher with 60 yards and a touchdown.

Toward the end of the game, Alvarez went with first-year quarterback Bevell. Bevell completed 3 of 5 passes for 37 yards and showed good composure.

As the clock ticked off the final seconds, the Wisconsin fans were jubilant, chanting "We beat the spread! We beat the spread!" It was as if the Badgers had won, and maybe, in a small way, they had.

The 17-point victory was the smallest in a home nonconference game since the Huskies played San Jose State in 1990 and Washington fans, coaches, and players left the game shaking their heads. It was a raggedy way to start the drive for back-to-back national titles.

The Washington game represented an understated turning point for Alvarez's program. National expectations were that Washington would humiliate the Badgers, yet the Huskies struggled while Wisconsin proved it was solidifying. And while moral victories are abhorrent to any coach, Alvarez took credibility away from Seattle.

Emerging from the locker room, Wisconsin players held themselves with a different air. No one was pleased with the outcome, but they had a sense of confidence and optimism that was absent after many of their previous losses.

The promise Wisconsin displayed at Washington was to be fully realized in its next three games.

Alvarez closed practice to the media for the week before Wisconsin's home opener against Bowling Green State. The conventional wisdom was that former Alvarez assistant Scott Seeliger was now assistant head coach to Gary Blackney at Bowling Green State and Alvarez did not need any more information filtering to the Falcons through news accounts.

The truth was that Alvarez and Childress had decided on Sunday to bench Jay Macias in favor of Bevell, whose performance in the Washington game they felt showed potential. They didn't need reporters telling the world about the shift.

The secret was well-kept and Bevell was unveiled in an auspicious manner. There were 57,758 people on hand at Camp Randall Stadium, the largest crowd for a home opener since Morton's first game in 1986.

It was a gamble, Alvarez knew, yet Badgers coaches felt Macias was unable to generate any offensive snap. The gamble paid off for Wisconsin as Bevell, less than four minutes into his first start, tossed a 49-yard touchdown strike to Terrell Fletcher.

In all, Bevell would throw 3 touchdown passes that day—including a 2-yard pass to Lee DeRamus and a 16-yard pass to Mark Montgomery circling out of the backfield. Four Rich Thompson field goals and a 21-yard interception return for Scott Nelson for a touchdown gave the Badgers a 39-18 victory.

Wisconsin's victory margin was the largest ever during the Alvarez era. More important, however, Bevell seemed to exude confidence in completing 11 of 17 passes for 142 yards.

The next week, Wisconsin completed its nonconference schedule against Northern Illinois. The game featured another player shift that would stick for the long run. Alvarez returned Brent Moss to tailback, after experimenting with him at fullback.

Moss's brutal running style seemed to make him well-suited to playing fullback, but he preferred tailback where he got more carries and a better view of the defensive line.

The shift would prove valuable late in the game.

Northern Illinois was more stubborn than its billing. The Badgers strained to build offensive rhythm and led by the disappointing margin of 3-0 at halftime on a 24-yard field goal from Thompson.

Northern Illinois responded to the opportunity with a field goal in the third quarter and a pair of fourth-quarter touchdowns. First, quarterback Rob Rugai connected with receiver Larry Wynn for a 19-yard touchdown and then running back Brian Cotton scored on a 1-yard run with 12:41 to play.

The Badgers helped feed Northern Illinois' momentum with 3 lost fumbles and 2 interceptions that took the edge off their 258-111 yard rushing advantage in the game.

Wisconsin, however, showed a surprising resilience. With 7:21 left, Moss chipped into Northern Illinois' lead with a 2-yard touchdown.

But the show wasn't over. Bevell, showing the same sort of composure as the week before, led Wisconsin on a drive that ended as Moss ran for 11 yards and a touchdown. The score narrowed Northern Illinois' lead to 17-16 and there was no question in Alvarez's mind about going for the 2-point conversion and the victory.

With 2:09 left, the slow-footed Bevell took the snap and rolled to the right. He looked for receiver DeRamus. But DeRamus was covered, so Bevell turned upfield and lumbered over the goal line on a play that seemed to take forever to develop. Bevell said he knew he made it to the end zone because when he was tackled the pile kept getting heavier.

The victory marked the fourth in five games dating to 1991, something the Badgers had not accomplished since 1984-85.

Alvarez saw that his team was starting to pay closer attention to the game plan. Before each game, coaches go over every point of emphasis and the last one is always: "Don't flinch."

"We talk about finding ways to win," Alvarez said after the game. "A win like this will pay some dividends down the road."

The dividends started to pay off a week later as twelfth-ranked Ohio State came into Madison a heavy favorite. The Badgers hadn't defeated a ranked opponent for seven years and it had been eleven years since they won a Big Ten opener.

At the team meeting the night before the game, Alvarez preached simplicity. No trick plays, no funny business. Just line up and smash your opponent in the mouth.

Before a national audience on ESPN, Wisconsin seized control of the line of scrimmage. "They stacked the line and challenged us," said Buckeyes tailback Raymont Harris, who rushed for 30 of Ohio State's 45 yards on the ground. "I thought their guys were very aggressive."

The Badgers' offensive line took particular joy in pushing around Ohio State noseguard Greg Smith, who they say trash talked his way through the Buckeyes' victory over Wisconsin in 1991.

Cory Raymer said even players on defense wanted to take a turn on offense to exact retribution. During the game at Camp Randall, Raymer said Smith did not make a peep.

Ohio State took a 10–3 halftime lead, but Moss's 2 third-quarter rushing touchdowns gave Wisconsin a 17–10 lead going into the game's last 15 minutes. Thompson nailed a 31-yard field goal to extend the Badgers' lead. But Ohio State, helped by 3 personal fouls on Badgers defenders, marched 76 yards in 13 plays and scored a touchdown as quarterback Kirk Herbstreit passed 3 yards to receiver Brian Stablein.

The Buckeyes' try for a 2-point conversion failed as Harris was stopped short by linebacker Gary Casper and defensive back Korey Manley with 4:29 left. Wisconsin ran out the clock and some of the 72,203 jubilant fans in Camp Randall streamed onto the field and tore down a set of goalposts. A beaming Alvarez walked off the field with his arm slung around Dan McCarney.

The victory was the first true jewel in Alvarez's crown, and it came on national television, something Rob Ianello said was worth at least 500 recruiting calls. And it further solidified Bevell as the team's quarterback. "He isn't pretty," said Alvarez. "But he gets the job done."

The Badgers were building a reputation for hair-raising finishes, and that carried over into the Iowa game the following week. But sparks flew between the two programs well before the game.

Alvarez, who worked under Head Coach Hayden Fry for eight seasons for Iowa, challenged Fry on the Hawkeyes' practice schedule. In a teleconference with reporters, Fry first said that Iowa players routinely run on Sundays, then backpedaled and said Iowa players enjoy Sunday as their mandatory day off.

Alvarez said if he tried that at Wisconsin, officials would count it as a practice day. An Iowa spokesman later denied any coaches were at the "Sunday shakedown," designed to see if players were physically up to playing.

The incident received national attention, irritating Fry, which seemed to please Alvarez. During pregame warmups, the two didn't speak, patrolling only their respective sides of the field. Asked about the tiff later, Alvarez said, "I have nothing to say to him."

Although the men have settled their differences and are on better terms, Alvarez admits they still keep each other at arm's length.

At Kinnick Stadium, the Badgers took a 22–15 lead on a 2-yard touchdown run by Moss with 3:54 left. But Iowa quarterback Jim Hartlieb came back to guide an 80-yard drive that ended when receiver Anthony Dean caught a 4-yard touchdown pass with 55 seconds to play.

Fry ordered a 2-point conversion attempt and Hartlieb spotted Dean along the rear of the end zone and put the ball up. Despite glancing off Casper's hand, Dean hung on and Iowa gained a 23–22 lead.

Alvarez said one of the officials came up to him with about 3 minutes left in the game and said it was the finest game he'd seen in some time. The Badgers' coach had to agree.

Wisconsin had one more chance. After Bevell was shaken up during the next drive, Macias came on and completed a crucial 22-yard pass to receiver Lionell Crawford at the Iowa 36. With 6 seconds left, the Badgers had one option: a 53-yard field goal attempt by Thompson.

This was Thompson's dream, to nail a long field goal to win the game. His dream, however, fizzled as Iowa cornerback Carlos James knifed through and blocked the attempt after Thompson received a low snap. But Thompson made no excuses. "Even if the ball rolled back there and the ball was on the spot, I should have gotten it up enough so it wouldn't be blocked," he said.

Before the week was out, Thompson would have his day and his dream. Wisconsin's next game was against Purdue, which ran off to a 16–6 lead in the third quarter at Camp Randall.

In response, Wisconsin rattled off 13 unanswered points and Macias again came in for an injured Bevell to set up the Badgers for a game-winning field goal. Facing a third and 11 on the Badgers' 49, Macias hit DeRamus with a 12-yard pass in a drive that positioned the Badgers for a 49-yard field goal attempt.

Out came Thompson, intent on erasing the stigma of the previous week. "I never dreamed I'd have a shot at it so soon," said Thompson. Seconds later, he got a clean snap and a solid kick that gave Wisconsin a 19–16 victory and a 2–1 Big Ten record.

Following losses to Indiana, Illinois, and Michigan State, the Badgers retained the Paul Bunyan Axe by defeating Minnesota 34–6 and headed into the final game of the season 5–5.

There was a flinty chill in the air as the Badgers boarded buses outside the North Shore Hilton to head to Northwestern's Dyche Stadium, an old dowager stadium where Wisconsin was throttled in Alvarez's first season.

The stakes in the finale were different now. A bowl game was on the table for Wisconsin for the first time since McClain's team lost in the Hall of Fame Bowl in 1984.

The crowd at Dyche Stadium was in stark contrast to the seething throng the Badgers faced at Husky Stadium to begin the season. Years of football futility had whittled away at Northwestern crowds, and Gary Barnett's inaugural season didn't do much to perk up attendance. An unsatisfying crowd of 28,265 showed up.

Wisconsin rallied from a 27–17 deficit on Bevell's 42-yard touchdown pass to DeRamus and a 2-point conversion. That narrowed the Wildcats' edge to 27–25. With less than a minute left, Bevell drove the Badgers to the Wildcats' 27-yard line.

Now, all the Badgers had to do was position the ball in the center of the field to set up a straight-on, game-winning field goal. Destiny was a carry and a kick away.

The Freedom Bowl's Anderson watched eagerly as the Badgers came to the line and Bevell barked out his signals. At the snap, Bevell whirled and handed off to sophomore fullback Jason Burns.

Almost instantly, something went wrong on the Badgers' line. Wildcats free safety Greg Gill saw an opening and swept in on Burns, intent on stripping the ball.

Gill wrapped up on Burns behind the line of scrimmage as the ball, and the Badgers' hopes of a winning season, tumbled to the turf and the Wildcats recovered. The Badgers' bowl chances were extinguished as Northwestern players rushed onto the field and embraced each other as if they had won a national championship.

"They had a great defense against the play," said Bevell. "It was a clean handoff. The guy comes untouched because he's a safety and no one is supposed to be blocking him. While Jason was trying to spin, he lost it. It was devastating."

Wildcats players made a point of getting in the faces of Badgers players, underscoring the magnitude of Wisconsin's fumbled chance at a bowl game.

Anderson left the press box at Dyche Stadium disappointed that the Freedom Bowl reunion game wouldn't come off. Instead, the selection committee went with USC and Fresno State. The Independence Bowl settled on Oregon and Wake Forest.

While Wildcats fans tore down the goalposts, Badgers players searched for answers. The accomplishments of the 1992 season didn't salve the wounds this game inflicted.

All of the politicking went down the toilet.

On the field, Badgers players were widely taunted by the Wildcats for blowing their bowl-game chances. "After the game, they were saying, 'You're not going anywhere,' and really rubbing it in," said Bevell.

As the Badgers climbed aboard the bus parked outside the arching ramparts of Dyche Stadium, players were hurting emotionally. But that hurt was part of the rebuilding; an undesirable, but effective way to harden the resolve of Wisconsin's returning players.

"I expected us to win every time we set foot on the field," said Joe Panos. "Even when we were 5–6, after the games we lost we were deeply disappointed. People thought we were used to losing.

"But we weren't. Not at all."

Breakthrough after Breakthrough

The program boiled with confidence after spring practice in 1993.

Coaches and players knew Wisconsin was performing at a level of competence unparalleled during Alvarez's tenure. The signs of improvement were abundant: Darrell Bevell was more confident and had better vision, the offensive line was pushing even the number one defense off the ball, and the running backs were far more productive.

And the Badgers had come up with their best recruiting class ever, ranked tenth in the nation. They had snared St. Paul, Minnesota, tailback Carl McCullough away from Minnesota and Florida State and assembled their most athletic class to date.

Reasons for optimism were everywhere.

Bevell's improvement at throwing the ball was crucial to unlocking Wisconsin's offensive potential. Alvarez's central offensive nostrum had not changed: run to set up the pass.

With a good passer and some sound running backs, that theory works. But in the 1992 season, Bevell completed just 51 percent of his passes. That locked the Badgers into a more predictable, run-dominated offense and enabled opposing defenses to key on the rush.

Brad Childress knew the Badgers couldn't vary their offense much with a passing game that produced roughly 50–50 odds of going into 2nd down with 10 yards to go. In the Big Ten, that's considered to be working in the margin, so the rush became the mainstay of the Wisconsin offense. And every defender in the Big Ten knew it.

If Bevell could improve his completion percentage, with the running backs

Wisconsin had, it would open up Wisconsin's play-action game in 1993. That would give the entire offense a new flavor, punch, and unpredictability.

Bevell came to Wisconsin before the 1992 season because of Offensive Coordinator Childress. Childress had coached him as a freshman at Northern Arizona in 1989 and saw immense potential in the way he led a team and in Bevell's emerging ability to throw the ball.

The son of the football coach at Chaparral High School in Flagstaff, Arizona, Bevell belongs to the Church of Latter Day Saints. As part of the teachings of his Mormon faith, he decided after his first season at Northern Arizona to embark on a two-year mission. He left organized football and went to some of the toughest neighborhoods in Cleveland for his ministry.

The demanding work toughened Bevell. Hundreds of doors were slammed in his face, guns were pointed at him, Rottweilers were turned on him, and insults were hurled his way as he carried his ministry from door to door in ragged, unwelcoming neighborhoods.

"I missed football a great deal. Every time I went by a stadium or watched little kids play Pop Warner, I got homesick for it and really wanted to play," said Bevell, who grew up playing two-on-two football with neighbor boys.

He wore out footballs throwing with fellow missionaries in vacant lots and tried to stay in shape, but his demanding schedule did not allow much time for athletics.

After taking the Wisconsin job, Childress maintained contact with Bevell and convinced him to become a Badger when his Mormon street work was finished. Alvarez liked the idea of having a twenty-two-year-old signal caller with Bevell's maturity and background.

The age advantage gave Bevell maturity, but his mission and redshirt year gave him the added benefit of having four years of eligibility remaining.

When Bevell arrived for spring drills before the 1992 season, the head coach was not in a joking mood after he saw what Bevell had to offer on the field.

Bevell's skills were caked in rust. His timing was poor, his reads virtually nonexistent, and he was out of condition. Here was a project.

"Barry looked at me like, 'What have you been smoking?'" Childress recalled.

But Childress stuck by Bevell, working on his technique and physical skills. Bevell made gigantic strides during the off-season. It was the sort of progress that University of Utah basketball coach Rick Majerus had told Alvarez to expect out of a Mormon athlete coming back from a mission.

Alvarez said Majerus, the former Marquette basketball coach, told him before the season that there is a drastic improvement between the first year a Mormon returns and the second year. His prediction was borne out in Bevell.

By the time 1993 spring drills rolled around, Bevell had made huge strides.

He was twenty pounds heavier, stronger, and with better vision. No longer solely focused on the onrushing noseguard, Bevell was reading coverages and anticipating pass routes.

Nothing could have pleased Alvarez more. "It was quite obvious that he was a different football player. He put on pounds, he almost doubled his strength, he understood the offense much better," Alvarez said.

And Bevell possessed a renewed commitment to be a strong starting quarterback and throw off some of the persistent questions about his ability and leadership.

"I don't think people had expectations for me," Bevell said. "They knew the quarterback had to be solid and let everyone else around him do their job. I felt the pressure was from myself, because I felt I could be better than just some guy doing his job."

"All the expectations came from me. All the doubting and questions came from everybody else," he said.

Childress liked the looks of Bevell going into the 1993 season. "He's improved athletically and is looking at things and not just trying to survive out there," he said. "He's gotten through the mechanics of it and can concentrate on what they're doing on the defensive side of the ball."

After a promising spring camp, most of the Badgers players stayed for summer conditioning, and the team drew closer personally. The young players got to know each other better in the weight room and running on the turf in the McClain Facility. The successful spring and the summer workouts tended to break down walls that had separated players in the past.

"The previous season, the team was sort of broken down into units. The running backs hung together, the linemen, the receivers," said flanker J.C. Dawkins. "But as time went on we started seeing ourselves as an offense and a defense. We were more cohesive, personally and on the field."

And Strength Coach John Dettman's conditioning program, though demanding, held the attention of the players.

For the first time, the Badgers offered a Tae Kwon Do class. The concept, used by several NFL teams, was aimed at increasing flexibility and Alvarez liked that idea.

Defensive tackle Carlos Fowler, at a lumbering 275 pounds, also took a shine to the new class. "Like it? He was one of the stars," said Alvarez.

Dettman, always searching for an innovation, traveled to the Dallas Cowboys' training camp and picked up tips that soon had Bevell at the end of his rope. Dettman paid special heed to Cowboys' quarterback Troy Aikman and his workouts.

Aikman had a quick, deep drop, something Bevell needed to work on. The Cowboys worked on that drop by attaching long bungee cords around Aikman's waist and applying either resistance or assistance as he made his drop.

Soon Bevell was in the McClain Facility at the business end of a bungee cord. He said the drills helped improve his drop and provided an interesting and challenging aspect to conditioning.

Joe Panos said the off-season program helped sow the seeds of success for the 1993 Badgers. "We were close to getting over the hump in those last two years," he said. "Finally, I saw the confidence over the summer. I knew it was going to be a different team because eighty-five of us stayed over the summer. The confidence level and the way we grouped together told me this was going to be a successful team."

Even at the Big Ten football meetings in Rosemont, Illinois, the first week of August, Alvarez was unabashed in his enthusiasm. While many coaches downplay their preseason expectations, Alvarez was boldly underscoring his.

"I thought we should have been in a bowl last year and if we'd done a good job coaching, maybe we would have," said Alvarez. "I didn't have a timetable. I didn't think going into the season, quite honestly, that we were ready to contend for a Big Ten championship. But I thought we could be a top-four team in the conference."

During the off-season, the Big Ten had signed an agreement to send the league's fourth-place team to the Hall of Fame Bowl in Tampa. That expanded Wisconsin's chance to land in a major bowl game, and Alvarez wanted to make the most of it.

The heightened expectations played into the hands of the UW as the contract for exclusive radio rights to Badgers football and basketball was being bid. In the final year of a five-year deal, Milwaukee's WTMJ paid $340,000 for the rights during the 1993 season.

But when WTMJ's bid was disqualified in early August for being filed late, the contract went to Learfield Communications of Jefferson City, Missouri. In 1994, it will pay $450,000 for the rights, a figure that balloons to $500,000 in 1996. The numbers brought smiles to faces across the Athletic Department.

Richter, a periodic visitor to football practice, gave an annual talk to the team at Holy Name Seminary during training camp. He was one of several speakers Alvarez lined up during training camp to address topics such as media relations, drug abuse, and gambling.

Each year, Richter saw the physical progress the team had made as he scanned the seminary's auditorium.

"Four years ago, I remember going out to the seminary to give a talk and seeing a lot of thin necks. Their shoulders weren't touching. There wasn't a lot of meat out there," said Richter. "The next year I went back and the shoulders were touching, necks a little thicker. The third year, I went back and the kids were sitting in every other chair. We knew we were making progress."

Alvarez loves the seminary and sees it as a privilege to train there. Besides providing a jolt of pure football for a couple of weeks, its monastic, self-contained atmosphere allows coaches and players to become immersed in the game.

It is a sweaty cauldron but the staff tries to find ways to lighten the two-a-day grind. One is the annual talent show, a Friday-night affair with mandatory participation. After all, if you can't act silly in front of 120 teammates, what kind of performance will you give before a crowd of 77,745 in Camp Randall Stadium?

The show features skits, impersonations of coaches, and even feats of true skill. A favorite is tight end Matt Nyquist's act, in which he juggles a football helmet, a shoe, and a bowling ball.

"This was a team that knew how to have fun," Alvarez said. "Football is tough. The great teams learn how to have fun and that's something this group learned how to do."

The 1993 camp was more enjoyable because he knew the Badgers' competence level had shot up after the 1992 season. Finally, there seemed to be a convergence of attitude, conditioning, and experience that pointed to success.

Alvarez's initial concern was building a sense of family on the team, breaking down the walls Dawkins noticed, and moving ahead with uniform goals.

"The first thing that came out of my mouth when we met at the seminary was: 'We're going to be a good football team. How good will depend on the chemistry we have on this team,'" he said.

Unquestionably, this was the best camp of the Alvarez era. The ragged edges of past years were gone. Virtually no one was on the ground in the crisply run drills and players took practice time more seriously.

"The seminary is hell," said Fowler, arriving at a theological contradiction. "But that's where this team came together, where guys started to rely on each other. It was hot and we were constantly picking each other up and keeping each other going."

During the first week of camp, when a fight broke out between players, Panos stepped in with a high-volume lecture about how this was wasting everyone else's practice time. The combatants slunk back to their units and practice went on.

"I like to get in a scuffle as much as the next guy, but we couldn't be beating each other up and wasting time. There was too much we had to get done," Panos said.

Coaches also were impressed at the work ethic players displayed. One morning during the second week of workouts, a fast-moving practice yielded forty plays during an inside rushing drill scripted for twenty-eight. That sort of efficiency was helping a still young team squeeze more repetitions out of limited practice time.

Preparations for the Badgers' opener against the University of Nevada's pass-oriented offense started with worries about Wisconsin's defense. Alvarez's idea of college football involved standing toe-to-toe with an opponent and slugging it out. Pass-happy teams made him nervous.

"I don't like this brand of football. I don't particularly like to play fast-break basketball," he said.

The slipperiness of Wolf Pack quarterback Chris Vargas, whose three-step drop and quick release played a role in several Nevada comebacks in 1992, was also a worry.

Fowler said the defensive line was worried about keeping pressure on Vargas until the Wisconsin offense showed it could play a ball-control game against the Wolf Pack.

Bevell erased many lingering questions about his skills as he threw for a school-record 5 touchdowns in what became a 35–17 rout of the Wolf Pack. And, for the first time, the 66,557 fans at Camp Randall Stadium saw evidence that new offensive weapons were emerging.

Dawkins, making his first collegiate start, had touchdown grabs of 49 and 16 yards. His early success was important, because it took some of the defensive pressure off Lee DeRamus, who had been seen as Wisconsin's only threat as a receiver.

It would be the only game of the 1993 season in which Brent Moss would rush for less than 100 yards; he gained 74 yards on 19 carries. That was partly due to Wisconsin's passing success and partly because Alvarez cycled in Terrell Fletcher and freshman Carl McCullough at tailback.

To Bevell, the game was a proving ground. He felt strongly that he needed to showcase his improvement for the public early to lift the cloud of skepticism that plagued him during 1992. "Everyone said that I was the missing piece, and for us to have a good team, I had to play well," Bevell said. "I felt I had to show everyone, the people in the stands, the media, that I could hold up my end."

The 5 touchdowns definitely made a statement.

"It got people off my back, but I knew I was going to have to keep doing that game after game," he said. "No one's going to remember 5 touchdown passes when you're playing your next game at SMU."

If there was a bugaboo that nagged players and coaches throughout the Alvarez era, it was the Badgers' horrendous record on the road. Going into 1993, Wisconsin was 1–12 in road games under Alvarez and that victory was the only road win by the Badgers since mid-1986.

The road triumph under Alvarez was the 19–16 affair at Minnesota, which was saved by Badgers defensive back Melvin Tucker in the game's waning seconds. Players and coaches were weary of trying to explain their lack of focus away from Camp Randall.

The Badgers' trip to Southern Methodist University in Dallas was geared to remedy that problem. But there were bad omens in the game, starting when football staffer Pat O'Connor was bitten by the SMU mascot, a Shetland pony named Peruna VII.

Aside from a cranky Mustangs mascot, Wisconsin faced a variety of new wrinkles in the game.

It was a night game before an Ownby Stadium crowd of 19,000, a tiny gathering by Big Ten standards. And it was hot, 93 degrees at the 7 p.m. kickoff.

No one on the Wisconsin roster had played a night game as a collegian, and they didn't much like it when they did. The Badgers arrived in Dallas Friday night and did not play the Mustangs until 7 p.m. Saturday. Wisconsin had plenty of time to get sluggish, especially in the heat.

The Badgers tried to combat SMU's throwing game by dropping into a nickel package that called for strong safety Reggie Holt to play inside and outside linebacker, as well as safety.

The skittish Badgers fell behind 13–0 at halftime. This time, though, the no-can-do attitude that prevailed at halftime of other away games was not prevalent in Wisconsin's locker room.

"We came out flat and at halftime, coach was pretty upset. He told us, 'You better wake up or you'll lose this game,'" said Fowler. "We woke up in the second half."

With 6:28 left in the game, Bevell's 25-yard touchdown pass to Dawkins gave the Badgers a 17–16 lead, and a 1-yard touchdown plunge by Fletcher in the last minute of the game gave Wisconsin a 24–16 victory. It was only the second time in seven years that the Badgers had won on the road.

Moss rushed for 181 yards, the first of a school-record 11 straight games in which he would break the 100-yard barrier.

Bevell said the game, often overlooked in the course of a season studded with more impressive wins, might have been central to Wisconsin's success.

"No question: the SMU game was one of the most important for us as a team," said Bevell. "It proved our composure, our savvy, and got the monkeys off our back about road games. That burden came off early and that helped us through the rest of the season."

The Badgers' nonconference season was a smorgasbord of varying offenses that forced the defense to make fundamental changes. Both Nevada and SMU liked to play basketball, spread the defense and throw.

The third, Iowa State, used an option-oriented attack, forcing more changes. Playing an option team imposes rigorous demands on the opposing defense. It requires strong discipline, since it is assignment football—everyone needs to perform a rigid assignment and free-lancing will immediately be exposed.

Before a sellout crowd at Camp Randall, the Badgers gained 448 yards and held the Cyclones to 225 yards. The Badgers' offensive line showed its potential, blocking the Cyclones several yards off the ball on virtually every snap. It gave Panos the sense that the line could be a featured unit before the season was over.

"We did whatever we wanted to do. I sensed that we had reached a milestone and there was no going back," Panos said.

The sudden rise in the popularity of the program was reflected at the gate. For Iowa State, the Badgers drew their first capacity crowd in eight years and the first sellout for a nonconference game since 1982.

Since he arrived in Madison, Alvarez's goal was to make Wisconsin season football tickets like those at Nebraska, where they are handed down from generation to generation. Wisconsin seemed to be headed in that direction.

"In the first couple of years, getting over the hump was hard," said Richter. "People were saying, 'I've heard this before. You're going to have to prove to me you're going to be successful.'"

Wisconsin's Big Ten season began in a driving rainstorm at Indiana University's Memorial Stadium. As Indiana students slid on rain ponchos down a rain-slicked hill at the north end of the stadium, the Badgers concentrated on sustaining their success on the road.

The victory at SMU proved Wisconsin could win under trying circumstances, but the Hoosiers entered the game as a more formidable opponent than the Mustangs.

Finally, after years of indecision, Alvarez swept the media out of his practices before the Indiana game. After allowing reporters to roam freely at previous practices, he gave them the boot, saying he would evaluate the policy later.

But the practices remained closed. Part of the reason seemed to be Alvarez's wish to close things down, but part may have been rooted in superstition— as long as the Badgers were winning, why tamper with success?

The expulsion of the media came at a good time for Alvarez. Wisconsin coaches were worried about Bevell before the Indiana game. Unbeknown to the media and the Hoosiers, Bevell had the flu and was only able to practice for one day during the week before the game. It showed in his 5-for-15 passing performance and 2 interceptions.

"It was weird; I was sick the week before and the year before I was playing hurt and I didn't play well in either year," said Bevell. "But even though I didn't have very many bombs all year, I had 3 in that game."

But this was a day in which the Badgers did not require a sturdy passing attack. The Hoosiers' top-ranked Big Ten defense against the rush was being thwarted at every turn.

Wisconsin's offensive line was expected to face its staunchest test at Indiana, against a defense that had allowed 86 rushing yards a game during nonconference play.

Methodically, however, the Badgers' line decimated the Hoosiers' defensive front, allowing Moss to rush for a season-high 198 yards. Fletcher fattened up on the line's success as well, gaining 99 yards and scoring a 57-yard rushing touchdown, in the rain-soaked 27–15 victory.

The triumph over Indiana set the table for homecoming against Northwestern. The word about this game had been out since summer.

Players and coaches had circled the Northwestern game on their calendars. Finally, the Badgers would have a chance to make Barnett's Wildcats pay for the season-ending embarrassment that deprived Wisconsin of a bowl berth in 1992.

Coaches operated under an overriding principle in the weeks before the game: "Humiliate Northwestern." Players also were eager to gain revenge for the previous season's heartbreaker.

"We went in with a hit list. Teams that kept us out of bowl games, we wanted them bad. They were basically Northwestern, Michigan, and Illinois," said Fowler. "I wish we could have played Iowa because Hayden Fry has this thing about Wisconsin teams never beating the Hawkeyes."

Bevell, too, was eager to play Northwestern. The purpose in playing the Wildcats this season was to run up the score. It didn't matter if it was 50, 60, or 70 points. The word was to aim high.

"This year, we weren't going to let up," said Bevell. "And it was very sweet."

Again, the Wisconsin offensive line was overpowering as the Badgers converted 10 of 11 third downs. Northwestern, however, converted only 1 of 10.

That allowed the Badgers to race to a 53–14 victory, gaining the revenge they'd waited a year to collect.

After five games, it was becoming apparent that Bevell's improvement was no fluke. In 1992, Bevell was pathetic running the naked bootleg, a play that can help open up the running game. He routinely missed receivers by throwing into the ground or over their heads.

But in 1993, Bevell's mechanics had improved so much that the naked bootleg yielded an 80 percent completion rate.

"I felt a new confidence because I knew what all the receivers were going to be doing," said Bevell. "I knew if we ran a certain route, Lee DeRamus might take an extra step. The communication was so much better."

A lot was riding on the Badgers' trip to West Lafayette. A sixth straight victory would give Wisconsin its first winning season since 1984, and the best start in eighty-one years. And it would continue a road winning streak, burying a negative that had haunted Alvarez since his arrival.

"We haven't won many games here period, let alone four straight on grass," Alvarez said of Wisconsin. "I'm not really much for those negative streaks. We're just building the program. They were negatives before we got here."

Early in the game, the entire Wisconsin bench held its breath after Moss was driven out of bounds near the Badgers' bench by a knifing blow by Purdue free safety Pat Johnson. Moss lay on the grass, trying to recover his lost senses as training staff whirled around him.

It was not the first time Moss had been knocked silly. His hat-on-a-hat running style invited occasional wallops that rendered him senseless and rubber-legged. A memorable one—at least for his teammates—came in a goal-line series in practice in which Moss was nailed by defensive back Jamel Brown. Bevell said Moss absorbed the hit, continued with the series, and went to the sideline after scoring a touchdown. Once there, he asked Bevell what just happened. "You scored a touchdown," Bevell said. Moss just nodded.

"You can't take him out of a game; he's just too tough. It is impossible," said Bevell.

Moss said the wicked tackle in the Purdue game helped spark his running once he was reinserted into the lineup. "It kind of woke me up. It was like, 'Hey, I'm ready to hit,'" Moss said.

It was the kind of tackle that Moss appreciated, a violent, brutally honest confrontation where there is a clear winner and loser. Later, after Moss ran for a touchdown, Johnson approached him.

"We met again by the goal line and he said, 'You brought it to *me* that time,'" Moss recalled. "That's the kind of game I like, where you get down and dirty."

Later, Bevell was hurt when his foot lodged in the rain-softened turf as he set up to throw and he was knocked backward by a Boilermakers defender. He stayed in for three more offensive series, but Alvarez and the training staff then decided Bevell should be examined at a hospital.

Bevell argued against going in the ambulance parked next to the field, but he was told it was the fastest way to get there, so he reluctantly clambered aboard. As Bevell sat in Purdue Hospital's emergency room getting treatment for his strained thigh muscle, in walked Purdue quarterback Matt Pike who was taken out with a shoulder injury. The two shook hands and wished each other luck.

"It must have been a tough day for number 11s," said Bevell, whose strained thigh muscle was of only momentary concern after he threw for 4 touchdowns before the injury.

After the gun, the 6-0 Badgers filed into Ross-Ade Stadium's concrete block visitors locker room. The 42–28 victory provided an emotional moment for players and coaches who had chased a winning season for so long.

Outside, reporters waited for access to the players and hooted at Jay Wilson, sports director at a Madison television station, who somehow was now in custody of the sledgehammer that Boilermaker Pete, Purdue's mascot, carries. Wilson, who tried vainly to find old Pete and return the waylaid sledge, gave up and slipped the hammer under some coats. A Purdue police officer who saw him tuck the tool away soon relieved Wilson of the trophy and restored Pete's image.

Inside the locker room, there was another trophy up for grabs. For the first time in nine years, Wisconsin had assured itself a winning season. Alvarez found himself surrounded by the hopeful, exuberant, and exhausted faces of winners for the first time in his tenure at Wisconsin.

Lamark Shackerford and Panos, the team captains, stepped forward to present Alvarez with the game ball. In a moment choked with emotion but free of flowery speeches, the Badgers beamed with pride.

And while much was made of Alvarez being presented with the game ball, few realized that Alvarez later returned the ball to Panos. Alvarez had savored the joys of coaching with some of the nation's most prolific winners, and although the 6–0 start was a monumental achievement, the coach believed Panos was the more fitting recipient of this trophy ball.

After his many years of grueling work on the football field, this was the first time Panos could call himself a winner and back it up with statistics. Despite his leadership and self-made ability, Panos had never experienced a winning season, not at Brookfield East High School and certainly not at Wisconsin.

"In the locker room, the guys were giving me crap about not coming from a very successful program," Panos said. "We gave the ball to coach because it was his first winning season, and he turned around and gave it to me because I've never been on a winner before. It felt great."

While he still had the team gathered in its locker-room sanctuary, Alvarez upped the ante. This was the first time that Alvarez felt he could say it out loud, although privately, with his team: The Badgers had a chance of going to the Rose Bowl.

"I said we were going for the brass ring," Alvarez recalled.

The reach for that ring got a bit longer the following week as the Badgers traveled to Minneapolis to play the University of Minnesota in the Hubert H. Humphrey Metrodome.

Preparations for the game against Jim Wacker's Golden Gophers started badly as Wisconsin's hotel reservations fell through in the days before the game and the team was shunted from a downtown hotel to one in suburban Bloomington.

Maybe it was an omen. Get out of town while you can.

The hype of the Badgers' fast start was tarnished in the first half against Minnesota. The Gophers ran to a 21–0 halftime lead as Wisconsin started sluggishly, especially on the offensive line.

As the roof fell in on the Badgers in the Metrodome, virtually no one noticed that Bill Callahan was nowhere to be seen along the sideline during the entire game. In the whole scheme of things, people usually do not stop to take an accounting of the whereabouts of the offensive line coach.

His absence, however, several weeks later ballooned into a major story that was to have profound consequences.

Callahan missed the game due to a one-game suspension meted out by the Big Ten after University of Illinois officials complained that Callahan was seen in their coaches' booth at Purdue's Ross-Ade Stadium three weeks earlier.

Sent to scout the Purdue-Illinois game in early October, Callahan was in the press box that day. An Illinois student manager told Head Coach Lou Tepper that she had discovered Callahan in the booth after the game. At every game, teams are allowed to have coaches watch the game from the press box from an enclosed booth connected by telephone to the sidelines. The booths usually are littered with playbooks and other game-planning and strategic documents. After games, coaches vacate their booths and return to the locker room, sometimes leaving behind material to be collected later.

So Callahan's presence in the booth raised the hackles of Illinois officials, who equated it with espionage. They fired off a complaint to Big Ten Commissioner James E. Delany, heightening the animosity between the two schools.

Richter felt that Illinois Athletic Director Ron Guenther or Tepper should have handled the matter personally, by contacting him instead of trotting off to the Big Ten.

Wisconsin officials tried to put a more benign face on the incident, indicating that all Callahan did was look at a depth chart posted on the wall in the booth. Some quietly indicated, however, that Callahan never should have put himself in such a compromising position.

Callahan, meanwhile, has repeatedly declined comment on the incident in hopes that it will die away.

Although Wisconsin officials took a low profile on the issue, the Monday before the game Tepper inflamed the situation with a little sermon. Speaking to reporters, he said he was willing to forgive Wisconsin.

That only inflamed matters, since Wisconsin officials felt there was nothing that called for Tepper's forgiveness.

Callahan's absence had a profound impact on the outcome of the Minnesota game, many players say. The sudden vacancy forced Alvarez to call on Running Backs Coach Jim Hueber to manage the offensive line as well. Along the sidelines, Hueber worked feverishly to keep both units working efficiently.

"I think it was a 14-point difference by not having him on the field," said Bevell. "The adjustments he can make are vital. Coach Hueber was coaching the line, taking care of his backs, and signaling plays in."

To Panos, Callahan's absence also was devastating. "It definitely hurt. We got screwed out of having the biggest part of our machine, Coach Callahan, help us out in that game. It hurt and we weren't ready for it," said Panos. "If coach was there, I think we would have gone undefeated."

Wisconsin's offense lacked the punch of past games and Bevell was struggling. Bevell and the line were under siege for much of the game, as the Gophers blitzed on almost every down and the offensive line struggled. That forced Bevell to make bad throws and he was intercepted 5 times, damaging the Badgers' ability to rally.

"It wasn't bad reads, it was bad throws," Bevell said. "I threw the ball well at times, but the interceptions killed us."

The Metrodome was bulging with college football fans that Saturday night. Typically, Minnesota draws about 36,000 fans for home games, but the heavy interest by Wisconsin fans resulted in a crowd of 64,798.

Bevell said the noise generated by the crowd made it difficult for the offense to hear signals. "The Metrodome is, by far, the hardest," he said. "Cory Raymer just could not hear me sometimes. I'm screaming and he's telling me to scream louder."

Despite the Wisconsin mistakes, the Badgers managed to move the ball in the second half and claw their way back into the game, but came up short, 28-21.

Alvarez refused to find any speck of hope, any lesson in the loss. "There's nothing good about losing," he said. "If you can't deal with adversity, then you're a loser."

The egg laid by the Badgers in the Metrodome instantly hatched into widespread skepticism by Wisconsin fans used to collapse and disappointment. Even though Wisconsin had its best start since 1912, the taste of failure was too fresh in many fans' mouths to believe the Badgers could overcome this loss.

The following Monday, Alvarez drove to Madison's west side for his weekly radio call-in show with WTSO's Matt LePay.

"A guy calls in and says, 'I'm a great Badgers fan, but people are saying you're going to lose your last five games,'" Alvarez said. "The guy hangs up and we go to a break and LePay says, 'That guy's not bullshitting. Everybody's saying that.' I said, 'We'll find out.'"

9

Michigan's Past, Wisconsin's Future

T he less said, the better.

As Wisconsin prepared to play the University of Michigan, the previous week's loss to Minnesota was almost a forbidden topic. At Sunday's team meeting, coaches clinically reviewed the film with players, then dropped the subject.

It was intended to be a signal to the team and the staff's reasoning was clear. Players knew they had given up the chance of an undefeated season in the mistake-riddled game and it would do little good—and could possibly harm the team's chemistry—to rub their noses in it. Besides, coaches knew that players were being hard enough on themselves about dropping to 6–1.

"The coaches did not mention the Minnesota game again. Ever. They structured practice the same. They didn't try to change anything, whether they were superstitious or whatever. Everything was the same. That told us they kept faith in us and we had to keep faith in them," said Scott Nelson.

The mood was somber at the meeting, but curiously focused and intense. That feeling of resignation, that here-we-go-again helplessness common in previous years, was supplanted with a renewed dedication. The fire was there and that buoyed both players and coaches.

"People had that look in their eye, not mad, but dedicated. We knew it was going to be a war and if we weren't ready, we knew we'd get our butts spanked," Nelson said. "It was the first time all year we'd had that losing feeling that was so much a part of this team in the past and guys were really down, but they weren't ready to give up this time."

Michigan's season had come apart at the seams, with chances for the Big Ten's first national championship since Ohio State's 1968 title hopelessly lost as the Wolverines lost 27–23 to Notre Dame; 17–7 to Michigan State; and 24–21 to Illinois the week before the Wisconsin game. The defending Big Ten champions had shocked even themselves.

"They thought they'd walk through the Big Ten this year with the talent they had, and maybe even compete for a national title. They lost a couple games they weren't supposed to lose and the week before we played them, they lost to Illinois on a last-second touchdown," said Nelson. "They were a little confused."

Apart from that, Michigan was banged up. Tailback Tyrone Wheatley, who had dueled with Brent Moss to become the Big Ten's leading rusher, was out of commission with injuries to his groin and shoulder. He was replaced by Ricky Powers. In a way, Moss was disappointed because he had viewed it as a chance to outshine the more publicized Wheatley.

Overall, though, Wheatley's injury was a boon to the Badgers. Not only did they get to play Michigan at home, but the Wolverines were off-balance and without a player touted before the season as a Heisman Trophy candidate.

One thing Alvarez had sold to his players all along was not to be cowed by tradition. The message seemed to be seeping in as Wisconsin prepared for the game. Players talked about not being intimidated by Michigan's past and making the game one of the moment, not one from the history books.

"We weren't playing Desmond Howard and Bo Schembechler. They were all gone," Darrell Bevell said. "It was important for us to remember we were setting our own tradition as well."

That was a key element of their attitude since Wisconsin's record against Michigan was one of humiliation. In a series that dated to 1892, the Badgers had posted an 8–41–1 record against Michigan. Going into the game, the Badgers had defeated the Wolverines just once (21–14 in 1981 at Madison) in 24 meetings since 1965.

This week, though, the tables were turned. For the first time in memory, Wisconsin was more highly ranked than Michigan, with the Badgers twenty-first and the Wolverines twenty-fourth. Conventional wisdom said the game would reveal whether the Badgers were worthy of all the attention after sailing through what many considered a soft schedule in their first seven games.

"We knew that if we did exactly as the coaches told us all week and not worry about the Minnesota game, we could take advantage of them," said Nelson. "We knew we had to play our best football of the year."

The Minnesota loss took some of the luster off of this game for the national media, who had flooded Steve Malchow's office with requests for credentials. After Wisconsin fell to lowly Minnesota, a fair number of those writers canceled their plans to come to Madison, taking a wait-and-see approach.

The first spectators into Camp Randall were the students, who jammed the section near the closed end of the horseshoe about an hour before game time. The early-arriving students crowded into the aisles and prepared to toss marshmallows at the Wolverines as they exited the visitors tunnel. All of the elements for a classic Big Ten clash were converging.

Celebrities du jour were Donna Shalala (who had departed earlier in the year to join the Clinton administration) and then-Defense Secretary Les Aspin. Shalala joked that it was the first time in the history of the world that two cabinet secretaries had attended a Badgers game.

Just the week before, President Clinton had remarked at a cabinet luncheon, "Donna's the only one here going to a bowl game," referring to Wisconsin's rising fortunes.

"There were a lot of dull looks at the table," said Shalala, who had arranged a speaking trip to Madison to coincide with the Michigan game. "They aren't a lot of football fans."

Just before the start of the game, the Wolverines infuriated Badgers players by huddling at midfield, on Camp Randall's red-and-white "W." Most Wisconsin players saw the action as a sign of disrespect that transcended simple trash talk.

"I didn't think we got any respect from Michigan," said Bevell. "It made a lot of guys upset. They come into our field, our house, and circle up on our 'W.' You don't do that at Wisconsin anymore. In the past, we might have laid down our hats and let them. We weren't going to do that. We were going to knock them in the mouth."

Lamark Shackerford also rapped the Wolverines for their theatrics, saying Michigan picked a poor way to try to intimidate the Badgers. In fact, he said, the stunt backfired: "If any team comes in and thinks they can call it up on our 'W' in the middle of the field and thinks we're scared of them. . . . I'd rather take the respect at the end of the game."

Respect was a delicate issue for the Badgers all season. Perhaps it had to do with shaking off the insecurity complexes of the past. The theme that emerged as the season drew on was: we don't get no respect. The Badgers used the theme to their benefit. Instead of simply whining about the lack of respect, they attained it methodically, game by game.

Cornerback Jeff Messenger was one of the Badgers' players who, coming into 1993, had received little respect. As a sophomore, his strong-side coverage tended to be soft and the media was not kind to the Marinette native who was one of Alvarez's first recruits.

This season, however, the Badgers put junior college transfer Kenny Gales on the wide side of the field. Gales, whose speed was superior to Messenger's, generally was responsible for covering the opponent's best receiver.

Messenger was shuttled to the weak side and faced split ends whose speed was more comparable to his own. Still, the soft-spoken Messenger felt he had something to prove in 1993, after his subpar performance was panned by sportswriters the previous season.

In the 1993 season, Messenger saw a chance to redeem himself. "I felt like I had something to prove, not just to everyone else, but to myself," he said. "I wanted to show I could bounce back from taking the criticism and put it in the positive and make myself a better player."

Throughout 1992, Messenger dreaded reading the Sunday sports section. His lapses in coverage often were highlighted and the season wore on him mentally.

"It's hard to take when people doubt your abilities, especially when you're giving all you can give," he said. "I went out there and busted my butt every weekend last season and I was in the paper every weekend because they'd find something I screwed up."

The criticism, though, forced Messenger to examine both his priorities and his play. That's something he said helped him to improve during the 1993 season, during which he led the Big Ten with 7 interceptions and led the Badgers with 6 passes broken up.

"I remember who said stuff, but there are a lot of things you just have to block out of your memory and go on," he said. "What is really important is how you feel about yourself and how the coaches feel about you."

This week, the coaching staff needed to rely on the secondary to make big plays. With Wheatley out, it was felt that Michigan quarterback Todd Collins would go to the air more often to exploit talented receivers such as Derrick Alexander and Mercury Hayes.

Michigan's offensive line was also a pressure point for Wisconsin. Although the Wolverines had been known for their line strength in years past, Coach Gary Moeller was depending heavily on inexperience in 1993.

After 1992, in which the Wolverines generated the most potent offense in the program's history, Moeller knew youth, especially on the offensive line, could dampen Collins's efficiency. He was right.

"I'm really concerned that we don't have the leadership up front," said Moeller. "We have to get better at controlling the ball for amounts of time. In fairness, we're young, but we're not where we should be at this point."

The Wolverines' lack of strength on the line gave Wisconsin another tangible reason to set aside Michigan's daunting tradition as the game approached. After kickoff, Wisconsin's defensive linemen got a feel for how raw the Michigan front was. Along the sidelines, confidence mounted.

"The feeling was: They had a tradition and they were resting on it. They were just guys. We weren't playing the Michigan tradition, we were playing the guys on the field," said Carlos Fowler.

As the game wore on, Fowler said that Michigan's offensive line started to crack. That was reflected in their inability to generate a rushing attack. At halftime, Michigan had 10 yards rushing on 8 carries and Wisconsin had 131 yards on 30 carries.

"They were a little easier because they were young guys," Fowler said. "These guys didn't put us in awe. They were a bunch of guys wearing blue and maize. If anyone was an awesome group, we were."

That's where Rick Schnetzky's improbable dream started to be played out.

A former prep soccer player who had never played football, Schnetzky came to the UW hoping to try out for the ice hockey team. But Wisconsin discontinued the junior varsity program and Schnetzky dropped out of competitive athletics for a year.

Then, while watching NFL games over Thanksgiving weekend in 1992, a pair of missed chip-shot field goals got Schnetzky thinking about football. "Dad looked at me and said, 'Hey, why don't you kick field goals?'" Schnetzky said.

Shortly afterward, he began a shrewd campaign to get noticed by the Badgers' coaching staff. Through trial and error, he found out when coaches took their daily jog in the McClain Facility and timed his kicking workouts so Alvarez and his assistants might notice.

"Hey, whatever it takes," Schnetzky said. "It felt natural, and I kept plugging away."

He went to Jim Bakken, the former St. Louis Cardinals kicker who now worked in community relations at the Athletic Department, for critiques and help in lobbying Alvarez.

Finally, Schnetzky was allowed to walk on with the Badgers and settled in as a backup to scholarship kicker John Hall. But Hall's season was rocky, as he missed 5 of his first 6 field-goal attempts, and Schnetzky started looking more appealing to Alvarez.

Schnetzky's first game experience was in the Northwestern rout, and only after the game was well under control did he come in to kick the last of Wisconsin's 53 points. That's why it came as a shock to Schnetzky when Alvarez pulled him aside the Thursday before the Michigan game and told him he would be the Badgers' field-goal kicker on attempts of less than 35 yards.

Although he had lobbied Special Teams Coach Jay Norvell for the chance to start, Schnetzky did not believe he would be put in for such a meaningful game. He leaped at the chance. Hall and his stronger leg, meanwhile, were relegated to kickoffs and long field-goal attempts.

Schnetzky was such a new commodity that Alvarez could not recall his first name during a briefing with ESPN announcers the day before the game. Whatever his first name, Alvarez liked Schnetzky's swing and his pluck. And with Hall's lackluster track record, the Badgers had little to lose in the experiment.

Before the game, Alvarez tried to reassure Schnetzky. "I told him he was going to have such a great day that they were going to build a statue of him in his hometown," Alvarez said.

By game time, Schnetzky (hometown: Mequon) was in a zone. Not un-
nerved, not squeamish. Just focused and intense.

"It doesn't matter if you're kicking in front of one person or 100,000
people. It's the same swing. A lot of people compare it to golf," he said. "If it
came down to 3 points, I felt I was ready to do what had to be done."

What had to be done came quickly for Schnetzky. The Badgers' first
possession went for 16 plays and consumed more than 8 minutes, but on third
and 4 at the Michigan 7-yard line Bevell's pass was tipped and fell incomplete.

Schnetzky trotted on and nailed his first collegiate field-goal attempt, a
25-yarder that put Wisconsin ahead 3–0.

The Badgers again went into a ball-control mode to start the second quarter. But after a nearly 10-minute drive that covered 83 yards, Wisconsin found
itself in much the same position. Bevell had overthrown Lee DeRamus in the
end zone on third down and Schnetzky came on again, this time making a
26-yarder as Wisconsin took a 6–0 lead.

Michigan's first significant drive of the game was fueled by Collins's 54-yard
pass to receiver Amari Toomer, who was ridden out of bounds by Nelson at
the Wisconsin 7-yard line. Four plays later, the Wolverines settled for a 22-yard
field goal by Peter Elezovic.

But Wisconsin's offense again responded, this time with a drive that ended
in a 12-yard touchdown run with just 38 seconds to play in the half. And there
was Schnetzky, hammering home the extra point.

The Badgers headed for the locker room at halftime with a gaping edge in
possession time of nearly 10 minutes. That was a crucial element of the game,
since the offense's dominance kept the defense rested for the second half.

That would pay dividends for the Badgers as the Wolverines' offense
showed signs of returning from the dead.

The Wolverines scored their first touchdown in the third quarter, as Collins
connected with Alexander on a 7-yard scoring pass that narrowed the Badgers'
lead to 13–10.

Even though the Badgers lacked the offensive punch they delivered in the
first half, Alvarez's rested defense helped pick up the slack. "In the second
half, they responded time and time again. They got big plays," he said.

The biggest came as the Wolverines were driving at the Wisconsin 32 with
10:57 left in the game. Collins, facing a stiff outside rush from his left by
linebacker Chris Hein, threw for Alexander along the left sideline.

Messenger looked back, timed his leap, and pulled the ball away from
Alexander at the Wisconsin 9-yard line and returned it 8 yards. Alvarez said
Messenger's timing was perfect, though it appeared from the sidelines that he
may have interfered with Alexander. Officials ruled it a clean play.

"When I saw the ball was high in the air, I was kind of worried about what
he was going to do, so I tried to get a little bit of my body on him, so I could

turn into him," Messenger said. "There was a little bit of contact, but we were both looking for the ball, so they weren't going to call it."

Another monstrous defensive play came on Michigan's next possession. With Michigan on the Wisconsin 28 with 5:14 left, Collins had to come up with 8 yards on fourth down. He dropped back, spotted receiver Walter Smith, and completed the pass, but an onrushing Hein stopped Smith for a 7-yard gain as the Wolverines sacrificed the ball on downs.

That allowed Wisconsin to run out the clock, with the game ending as Bevell dropped to one knee at the Michigan 20 as exultant Wisconsin fans prepared for the traditional Fifth Quarter band concert.

"You think of the people who said we were never going to do it, and watching the clock run down it was an incredible feeling knowing we'd knocked the champions out," said Bevell. "Here we were: a team from Wisconsin that nobody thought could play with the big boys."

Messenger's interception teamed him with Schnetzky as the two vindicated heroes in a game of monumental importance for Alvarez's surging program.

So Schnetzky, whose name the coach could not recall and who shared a jersey number, 98, with linebacker Yusef Burgess, left the field that day with more than half of the Badgers' scoring output.

"I'm just glad the coaching staff had the confidence in me and let me do my job," said Schnetzky, whom public address announcers at Minnesota confused with Burgess.

Schnetzky never did ask for his own jersey number. "I'm happy with 98; that's just fine."

Messenger, meanwhile, said the victory set the stage for the remainder of the season and cemented the Badgers as a national power. "People were giving us all this stuff about how we couldn't win the big game. We were 6–1 and didn't feel like we got much respect," said Messenger.

It was another game that supported Alvarez's conviction that these Badgers were resilient and dedicated to maintaining the standards set early in the season. They had proven that the Minnesota game was the fluke, not the victory over Michigan.

"We were not a peak-and-valley team," said Alvarez. "This was a team that believed in themselves. They believed in the plan we gave them. Regardless of the doubters, regardless of whether they were underdogs or favorites, regardless of what people said or what they had to overcome."

The Wolverines left the game deflated and searching for a remedy to their flat offensive play and lack of emotion.

"After the Wisconsin game, we were really down," said Michigan tight end Marc Burkholder. "We knew we could play football better than what we were showing. So it was just a lot of frustration and built-up emotion. We really wanted to show, and continue to show, that we are a good team."

Just three weeks later, the Wolverines would prove how tough they were, to the delight of Wisconsin fans everywhere. For the moment, though, Michigan was beaten, and the Badgers were in heaven.

Hell waited in the north end zone.

10

Heroes in Hell

Mike Brin was one of the first Wisconsin football players to sweep into that hell.

A walk-on receiver, his name was barely known to sportswriters who covered the program daily, much less by fans. By week's end, however, Brin would be known nationally as a selfless hero in the face of a major disaster.

Following the victory over Michigan, chaos cast a riotous shadow across the sometimes-rowdy, 12,500-seat student section at Camp Randall Stadium. As if someone had yanked the stopper out of a giant sink, the students gushed downward in a terrifying rush toward the end zone. Their motives were clear: to celebrate, preferably from the goalposts, one of the most historic victories in the program's history.

The result of their advance, however, was a frightening, incongruous, and tortured scene that ended with dozens hospitalized after a stampede toward the AstroTurf and the virtually indestructible goalposts. People climbed over people, while fans were lifted from the stands and carried yards away. It was a ghastly picture of uncontrollable dimensions, an unthinkable but ever-mounting price to pay to dance the polka on the 20-yard line.

The consequences of the rush weren't always clear to other students who were whooping and dancing for joy yards from where fans lay breathless and crushed in a steadily growing pile of revelers who had collapsed the stadium fence.

What had been a golden moment for Badgers football was, within seconds, wrenchingly transformed into a major disaster requiring emergency medical teams from eight Madison-area communities. In all, sixty-nine people were hospitalized, four in critical condition.

Videotapes of the onrushing students show a wildly out-of-control crowd. Within seconds, the top third of the stadium bleachers had emptied as the rush began. Because the student section is in a corner of the closed end of the horseshoe-shaped stadium, the rush was like pouring water through a funnel. Trouble was, the funnel was plugged.

The student section aisles began to clog up at about 2:26 p.m. Fifteen minutes later fans in the upper parts of the stands began a forceful push toward the field as many of the 77,745 people in the sold-out stadium counted down the final seconds. Along with the countdown came these chants in the student section: "Rush the field," "Take the field," and "Storm the field."

Almost simultaneously, a cast-iron safety fence in Section Q collapsed under the force of the crowd. Just before the game ended, isolated students were seen leaping the fence past UW police officers and heading for the field and the north goalposts. They dodged through band members and sports reporters.

Police and most members of the crowd seemed unaware of the fence's collapse and the injuries it caused. Other sections also gave way under the mounting pressure of the exultant students, compounding problems. Two police officers reported seeing the damage from the compacted crowd only after the chain link fence surrounding the field had given way to the pressure.

Although dozens of students poured onto the field, others were helpless, some turning blue from a lack of oxygen.

Just after 2:41, the Wolverines began to file off the field through the visitors tunnel with extra police protection because a player had been cut during pre-game warmups by a coin-filled marshmallow hurled from the stands.

UW Police Detective David Williams was one of many officers trying to secure the tunnel that Michigan used to enter and leave the field. One unidentified fan squirted mustard through a mesh grid protecting the tunnel area and onto several Michigan players and coaches.

At halftime, one Michigan assistant coach sustained a minor cut as a fan tried to snatch his clipboard as the team left the field, police reports show.

After the Wolverines had left the stadium following the game, police attempted to open the walkway gates to allow students through, but the pressure on the gates and adjacent chain link fencing was too great and both the fence and the gate collapsed.

According to UW Police Chief Susan Riseling, the rush became uncontrollable for officers in the stadium. Some students interviewed by UW police in the days after the surge said they were lifted off their feet and carried at least twenty rows by the force of the exuberant crowd.

Then, just before 2:43 p.m., Riseling gave a "Code 1000" order for police to pull away from the perimeter of the field. She also asked stadium announcer Jack Rane to plead with students to disperse. Rane warned the crowd that there were "pulseless non-breathers" in the pile and beseeched students to pull back so emergency crews could work. By this time, some officers had begun to rescue students trapped beneath the pile. In another minute, more

No field mouse, Alvarez assumes a pit-bull stance as he barks orders to his 1993 Badgers. He's flanked by two longtime pals who followed him to Wisconsin from the University of Iowa, tight end coach and master recruiter Bernie Wyatt, left, and defensive coordinator Dan McCarney, right. At far right, wearing the headset is offensive line coach Bill Callahan.

The season started brightly for the Badgers as they dominated the University of Nevada 35–17. Part of the reason was harassment administered by Wisconsin outside linebacker Bryan Jurewicz and the rest of the Badgers defense to Wolf Pack quarterback Chris Vargas.

Senior free safety Scott Nelson picked off a pass by Nevada quarterback Chris Vargas and returned it 44 yards. It set up a failed 37-yard field goal attempt by Badgers kicker John Hall, a sign of more troubles ahead for the first-year kicker.

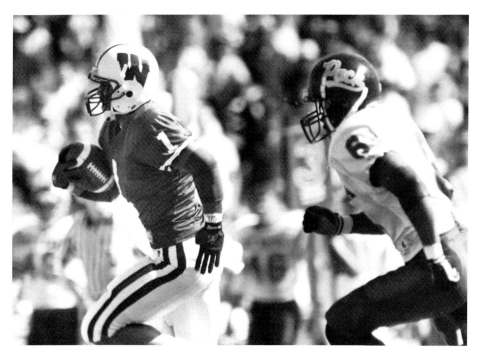

Dawkins kept Nevada's young secondary scrambling to catch up as he caught three balls for 85 yards and two touchdowns. For the day, Badgers quarterback Darrell Bevell had five touchdown passes, as he set a school record.

Wisconsin quarterback Darrell Bevell, after a rocky start in 1992, was third nationally in passing efficiency and became the first UW quarterback since Ron Vanderkelen in 1963 to win all-conference distinction.

A linchpin of the Badgers offense
was the sure-handed performance
of tight end Mike Roan, an Iowa
City native. Although Alvarez's
arrival at Wisconsin signalled a
halt to the University of Iowa's raid
on top Dairy State prep talent,
Wisconsin pulled Roan out of Iowa
coach Hayden Fry's backyard.
(BILL OLMSTED)

Vision was a key to Bevell's
improvement at quarterback in the
drive for the Rose Bowl. In his first
year at Wisconsin, he was more
concerned with watching onrushing
linebackers than reading coverage.
(BILL OLMSTED)

As a junior, split end Lee DeRamus broke the school record with 920 yards receiving set by Al Toon a decade earlier. For his career, the New Jersey native is second on the list behind Toon and is on pace to break the record as a senior. (BILL OLMSTED)

An unknown in the Badgers' defensive mix before the season was inside linebacker Eric Unverzagt (47) who stepped in for the first time as a starter. His three top games came against the Badgers' best-rated opponents. Here, he jolts the Iowa State option game with a tackle. (BILL OLMSTED)

Lamark Shackerford waited by his mailbox after his high school career for a Division I scholarship offer that did not come until late June. By his senior season, the noseguard was a first-team all-Big Ten choice who finished his career with 27 tackles for loss.

Wisconsin players rush to congratulate Dawkins after he caught a 25-yard touchdown pass from Bevell to put Wisconsin ahead 17–16 at Southern Methodist with 6:28 to play. The Badgers went on to win 24–16, logging their first non-conference road victory since 1985. (THE MILWAUKEE SENTINEL)

In his first season as a starter, flanker J. C. Dawkins built a solid reputation as a possession receiver with enough speed to break some big plays. The high school teammate of tailback Brent Moss, Dawkins finished the season with 508 yards receiving and four touchdowns.

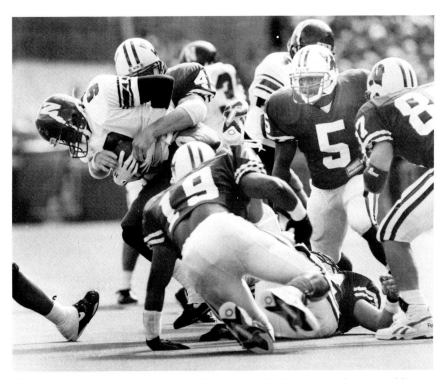

Wisconsin's homecoming proved to be a headache for Northwestern as the gang-tackling Badgers rolled to a 53–14 victory.

The Badgers came into the Northwestern game hoping to exact revenge for their narrow loss at Dyche Stadium in 1992. Tailback Terrell Fletcher helped rub salt in the wound by rushing for three touchdowns.

Badgers senior fullback Mark Montgomery scores on an 8-yard run during Wisconsin's rout of Northwestern. Known as a strong blocking back, Montgomery was drafted in the seventh round by the Philadelphia Eagles.

UW defensive tackle Mike Thompson swoops in for one of his five sacks against the Wildcats. It was a game that marked his full recovery from injuries that nagged him earlier in the season.

Hard-hitting Wisconsin tailback Brent Moss exploded on the college football scene in 1993, rushing for a school-record 1,637 yards and scoring 16 touchdowns. Moss's aggressive running style resulted in a string of 11 games in which he gained 100 or more yards. He entered the 1994 season being prominently mentioned as a contender for the Heisman Trophy.

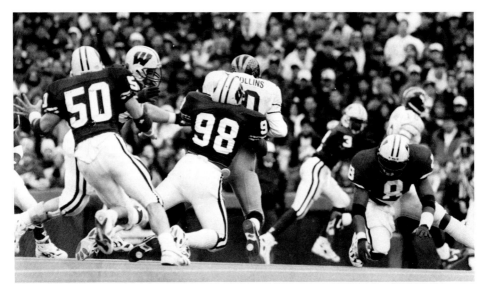

Defensive pressure helped the Badgers notch their first victory over Michigan in 12 years, a 13–10 nail biter. Here, linebacker Yusef Burgess brings down Wolverines' quarterback Todd Collins. Pressure like this helped stave off a Michigan drive late in the game and preserved the victory.

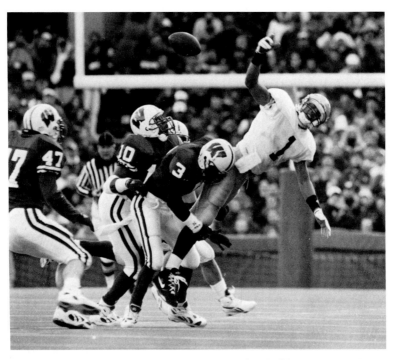

Michigan receiver Derrick Alexander draws a crowd in the Wisconsin secondary, as Badgers' cornerback Kenny Gales (3) makes a tackle with the help of strong safety Reggie Holt (10).

Fullback Mark Montgomery struggles to gain yardage on fourth down as he is driven out of bounds by a Michigan defender.

The wave of students that surged from the stands in the north end zone after the Michigan game resulted in a bizarre scene mixing horror with dizzying, claustrophobic, and perilous celebration that left some unable to breathe, crushed by the crowd.

Fans and paramedics administer aid to one of the dozens of fans who were injured following the crowd surge.

Thompson exhorts the capacity crowd at Camp Randall Stadium after the Badgers stop an Ohio State drive late in the game. (AL HOCH)

Hard-headed football was the hallmark of the Ohio State tie, which helped propel the Badgers to Pasadena and sink the Buckeyes' Rose Bowl hopes. (AL HOCH)

Sharing time with Moss at tailback, Fletcher was hounded by the thought he could do better. A devilishly fast outside runner, Fletcher's perturbation was compounded when he missed the 1,000-yard plateau by four yards. (AL HOCH)

Many eyes were trained on senior inside linebacker Yusef Burgess (98) as the 1993 season got under way. Despite never having been a regular starter, Burgess emerged from obscurity and finished the season as the Badgers' top tackler and led the Big Ten with five fumbles caused in the regular season.

Matt Nyquist proved to be one of the Badgers' most versatile players, starting at fullback and moving to tight end. As a second tight end, Nyquist scored touch-downs on four of 10 catches in 1993. (AL HOCH)

Fletcher's recruitment to Wisconsin after a top-notch prep career in Missouri helped Alvarez and his staff break an early recruiting logjam and press ahead to become one of the top recruiting staffs in the nation. (THE MILWAUKEE JOURNAL)

The celebration begins along the Wisconsin sideline in the waning moments of Wisconsin's 41–20 victory over Michigan State in Tokyo. The triumph at the Tokyo Dome assured Wisconsin's return to Pasadena for the first time since 1963. (THE MILWAUKEE SENTINEL)

Wisconsin turned the tables on the Bruins, who entered the game with the nation's best turnover margin. During the game, the Badgers forced UCLA into six turnovers including this fumble by receiver J. J. Stokes which was recovered by Shackerford (62). (THE MILWAUKEE SENTINEL)

Following his stunning and pivotal 21-yard touchdown run, Bevell is hoisted aloft by gleeful offensive lineman Joe Panos at the Rose Bowl. (THE MILWAUKEE JOURNAL)

fencing tumbled, more students were injured, and mutual aid calls for ambulances from eight neighboring communities went out.

A countywide disaster plan went into effect and ambulances cycled in and out of the stadium quickly, with about eight on the field at any time. Paramedics huddled over the injured and conducted triage on the field. Madison's hospitals—University, Meriter, and St. Mary's—beefed up staffing, asking off-duty medical personnel to report for work.

The Badgers' training staff, led by Dennis Helwig, virtualy emptied their state-of-the-art training room of backboards, tape, bandages, and other medical supplies to aid the injured. The training staff helped to treat victims on the field as well.

From on the playing field, the scene was staggering, as the piles grew taller and screams of people trapped below were muffled but harrowing. Some were trapped below the railings and chain link fencing, which worsened their injuries. As the surge continued, it appeared from field level that the fans in the student section were slowly rocking back and forth as if they would all tumble from the stands.

Seeing this, some reporters and players fought through crowds and up the tunnel to safety. As the surge worsened, fans continued to hang over the walls of the tunnel to slap high-fives with anyone passing by.

Students continued their downward thrust, climbing over one another in an effort at first aimed at getting to the field, but later designed to save their own lives.

Police waved frantically for spectators to draw back from the pile, but the surge of seventy rows of victory-crazed spectators continued. Delirious fans who made it past officers onto the field weaved between members of the UW Marching Band, who were preparing to take the field for the Fifth Quarter, the traditional postgame concert that wouldn't take place this day.

An elated Brin was leaving the field with his teammates when he noticed the scene and acted purely on instinct, plunging into the crowd to help victims. It was part fate and part dreams that put him there that Saturday afternoon.

As a quarterback at Highland Park High School in suburban Chicago, Brin was recruited by a few Ivy League schools, notably Princeton. But the interest cooled after he injured his knee his senior year. Brin had a choice to make: give up football or try walking on with a Division I program. "I figured if I wasn't going to be a star, I might as well play out a dream and play on a Big Ten team," he said.

The Badgers' coaching staff encouraged his interest and worked him out for a season at quarterback before shifting him to wide receiver in 1993, a position where they felt he might be able to contribute. His biggest contribution, however, didn't come on the field. In fact, he didn't play a single down in 1993.

His impact came as he walked off the field, dizzied with the joy of having defeated the Wolverines. But the joy was soon to fade for Brin and other Badgers players. Brin, a pre-med student, had learned mouth to mouth resuscitation from his brother, Keith, a lifeguard, and was soon called upon to use his skills.

Brin noticed the crisis as he approached the tunnel the Badgers use to leave the stadium. The crush of fans was straining the chain link fence that security personnel use to provide access to the tunnel. Sophomore Aimee Jansen was pinned against the fence, her feet off the ground, and had difficulty breathing.

"We were going up the tunnel and I was with Brent Moss and John Hall and we saw Aimee Jansen bent over a fence and people yelling for paramedics," said Brin. "Once I saw Aimee, it hit me what was happening."

Brin reached over the fence, grabbed the woman by the leg, and pulled her over the fence. He dragged her a short way up the asphalt-floored tunnel and made sure she was breathing and conscious.

Jansen was seated in the lower rows near the tunnel when the surge started. The advance pulled her friends to the right as she was carried to the left.

"People started to yell 'Storm the field!' and that's when the push came. I didn't hit the fence right away, but when I did, my breath was going and things were getting fuzzy," she said. "I remember looking at people and hearing them scream. I remember someone yelling, 'She can't breathe!' Then I reached out and grabbed his jersey, number 3. I was just trying to take small breaths and keep the oxygen flowing."

After Brin pulled her clear of the crowd and into the tunnel, Jansen said she headed, bewildered, to the field to try to escape the crowds. Later, she and a friend went to a hospital to visit a friend who was injured in the rush and to have bruises on her legs and right arm examined.

Jansen still has trouble being in crowds, though she joined a group of friends for a bus trip to the Rose Bowl and said she had no fears of the crowd there.

After he helped Jansen, Brin leaped over the tunnel's concrete wall and began to aid others. Nearby, he spotted two women on top of each other, both unconscious and turning blue. One was Sari Weinstein and the other is still unknown to Brin.

"After I gave mouth to mouth to the one girl, a paramedic helped stabilize her and I went over to help Sari out. At one point, she started to swallow her tongue and I tried to keep her breathing," said Brin. "I was in shock. You don't see things like this outside the movies."

The scene seemed surreal as he struggled to keep the women alive. After Brin started to work on Weinstein, he was confronted by the anomalous, inexplicable behavior of the crowd. Fans continued to push down from the bleachers all around him, though not with the same volume or vigor.

"They were running by, telling me, 'Congratulations, great game!' and I'm sitting there with a girl who was half dead," Brin said.

UW police officers at the scene reported the same sort of grotesque behavior. Riseling said one of her officers had fans steal his hat and badge as he tried to keep count of compressions while administering CPR. Another officer giving CPR was suddenly ringed by people dancing the polka.

Police Officer Steven Rogers watched as the crowd swelled and finally collapsed the chain link fence separating fans and field. "For a very short period of time, we tried to order them back. Then, the crowd became completely unmanageable and many members of the crowd began leaping and climbing the fence," he said.

The fury of the churning throng was an imposing sight for officers who tried to maintain some sense of order. Madison Police Officer Tara Dommershausen surveyed the crowd from inside the fence in front of Section O. "As I looked up at the stands, I noticed that bodies were wall-to-wall and that there was a swaying movement in the crowd," she said.

Her yelling and pleading with students to back off did no good. As she stood about four feet away from the fence, it gave way. As she started to pull students free of the mounting pile, she said the students were stacked six deep.

"I was continually yelling at people to stop pushing and that they were hurting people. The crowd would not stop pushing as people were continually going down under pressure from behind," Dommershausen said. "It appeared that students did not care about their friends or fellow students and the most important thing to them was getting onto the football field."

The advancing crowd forced her to keep backing up, until she was near where members of the marching band were witnessing the melee on the turf inside the fence and north of the end zone.

A saxophone player was looking for help with nose and mouth cuts he sustained when he was punched by an onrushing fan as he prepared to play. And other members of the band were shaken by the scene unfolding before them.

"I ended up with my back directly to the UW band and had band members coming up to me crying and telling me to keep the crowd away from them," Dommershausen said.

She had the musicians huddle together around their instruments to protect themselves and their property. Then she turned to find a male student carrying a woman who was purple and not breathing. After Dommershausen started chest compressions, an off-duty physician took over the CPR effort.

As emergency crews began to take command of the situation, Badgers players filtered—dazed, horrified, some in tears—back to the locker room. "It was a helpless feeling in the locker room. I think everyone felt empty and confused. You saw all the people who were helpless and you felt the same way. It was disbelief," said Brin.

Backup center Brian Patterson and offensive linemen Joe Panos and Joe Rudolph also plunged into the sea of humanity, pleading with fans to step back and pulling the injured from the heaps of students and lifting them to safety. Panos cried as he pulled the injured from the stack. Those hurt tended to be women, who were less likely to be able to resist the forceful rush.

"We were pulling dead weight out of there, pretty much. There was a lot of people unconscious and passed out. When Joe pulled them out, me and Rudy passed them over the gate," said Patterson. "One girl . . . was laying on the ground with blood coming out of the corner of her mouth. I've never seen anything like it before in my life. There has to be something done to prevent it.

"There were probably twenty people stacked up where I was. The sad thing about it is only the strong survive in a situation like that. It was mostly girls on the bottom of the pile, because everyone else was strong enough to get out."

Most of the Badgers players were unaware of the tragedy unfolding in the stadium when they appeared for postgame interviews in the weight room of the McClain Facility. In fact, Alvarez was in the dark about the events in the stadium until he was leaving the locker room to join his wife, Cindy.

"I've got a daughter who was sitting in the second row of the student section, and as soon as my wife and I found out as we were leaving, she said, 'I wonder how Stacy is?'" Alvarez said. "I said, 'Don't worry about Stacy, she was on my back at midfield.' All I could think about that night were the students in the hospital."

Patterson said the jubilation of the victory lasted only seconds as players helped the injured in the north end zone. "It wasn't too much of a high left when we got back to the locker room," said Patterson grimly.

Panos was shaken afterward, sullen in his disbelief. "The win means nothing," said the lumbering but pensive lineman. "I'd give up that win in a second if it saved someone's life."

In its aftermath, the destruction was the petrifying testament to the ferocity of a mob. The two-inch welded iron pipes that made up the safety railing were ripped from their concrete moorings and twisted beyond recognition. Yards of chain link fence were down in that corner of the stadium and Richter stood, stunned and ashen, next to an ambulance as one of the last victims was ministered to on the field nearby.

"It's a tragic scene. It just started at the top and tumbled down, and just basically collapsed the fences. It was just a mass of people coming down and nothing could stop that momentum," he said. "Nothing."

Brin showered, dressed, and went back to his apartment on Regent Street, two blocks away. All night he struggled with his emotions and the indelible pictures of agony that kept running through his head.

"That night, I was depressed. We had just beaten Michigan and everyone was so happy. Then it just disappeared and it was all so serious and sad. You went from feeling so happy to feeling nothing at all," he said. "Rumors were floating around that one of the girls had died. I didn't know if it was one of the girls I helped out. If it was, there were images in my mind that were just haunting me."

Throughout the coming week, Brin tried to forget the incident. That was a challenge, since reporters from all over the nation were hounding him for interviews. The reserve player who had not been interviewed about anything since high school was suddenly a hot commodity.

"It was annoying. I'd wake up every night sweating, having nightmares about it. I didn't want to deal with it. I didn't want to talk about it. Yet, every night I'd get calls from reporters," said Brin. "I wish the press didn't make such a big deal of it, because I didn't do it for the press."

An earnest kid who rooms with reserve lineman Al Gay, Brin had labored hard to get on the field. He prefers talking about the team.

Yet Brin could not outrun the personal fame being foisted on him. By Wednesday, *People* magazine gathered Weinstein and her parents and Jansen for a photo shoot at the stadium. "It was a strange feeling, and there were a few tears, but it was relief to see them and to see that they were doing all right."

And on Friday, Brin was named person of the week by Peter Jennings on ABC's nightly news. In mid-December, Brin and Jansen were flown to Los Angeles to appear on the "Vicki" show, with talk-show host Vicki Lawrence. During the show, Lawrence jokingly called Brin "luscious lips," a reference that continues to haunt him among teammates.

All the attention had Brin feeling sheepish. "The last time a reporter asked me a question, I was in high school. Now I'm in college, playing at Wisconsin, and I'm getting interviewed for what happened after the game, not during it," he said.

Although empty liquor bottles littered the stands, UW officials downplayed the contribution drunkenness might have made to the tragedy. In recent years, the university has made a concerted effort to stem alcohol consumption in the stands and extracted marked cooperation from students.

According to Dean of Students Mary Rouse, in the mid-1980s drunkenness and misbehavior were much worse, with one student convicted in Dane County Circuit Court for throwing a piece of bleacher seating over the top of the edge of the stadium to the asphalt below. The student was fined and ordered to clean toilets at the stadium the next season.

Rouse sits in the student section where she carefully watches behavior and she pooh-poohed alcohol as the cause. Richter joined her in dismissing alcohol as the demon in the episode.

There was other evidence of substance abuse as well. Before the Michigan game, UW Police Detective David Williams said he was struck in the chest by a metal tube, used to store nitrous oxide gas, that was hurled from the stands. Later, he found about ten other tubes in the end zone.

The events were out of context with recent history at the stadium. Riseling still has a pre-surge local newspaper story hanging on her refrigerator that details how well-behaved 1993 crowds had been and how the number of police citations had plummeted.

In the inevitable finger-pointing that followed, some students tried to blame the police, at least in part, for the injuries because of the way the surge was handled. They claimed that police at the fence wrongly stopped the surge, which worsened the congestion.

"When you have a mob mentality, the mob is always to blame," Paul Gibson, an advertising major who was at the fence, told *The Milwaukee Journal*. "But you don't try to stop them. With 8,000 people, you can't fight them."

Riseling defended security at the stadium, saying no amount of police could have stopped a crowd surge involving 12,000 people. She doubted there was a plan available to stop such a surge from occurring.

"Everyone wants to assess blame for this," said Riseling. "No one wants to believe it's beyond our control. This was not an act of nature. It was a human phenomenon. People believe if you assign blame, it won't happen again."

Riseling viewed the videotapes hundreds of times during the department's investigation. Backward, forward, frame by frame. Seen in stop-action, their horror is magnified. Faces awash in euphoria drain to sheer terror as the crush intensified.

Riseling does not attribute the incident to any sort of malevolence on the students' part. "It was an act of celebration. I don't think there was any intent to injure. The people who made it to the goalposts had no idea what was happening on the fence line," she said.

Christopher Smith, a fourth-year medical student, eventually made it to the field and was struck by the carnage. "Everyone was going nuts and running on the field, but we had no idea people were getting trampled," he said. "When we got down there, it was like a battlefield."

He and a friend began aiding a woman whose back was injured, but were soon summoned to help a woman who'd stopped breathing. Smith administered CPR to a woman identified as Brenda Dickenson for about two minutes before she regained consciousness.

Cheryl and Joel St. Marie had driven from Appleton and watched the Wisconsin victory from fifty-yard-line seats in row sixty-eight of the east stands, not far from the student section.

As they left the stadium, they heard the public address announcer talking about people hurt on the field, but they paid little attention. They were in a hurry to meet their daughter, Daniele, an eighteen-year-old freshman, in front of the Regent Apartments, a block from the stadium. The family had planned to go out for dinner.

The wait lengthened as the St. Maries heard, but ignored, the scream of ambulance sirens that wailed throughout Madison's near-west side after the tragedy. Their anxiety grew as Daniele failed to show up. The St. Maries searched nearby parking lots and called her room, with no luck.

They waited for nearly an hour before returning to the stadium and speaking with police. Officers told the St. Maries to check in person with the three local hospitals.

"We were in a state of denial," said Cheryl St. Marie. "It couldn't be our daughter involved."

Yet, when the St. Maries inquired at Meriter Hospital, five blocks from the stadium, staff members rushed them to Daniele's bedside in the intensive care unit. "She was in a comatose state. This just can't be happening," said Joel St. Marie.

Daniele was breathing with the aid of a respirator and the St. Maries stayed at her side through the night. Finally, on Sunday, Daniele started to awaken and show signs of responsiveness.

"She didn't even recall the game," her father said. "She said, 'Did I miss the Fifth Quarter?'"

Daniele's recollection of the event is hazy. She sat about halfway up in the student section and was carried some distance from her seat before being caught in a pile of students and deprived of oxygen.

"I'm one of the lucky ones, because I don't remember much," she said. "The thing that scared me the most was waking up and seeing the tubes and all the medical gear. And the look on my parents' faces."

The parents of another victim, senior pre-med student Sari Weinstein, also were in the stands when the surge began. Like the St. Maries, the Weinsteins were unaware of the magnitude of the event. They assumed that a fan had suffered a heart attack when the first calls for help were made. Not until later did they learn from their son that Sari was in the hospital.

They found her in the emergency room, heavily sedated. When she awoke, Weinstein remembered only the surge and being in the hospital, according to her father, Everrett Weinstein.

Nineteen-year-old student Heather Greenfieg was trapped at the safety railing in the stands. From her seat in the second row of Section P, she also recalls the chants of "Storm the field!"

Greenfieg told police a sudden push pinned her to the railing, with one row of students in between. She felt the bar flex, then break, as she tumbled to the walkway below, face down and spread eagle. Feeling like she was drowning, Greenfieg blacked out and woke as two men carried her to a weight room just up the tunnel walkway for treatment.

Sara Woboril, a junior from Dousman, had been seated in an aisle in Section P when the surge began. The unyielding force of the crowd carried her down the aisle, as she struggled to control her own movements. Finally, she fell on the concrete steps.

"Everything was in slow motion," she said. "My friends tried to stop people from trampling me, but I couldn't get up. It was all closing in. The force of the crowd was too much. I was gradually being smothered and there was nothing I could do. I couldn't breathe anymore. It was the most terrifying feeling."

Deprived of oxygen, Woboril passed out but regained consciousness after the pile of people lying on top of her was disassembled. Her back and hip were injured and Woboril couldn't move. She was rushed to UW Hospital, where physicians first feared she had fractured several vertebrae. She was lucky, however, because the injuries proved to be severe bruises. She still experiences back and hip pain from time to time.

The incident, however, hasn't dampened Woboril's enthusiasm for UW football. When the Badgers played Ohio State the following Saturday, Woboril, only three days out of the hospital, was there, seated in the handicapped section.

"Football is a part of me. My parents have been going to Badgers games for nineteen years. I attended my first game four days before I was born. I wasn't about to stop coming," she said. "But when I go to the student section now, I want to sit in the top row."

Those feelings are shared by Elizabeth Kassis, a freshman who was with Jansen in the stands that day. Kassis, buried beneath a pile of students, was revived by Dave Schroeder, who administered CPR.

She was listed in critical condition at the intensive care unit of UW Hospital and remained there for three days. "I can't remember anything but waking up in the hospital," she said. "I'll be back at Camp Randall, but I'm going for the top rows, too."

Kassis joined Jansen on the bus trip to Pasadena. "It was exciting," said Kassis, who was not able to attend the Ohio State game because she was recovering at her parents' home in Antigo. "I was glad we went and I never felt scared."

The actions of police were heavily scrutinized in the coming days, but Riseling said she is confident her officers acted appropriately. "One of our officers said to me later, 'It's not the guy with the gun that gets to you, not the riots or the situations you find uncomfortable, but it's the second-guessing that eats at you.' We do things in seconds that people take a lifetime to criticize," she said.

The UW police have been inundated with calls about the incident, which crowd management experts have told Riseling is unmatched in its character. "Every major university with a football team wants to know what happened. They've never seen such a mass movement of people," said Riseling.

The legal consequences of the crowd surge are likely to be felt in Madison for some time. Thirty-five notices of claim, the first step toward suing a government agency in Wisconsin, were filed against the state by the March 1 deadline.

In the weeks after the crowd surge, Riseling received numerous letters making crowd control suggestions. One recommended building a sort of cage for the student section, a twelve-foot fence topped with barbed wires, similar to those used at some European soccer venues.

Another was more placid, though offbeat, in its intent. The letter writer suggested that the UW hand out 12,000 kazoos to students entering the stadium. Then, the UW band would line up in the aisles and play, accompanied by what might be the largest kazoo band in the world.

"They apparently thought the students needed something to do to stay out of trouble," said Riseling. "They even thought we'd end up in the *Guinness Book of World Records*. Trouble is, they already throw marshmallows. What would they do with kazoos?"

Riseling, herself a football fan, said the circumstances simply combined to create a combustible atmosphere that was out of anyone's control. "We had just lost to Minnesota, and people expected this team to fold," she said. "I was even psyched. You could feel that building. The Rose Bowl was within reach. People believed in it for the first time in thirty-one years."

"Nobody left as the game concluded. It was a moment to behold. I'll bet you that 60,000 of the 78,000 thought, 'Wouldn't it be great to charge onto the field?' The students had that thought and acted on it.

"Unless we can stop them from thinking that thought, it could happen again."

In the days after the surge, Chancellor David Ward called for an independent investigation into stadium safety. A few weeks later, Milwaukee businessman George Kaiser was appointed to manage the inquiry.

Late in April of 1994, Kaiser issued a seventeen-page report detailing forty-nine recommendations to improve safety, but assigning no blame for the incident.

In large measure, Kaiser's report also dealt with changing traditions in the stadium and reinforcing appropriate behavior by fans.

The inquiry found that, over the years, the UW has had a "laissez-faire" policy toward rules enforcement in the student section and that during the Michigan game overcrowding in that section ranged from 800 to 2,000. There was no evidence, however, that the Athletic Department oversold the section, Kaiser said.

Other recommendations included increasing the number of reserved student seats, seating the band inside the chain link fence, and tightening controls on student season tickets to assure they are not used to allow more than one person into the stadium. The report also called for UW Police to upgrade videotape capability by providing more cameras with zoom lenses to monitor the crowd.

Although Wisconsin students tend to balk at reserved seating, the UW is one of only two Big Ten universities (Northwestern is the other) that allow 100 percent general admission seating in the student section and most require reserved seating.

"There is also anecdotal evidence that students and others migrate to the student section from other areas of the stadium," the report states.

In addition, the report called for students to be removed from Section Q, which surrounds the tunnel visiting teams use to reach the locker room. That, Kaiser said, would reduce the chance objects would be showered on opponents.

To implement all of Kaiser's recommendations, it would cost an estimated $300,000, but officials seemed willing to consider many of the changes—including expanding the student section to 14,178 to accommodate increasing demand.

Although the memories of the crowd surge are likely to stick for a while, university officials are keenly aware that the institutional memory of the student population is short. They plan to reinforce stadium safety with students not just on game day, but in freshman orientation and other campus-wide forums.

"We're going to have to be very sharp and clear on our expectations," said Rouse. "We recognize that they have a great potential as a twelfth man, but we must enforce those high expectations."

11

The Purist's Game

O ut of the gray, cutting cold of the Sunday after the Michigan game, Badgers players filed grimly into the McClain Facility for their weekly meeting.

From the outset, this meeting had a darker tone, a cadence restrained by the postgame tragedy just twenty-four hours earlier. Players wondered if the students they helped pull out of the piles at Camp Randall Stadium would live or die. A psychiatrist was on hand to counsel them, if need be.

Richter spoke to the team about the importance of putting the events behind them and openly discussing their feelings.

"We did some great things," he said later. "Some were in the football game, some were after the football game. We are very proud of how those who were still on the field handled themselves. It was a focus forward. We have to deal with that and get them over that."

Alvarez was quietly worried about the effect the incident would have on his team, especially watching the faces of players as they arrived for the meeting. "There's Joe Panos and he walks in and he's just pale. He's in shock. It's obvious. And Joe Rudolph and a bunch of those guys, they're all in shock," he said.

Dr. Bruce Harms, of the UW Hospital, told the team that all of the victims of the surge would recover. There was a collective sigh of relief at Harms's news. "It was like somebody lifted a house off my shoulders," said Mike Brin.

The news also unburdened Alvarez and his staff. Outside of being relieved for the victims, Alvarez knew his team now would come back together. One of his fears during those twenty-four hours was the explosive effect that a student's death might have on the chemistry of this team.

"How the hell do you handle that?" Alvarez asked. "Put yourself in their place. They think they're *dead*. They show up Sunday and they still think they're dead.

"If one of those kids didn't make it, I don't know if we could have survived it. That was brutal. Michigan and Ohio State back to back is hard enough, let alone throwing something like that in."

On the advice of therapists, Alvarez limited media questions about the incident to a news conference the following Monday in the W Club Room in the stadium. Panos and Brin answered reporters' questions, but during the week that followed the subject was off limits.

Players were told not to answer questions about the incident and reporters were told not to ask. Alvarez said university mental health professionals told him to impose limits since the incessant reliving of the incident was not healthy.

Besides, the fifteenth-ranked Badgers were preparing to play unbeaten Big Ten leader Ohio State, an undertaking Alvarez expected would require all of their concentration.

With the sold-out Ohio State game looming the next Saturday, UW officials worked feverishly to devise an interim plan to help improve crowd control. They spent $7,000 to replace sections of damaged fence and railing and added six gates with quick-release latches near the student section to help relieve crowd pressure if needed.

In addition, they moved the Badgers' team entrance to a larger tunnel to the north between Sections L and M. The tunnel used by the visiting team was covered and fencing was added to protect opponents' players and coaches and camera access was restricted in that corner of the end zone.

The university also moved the band from 400 seats in the student section to a twenty-yard-long strip of unused turf in the north end zone. And students were forced to exchange their season passes for game tickets beginning the morning of the Ohio State game. The season passes are not stamped or canceled when a student enters the game, so often they are passed to friends outside the stadium who want access, and that eventually leads to overcrowding.

Some players used Monday, their day off, to gather themselves and put the incident behind them. Panos, Patterson, and Tyler Adam went hunting on Patterson's grandfather's farm in Sauk County. "It was a good tension reliever to go out and hunt squirrels and just get away from here," Panos said.

After students exchanged their season passes for tickets, many milled about outside the horseshoe end of the stadium waiting to take their seats. When the gates were opened at 11 a.m., many of the first to enter the stadium confounded onlookers. They took seats in the lower rows, where many of the injuries took place the week before.

The press box was bulging with college football writers from across the nation, munching frankfurters, potato salad, and ice cream. The same reporters who canceled out on the Michigan game following Wisconsin's loss to Minnesota hopped back on the bandwagon. This was to be one of the nation's featured games.

The *Los Angeles Times, Boston Globe, Dallas Morning News, Washington Post, USA Today, Chicago Tribune,* and others clamored for access and were gladly accommodated. Sports Information Director Steve Malchow was scurrying to find room for the media in a press box heavily populated with well-heeled boosters.

It was an ironic situation, since only three seasons earlier Malchow had been driven to twist arms at Milwaukee television stations to get assignment editors to send crews ninety miles west to cover Badgers games.

Aside from the sportswriters, there was a bevy of reporters interested in roaming the stadium's student section to do follow-ups on crowd behavior and whether the UW's interim safeguards were working.

University public relations people tried to establish press pools to accommodate the writers, though some bought tickets and sneaked into the student section for an unvarnished look of their own.

No one could remember when Wisconsin football had commanded this much attention.

Ohio State came into the game 8-0, with a third-place ranking in the polls. Those numbers kindled hopes in Columbus that the Buckeyes would win a national championship for the first time since quarterback Rex Kern led the Buckeyes to the number-one spot a quarter-century earlier.

Buckeyes tailback Raymont Harris boasted of the following the Buckeyes had found after taking early-season criticism. "They can jump on the bandwagon now, if they want to, but it's getting kind of full," he said.

After Wisconsin's 20-16 upset of twelfth-ranked Ohio State the previous year, the Buckeyes felt they had something to prove and the Badgers wanted to demonstrate that 1992's victory was not a fluke.

Illinois Coach Tepper, after viewing films of Ohio State's 51-3 trashing of Northwestern a week earlier, said teams can ill afford to scrap a rushing game even if Ohio State stops it. The Wildcats tried a one-dimensional approach and they came up empty. "They just chose to throw it and that was like putting bloody meat in front of a tiger," Tepper said.

After all of the pregame tub-thumping was finished, the game kicked off before a national audience on ABC. It was the sort of purist's game Alvarez savored: smash-mouth, Big Ten football. Strength on strength, man on man, in a high-stakes game that was key to winning the conference championship.

"When you talk about Wisconsin football now, you talk about a team that is physical, a team that is hard-nosed, a team that's blue-collar," said Alvarez. "There was nothing fancy about the way we went about our business, the way we went about winning."

Offensive planning for Ohio State and all of Wisconsin's other games was fundamental, seldom straying far from the Badgers' basic strengths.

"If Brad or other offensive coaches would come up with one reverse, we'd think it was a tremendous exotic involved in the game," said Alvarez. "It wasn't fancy. But that's what we're all about. That's the principle we built our program on: being tougher than the other guy."

The challenge Ohio State offered was the antithesis of the pass-happy note on which the Badgers started their season. It was Alvarez's brand of fight-to-the-death football.

In preparing players for the Ohio State game, Wisconsin coaches regarded the Michigan victory in the same way as they did the loss to Minnesota. They refused to dwell on the victory or immerse themselves in self-congratulation.

"They said, 'We played a great team, we beat a great team. Now we have to play an even better football team,'" said Scott Nelson. "The game was key to the rest of our season. We knew that if we came back after the great Michigan win and played our worst game, we still had two games left."

One of the remarkable facets of this Badgers team was the contribution made by walk-ons and players recruited in the chaotic month after Alvarez arrived. Some of the players who now anchored one of the nation's best football programs were either lightly recruited or drew no interest at all from Division I programs.

And many of those were Wisconsin athletes. Against Ohio State, ten Wisconsin players started and another, outside linebacker Chad Yocum, had been nursing a back injury since early in the season. Three of the state starters— Panos, linebacker Chris Hein, and punter Sam Veit—were walk-ons.

Among them, Panos is probably the most celebrated case. He spent his freshman year as a defensive lineman at tiny UW-Whitewater, a Division III program about forty miles southeast of Madison. He came from a losing program at Brookfield East High School and drew virtually no interest from Division I programs during recruiting.

But Alvarez's arrival at Wisconsin intrigued him. The talk of keeping the state's best football players at the UW led Panos to think there might be a chance for him to live out a dream and play for a Big Ten team.

He drove to Madison and offered to walk on if the Badgers would have him. Alvarez agreed and Panos spent the 1990 season as a redshirt, working with the scout team.

"I believed in coach," said Panos. "All I wanted to do was be a Badger. I was small. I was short. But I grew two inches and put on thirty pounds. I walked on as a defensive lineman, but they needed me on the o-line and the next thing you know, good things happened."

In 1991 he started nine games, five at center and four at right guard. The next year he was shifted to right tackle, started all eleven games, and became one of the Big Ten's most consistent blockers, grading out at 90 percent or better in seven games.

He was single-minded in his work in the weight room, surpassing all of his linemates in strength, with a 460-pound bench press and a 645-pound squat.

Born Zois Panagiotopolous on January 24, 1971, to Greek-immigrant parents living in Montreal, Panos is attached to his ethnicity, but is not a scientist about his background. Asked what his given last name means, he shrugged and asked, "Son of Panos?"

His parents, who own Ma Fischer's restaurant on Milwaukee's trendy east side, missed only one game during the Badgers' 1993 season—the loss to Minnesota. They traveled to Tokyo and to Pasadena as their sense of pride in Joe and the Badgers swelled.

"They're in love with the game, with the red and white," said Panos, who in May 1994 became the first in his family to graduate from college.

Throughout his Badgers career, Panos was relentless in his optimism and had a work ethic that was widely respected among his teammates. Before the 1993 season, his teammates made him a co-captain.

Alvarez said Panos's maturity and leadership made him one of the best team captains with whom he had ever worked. Each week, Alvarez would have his training-table meal with the captains and discuss team affairs.

From the outset, Alvarez said, it was obvious that Panos took his role seriously and not simply as someone who was designated to be on hand for the coin toss at midfield.

"Coach Alvarez, I put him so high on my list," Panos said. "He's a great man, a great coach, and I think the world of him. He put the trust in me and that motivated me to take our team where he wanted us to go."

Panos said the role came naturally. He was quick to step in to settle fights on the field or mediate disputes off the field. The team held Panos in high regard, and took note of his self-made status.

"It makes a difference if people respect you," said Panos. "There's some people here I don't like but I have a great deal of respect for and there are some people I do like and I don't have any respect for. A leader has to have both. You have to like the person and respect them."

Hein was also a success story. Coming out of Plymouth High School, his only scholarship offer came from Grand Valley State, a Division II school in Michigan. Instead, he decided to walk on in Alvarez's first season.

Despite never having started before the 1993 season, Hein showed he was a Big Ten-caliber player, making a pair of key defensive plays in Wisconsin's victory over Michigan.

"It was a hard fight going from a walk-on to a starting position," said Hein. "Walking on, a lot of people think you can't do it. Obviously, someone thought you didn't have what it takes."

Hein thanks his parents, Dave and Marge, for supporting his decision to come to the UW and bypass the small-school scholarship offer.

"Recruiting isn't exactly a science, but when you're a walk-on, it's kind of degrading," he said. "You have some tough times, but there never came a time when I seriously thought about throwing down my pads."

Each of Camp Randall Stadium's 77,745 seats was filled before kickoff as football fans hunkered down in snow flurries driven by a northwest wind.

Throughout the Ohio State game, Buckeyes Coach John Cooper relied on an odd system of quarterback rotation which the Buckeyes had used in previous games and one that may have hurt the Buckeyes' performance early on.

Ohio State had developed momentum in the first quarter, as starter Bobby Hoying directed the Buckeyes to a 7-0 lead on a 70-yard drive. Then Cooper inserted senior backup Bret Powers who led two failed series.

That opened the door to Wisconsin and Darrell Bevell led a 42-yard drive that ended with his high-arching, wobbly pass to Lee DeRamus in the end zone to tie the game at halftime.

Although the Badgers took a 14-7 lead on a 3-yard touchdown run by Brent Moss in the third quarter, 2 fumbled snaps by Bevell hurt Wisconsin's cause. One fumble came when the Badgers were threatening at the Ohio State 14-yard line.

"I keep hitting myself for the fumbles," said Bevell. "I should have been pulling the ball into my gut."

The game turned on two series. Ohio State's crucial possession came on a drive in which Powers finally came to life, completing passes of 15, 47, 11, and 26 yards. The 99-yard drive spanned just 46 seconds and ended when Powers hit split end Joey Galloway on a 26-yard touchdown pass to tie the game 14-14 with 3:48 to play.

During the drive, Powers picked on cornerback Donny Brady, a junior college transfer who came in after Nelson left the game with cracked ribs. Jeff Messenger was moved to free safety to cover for Nelson and Brady stepped in at corner.

Along the sideline, the injured Nelson, the old hand, tried to bolster Brady's spirits and those of the other defensive backs.

"I was more of a player-coach," said Nelson. "I was trying to help them out a little bit. The hardest thing was trying to get Donny to hold his head up. The whole secondary got together and said, 'That was one series, four plays. If they keep trying to go with four-play drives, we're going to beat them.' "

As the Buckeyes' surgical drive was under way, Bevell was on the phone to Brad Childress in the press box. The two were mapping the next series of offensive plays in serious, intense tones. Bevell's attachment to the telephone was a running joke among players all season.

But it also demonstrated the close communication that developed between Bevell and Childress. "Everyone's always saying, 'What are you doing on that phone?' If you watch me, after every series I go to the phone. We have great communication," Bevell said.

Bevell gets the sermon first, then the plan. "After he yells at me, screams at me, or pats me on the back, we go through the next series. We'll go over each pass and he'll tell me what coverages he's seeing and some of the defenses they're running," he said.

Wisconsin got the ball back and moved it to the Ohio State 15-yard line on third down with 7 seconds left before sending in the field goal unit. Some questioned Alvarez's handling of the drive, suggesting that he should have called timeouts and preserved the extra down. The way Moss was running, Alvarez's critics said gaining a first down and continuing the drive was a better bet.

Alvarez, however, decided not to chance giving the ball back to the Buckeyes with 25 or 30 seconds left after the way Powers moved the team the previous series. He contended that the Badgers were not going to pile up any rushing yardage with Ohio State sending eight men to the line.

"I liked my chances of kicking a chip-shot field goal," Alvarez said. So in came Rick Schnetzky to attempt a 32-yard field goal to win the game. Trouble was, Ohio State's Marlon Kerner had seen a chink in the Badgers' kicking unit all afternoon. He felt the Badgers were leaving themselves open to a blocked kick by allowing their ends to step out.

At the snap, Kerner knifed past Badgers corner man Matt Nyquist, stretched, and blocked the kick with both hands. "It was, 'Please, please, please, let me block it.' Then, 'thank you, thank you, thank you,'" he said.

After reviewing films, Alvarez said the block did not appear to be Nyquist's fault, since he was following orders to keep his outside foot "in cement" to secure the inside gap. Nyquist moved his foot about three inches. Instead of blaming Nyquist, Alvarez lauded Kerner's athletic play.

"A couple of inches? Whether that makes a difference or not, I don't know. The kid made a great play. Sometimes we have to give others credit, too, instead of looking to point the blame," said Alvarez.

After the game, Badgers players were numbed. "No one knew how to react," said Nelson. "We had the opportunity to take it and we didn't. It hurt us more than it hurt them at the time because of the won-loss record."

Buckeyes players, however, were jubilant. They had preserved their league-leading record and although they fell to fifth place in the national rankings, their Rose Bowl hopes were still alive. In fact, the following week, after a hard-fought game at Indiana, victorious Ohio State players were seen along the sidelines holding roses.

Carlos Fowler was struck by the relief shown by the Buckeyes in the moments after the game. "We were on the field crushed," he said. "They were happy and complacent. It was like they won the game. We looked at the game as a defeat. That told me that if we kept fighting, we'd be in the big dance and they wouldn't."

The additional security measures kept the aisles meticulously clear and, with the painful object lesson of the previous week, there was no crowd rush and the fans were generally well behaved. But fans, surprisingly, continued to throw marshmallows at the opposing team, some laden with coins.

After the Ohio State game, Buckeyes Coach John Cooper angrily displayed a wad of coin-laced marshmallows that pelted players as they left the field. The missiles continued to rain down on opponents even after the incidents of the previous week.

Cooper called those hurling the missiles "asinine." "No football team should allow throwing marshmallows with all those coins in them," he said. "Marshmallows are OK and fun, but when you start throwing coins, that should be stopped."

Like Fowler, Bevell noticed the Buckeyes' relief as they filed out of Camp Randall after salvaging the tie. "They felt they still had everything in their hands, because they snuck out of here," Bevell said. "And they did sneak out of here."

Pork in
the Rosebush

The coaches' goals for this game had changed.

At the outset of the season, Alvarez privately circulated a list of goals for his assistants that included a simple, "Beat Illinois."

After the Bill Callahan affair and all of the media attention it had drawn in the week before the game, the directive had been bluntly altered. "Beat the shit out of Illinois," were the new marching orders.

After the whole affair, Alvarez and his staff regarded Illinois Coach Lou Tepper as an irritating pipsqueak. The way they saw it, the game at Champaign's Memorial Stadium would have a lot to do with settling scores.

Although the game carried its own prominence as far as determining the course of the Badgers' season, a slew of underlying animosities ached to be settled.

Coaches were driven by the Callahan affair while players stewed about their 13–12 loss to the Fighting Illini the previous season. The loss was central to keeping the Badgers out of a postseason bowl game, and the contest featured plenty of trash talking. Wisconsin players had not forgotten.

And Kevin Cosgrove, Brad Childress, and Callahan—all former Illinois assistant coaches—had yet to defeat their former employer while at Wisconsin. That added another dimension, another motivator, to Wisconsin's side of the ledger.

Beyond that, Richter was angry with Illinois Athletic Director Ron Guenther over his conduct regarding the Callahan episode. And, of course, Richter yearned to have Wisconsin return to the Rose Bowl.

If ever a game was decided on testosterone levels, it was this one.

The stakes in Champaign were simple. The Badgers needed Michigan to defeat fifth-ranked Ohio State in Ann Arbor, then the Badgers had to win out to go to the Rose Bowl.

The week before the game, Tepper added fuel to the smoldering Callahan saga. In a conference call with reporters, Tepper voiced hope that the relationship between the two schools could be repaired.

"We, as a football staff, are tolerant and forgiving," he said. "If I find anyone who would have repeated, willful violations, then it's my obligation to turn them in. But I don't have any desire to have continued animosity with Wisconsin."

Wisconsin coaches, of course, did not believe they needed Tepper's forgiveness, but they kept a low public profile on the issue.

Throughout the season, Wisconsin benefited from timing. Their three bye weeks came when they needed them most, allowing them to heal and plan.

Now the schedule of network television was playing into their hands. ABC decided to broadcast a Big Ten doubleheader and scheduled the Michigan-Ohio State game first, to be followed by Wisconsin-Illinois. Badgers players and coaches were able to watch much of the first half of the Michigan-Ohio State game in their hotel rooms before boarding buses bound for the stadium.

It was an unpredictably lopsided game. At halftime, Michigan led 21–0 over a Buckeyes team that had abandoned all the principles it used to seize control of the Big Ten. Wisconsin players left their hotel rooms knowing the Wolverines were upholding their half of the bargain. Now the Badgers needed to seal the deal.

With the day of reckoning at hand, however, about a dozen players found themselves stuck between floors in an elevator at the University Inn. The breakdown caused major concerns for the players trapped inside, especially Joe Panos, who is claustrophobic.

"The biggest game of any of our careers, and here we were in the hotel elevator," said Panos. "I started to sweat and I took off my jacket and tie and unbuttoned my shirt. I can't stand small spaces and it seemed like we were in there forever."

The players on the elevator probably had themselves to thank for the mishap because the beefy bunch overloaded the car by about 1,000 pounds, Panos said.

After about twenty-five minutes, maintenance personnel freed the players and they arrived at the team bus in time to hear that Michigan retained its wide lead over Ohio State.

It was Pork Day at Memorial Stadium, the day when Illinois pig farmers show off their finest products, serving pork sandwiches in the stadium and press box. Even network TV got involved in the festivities as ABC's Roger

Twibell did a mock interview with a sow outside the red-brick behemoth that is Memorial Stadium during a break in the Michigan-Ohio State game.

During pregame warmups, the word started to filter out. Michigan had upset Ohio State 28–0 and the door was open for the Badgers: win and Wisconsin would go to the Rose Bowl for the first time since the Kennedy administration. There was a perceptible change in intensity. Players, while not tight, were more square-jawed, their gazes focused.

"Now we were playing for the whole ball of wax," said inside linebacker Eric Unverzagt. "If it wasn't for the Rose Bowl, we'd be more distracted, but with that much at stake there was no problem with focus."

Lee DeRamus said the news was a welcome relief, as the Badgers' destiny was put back in their own hands.

"Once you heard the score, your heart started to beat a little faster. You could see it in everybody's eyes in the locker room: They lost! Let's go,'" he said.

Although Alvarez debated whether to use the score of the Michigan-Ohio State game as incentive, the 28–0 result was like waving a red cape in front of a bull.

"It was a big motivator for us. The table was set and people had fire in their eyes," said Carlos Fowler. "This chance came around once in thirty-one years and we weren't going to let it slip through our fingers. No way."

As players stretched before the game, Alvarez and Tepper did not cross paths. As Tepper looked for Alvarez at midfield, Alvarez patrolled the field near the 5-yard line and ignored Tepper.

Going into the game, Alvarez lectured the defense on containing Illinois' sophomore quarterback Johnny Johnson. Johnson had shown a solid ability to scramble and make plays happen on his own.

The first part of Alvarez's defensive game plan was to disguise defenses, making Johnson read on the run, and bring pressure from the outside to contain him. Do that and the Badgers had a solid shot at winning their first game at Memorial Stadium since 1970.

And on offense, Wisconsin needed to do what it had done all season—run the ball effectively. The offensive line, especially in light of the Callahan affair, was primed for battle.

During team meetings leading up to the Illinois game, coaches asked players to disregard the controversy and simply focus on their jobs. Players, however, saw things far differently.

Panos met independently with offensive linemen to discuss the line's reaction to the brouhaha. Callahan is revered among his players for his fierce competitive edge, and his players felt they owed him a victory against the Fighting Illini.

"Coach Callahan told us not to play for him, but to play for ourselves to get where we wanted to go," Panos said. "I took the guys aside and said, 'The old man has been with us through good times and bad. These guys are bad-mouthing him and we have to go out there and get this game for him.'"

Brent Moss said coaches tried to downplay the off-the-field controversy involving Callahan in the days before the game, but it remained a strong undercurrent as the Badgers prepared. "That's the coaches. The coaches can't go out there and play the game," he said. "They said: 'This is our business. You just go out there and play.'"

Panos, however, said Callahan seemed to put more effort into polishing the line for its game at Memorial Stadium. While not much was said about the controversy, the linemen knew its significance.

If that were not enough incentive, Wisconsin players were furious with brash comments by Illinois defensive players who indicated they would hold the Badgers to less than 100 yards in team rushing.

"We were ready to dominate. You don't go into a fist fight with your hands down. You try to take them out right away," Panos said.

Defensively, the Badgers employed a zone, which was simpler and more straightforward, making it easier for younger players to absorb. It does not feature the complex pulling and trapping schemes that take time and talent to master.

It does require physical dominance and the ability to match up well on the line of scrimmage. After two years of building depth, Callahan, Childress, and Alvarez saw promise in the scheme.

Callahan, a former quarterback at Illinois Benedictine, said the scheme involves a minimalist approach to the game suited to the defensive player. "Defensive guys like it because it's essentially assignment football and that's the way most defenses are built," he said.

Since numerous defensive principles are involved, Callahan had to sell the transition to many of the Badgers' starters who made the leap from defense to offense. He tried to show them the built-in advantages of playing with a defensive mindset while knowing where the play was going and what the snap count was.

The first flickers of real offensive-line power came during the Iowa State game, when the line was able to block the Cyclones' defensive front several yards off the ball. That game proved the scheme and the players had matured and could prosper under the system. There was progress in virtually every game thereafter.

One element that made zone blocking so attractive to Callahan was the way it suited the defensive inclination of his linemen. Each starter had been recruited as a defensive player or had been shifted from defense.

Also making the conversion to offense were guards Steve Stark and Joe

Rudolph, and 300-pound tackle Mike Verstegen, who moved from outside line-backer in 1992.

For Verstegen and the Badgers it was a profitable move. That season, he started in all eleven games and played in 779 snaps, the most of any offensive lineman.

Rudolph, also recruited as a linebacker, switched to the offensive line in 1991, and made a solid contribution in 1992 and was coming of age in 1993.

Like Panos, Cory Raymer came to Wisconsin as a defensive lineman but soon made the shift to the offense. At first, Raymer despised the move, prefer-ring the more open game played on defense. The more the coaching staff saw of Raymer, though, the more convinced they were that he could be an all-Big Ten center.

Raymer started piling up experience as a freshman. It is rare for first-year players to start on the offensive line, much less at center, but Raymer was forced into the role. As a freshman in Wisconsin's 1991 game at Purdue, Raymer heard Callahan asking, "Where's Raymer?"

"I didn't know whether to put up my hand or hide," said Raymer.

In time, however, he became a mainstay on the line. As a sophomore, he was selected for honorable mention on the media's all-Big Ten team. Then, in his junior year, he was a first-team all-Big Ten pick, the first UW center since former Pittsburgh Steeler Mike Webster to earn that honor.

During his career, he was part of a line that made it possible to increase rushing yardage by 156 yards a game—a 165 percent increase—and to boost total offense by 214 yards a game.

Players also favored the zone scheme for its simplicity. Panos said the scheme also helped build closeness among offensive players. "I have to believe in the guy next to me and so does he. If one of us breaks down, then the whole machine stops. It instills trust and confidence in one another," he said.

As a result of their success, the offensive linemen were enjoying their newfound prominence. Usually ignored as the worker bees of any football team, these guys had taken on a luster uncommon even among the pros.

"I go down to walk in the mall and people say, 'There's Joe Panos, the o-lineman,'" Panos said of his season-long celebrity. "I say, 'What are you following a big, sloppy goof like myself for?'"

Raymer, always one to spin a creative metaphor, said the publicity the line was generating was a side benefit.

"Whatever people from the outside think of us, that's just have your cookies and get the ice cream, too. We're out there to have fun," said Raymer.

Panos was something of a morale officer for the team, always willing to offer the Bowen Court apartment he shared with backup guard Tyler Adam for a party. Raymer called it the "Panos Party House."

Wisconsin's offense spun on the line's ability to block and stay on those blocks. The gaping holes opened rich opportunities for Moss and Terrell Fletcher to do serious damage in the rushing game.

Darrell Bevell and the running backs were the first to sing the praises of the line. "Usually, they're the guys who don't get any credit, but they deserve it. They're what's running this team, and running the offense," he said.

Fletcher also went out of his way to laud the work of the line during the season, something that helped breed a kinship between linemen and the running backs. "On a lot of teams, the backs don't give the credit to the offensive line the way we do and have the sort of respect for those guys that we have had," he said.

Playing the nation's fourth-best defense against the rush, Wisconsin's offensive line made good on its private pledge to dominate the game. Illinois defenders were on their heels for the entire contest, as Wisconsin piled up 301 yards on the ground. "Coach Callahan prepared the line like never before," said Panos. "We knew exactly what was going to happen after watching countless hours of film. And we stuck it to them. We were playing the best we could play."

For the running backs, the Illinois game was a microcosm of the season, with each gaining over 100 yards and scoring a touchdown. Moss and Fletcher had shared time at tailback with grace and no small measure of cooperation. They were rotated regularly and the two did not become involved in the chippy locker-room jealousies that can detract from team cohesion.

Both backs shared information on opposing defenses and coached each other to perform better throughout the season.

"It kept us both fresh. We were both healthy all year and we each bring a new face to the offense and no one quite knows what to expect when we come in," Fletcher said. "He lets me know what's going on and I tell him. We get together before each series and talk it out."

Still, Fletcher was seldom satisfied with his play during 1993. Although the team was performing well and gaining accolades, Fletcher was often bummed out about his own contributions.

"It was weird. The whole season was a different experience. I was having so much success. But at times, it seemed like I wasn't as happy as I could have been. I was happy for the team, but I felt I wasn't playing as well as I could have been playing," said Fletcher.

"I felt like I had more to offer when I had the ball. Even if I had a good run, I felt there was something I could have done to make the play better. It bothered me all season," said Fletcher. "Like Coach Hueber said, I'm probably my own worst critic,"

Fletcher, Missouri's prep player of the year, was one of the Badgers' major recruiting catches in 1991, a player who helped the Badgers break through to other top players nationally. Fletcher almost chose Ohio State, because another St. Louis area tailback, friend Butler Býnotè, chose the Buckeyes.

"I knew what was best for me deep in my heart. Frankly, the 1–10 record didn't jump out and grab me, but I knew the place where I belonged and the only thing that swayed my mind was the fact that Butler was at Ohio State," said Fletcher.

Both Fletcher and Alvarez agree that under ideal circumstances, Fletcher would have redshirted in his freshman year to gain experience at the college level. The Badgers' wafer-thin depth, however, forced Alvarez to use Fletcher as a true freshman.

"My first year, everybody had to play for this team to get better," said Fletcher. "All of a sudden you realize, you're not physically mature and another year of seasoning would help a lot. But that wasn't the role I was supposed to take on."

Fletcher gained 446 yards on 109 carries and became the first true freshman to lead the Badgers in rushing since Ameche in 1951. Injuries hampered Fletcher in 1992, limiting him to eight games and 496 yards.

But in 1993, the speedy outside runner made it to within a hairsbreadth of every running back's goal: 1,000 yards. Fletcher finished the season with 996 rushing yards and a 6-yard average.

"It would have been nice to get 1,000 yards, but if I had done some things to make better runs earlier in the season, there would have been no doubt," he said. "Coming up short gave me more drive to come back and get the 1,000 yards."

Animosities ran high throughout the game. At halftime, as the teams left the field, a heated exchange was started by a member of Tepper's staff who taunted Callahan about chop blocks by the Badgers. There was concern on both sides that the trash talking could erupt into a fight. The incident stayed verbal, however, and afterward Alvarez wrote to Tepper, complaining about the incident.

The sparring went on after the season, as Tepper invited Callahan, Cosgrove, and Childress to a tenth-anniversary reunion of the 1984 Rose Bowl team, but said they wouldn't be allowed in the football offices. All declined the invitation.

Wisconsin's offense bullied the Illinois defense all afternoon, as the Badgers cruised to a 35–10 victory. Bevell said the line was an inspiration to the rest of the team: "We just knocked them in the mouth. As the game went on, we noticed they were getting tired and folding a little bit and we just kept pouring it on."

Tepper was amazed at the production of Wisconsin's offensive line against what he thought was a solid defensive front.

"We never really had a grasp up front of being able to stop the inside zone play that they ran so very well," Tepper said. "It's not an unusual scheme; it's something they've done quite consistently. But we did not, despite changes in fronts and change in coverages, stop that particular play."

The level of play by Wisconsin's line awed the Illinois defense. Illinois linebacker John Holacek said: "They are tremendous at staying on their blocks and keeping their blocks. I have never seen anything like that before."

Meanwhile, the Wisconsin defense followed its game plan as 15 of Johnson's 27 passes fell incomplete. Illinois tried to build momentum deep in Wisconsin territory as it trailed 28–10 early in the fourth quarter, but Johnson was sacked by defensive tackle Mike Thompson for a 19-yard loss. "That was amazing; he just kept running and running," said Thompson.

Fowler, who came to Wisconsin after playing prep football in the central Illinois farm town of Pontiac, seemed to excel at playing Illinois. In 1991, he recovered a fumbled pitch to score a touchdown. A year later, he fell on an errant snap to score another touchdown.

"Playing Illinois always gives me something extra, because I'm an Illinois boy," said Fowler. "I told the team I wanted this game so bad. I turned it over to the offense and said, 'I'm not scoring any touchdowns this time. I'll take care of the quarterback.'"

After the game, players gathered in the visitors locker room in the northwest corner of Memorial Stadium and presented the game ball to Callahan. Tears welled in the eyes of all three former Illinois coaches, who had never defeated the Fighting Illini since coming to Wisconsin.

Outside the locker room, Unverzagt stood with a single long-stemmed red rose, beaming. "It's been a long haul," he said.

And for the first time, Alvarez named an entire unit—the offensive line— as the Badgers' offensive players of the week.

The theme Alvarez harped on at the seminary during two-a-days, chemistry, seemed to have solidified and was showing prolific results.

Wide receiver J.C. Dawkins said in his first two years the team was fractured into units and cliques. But by 1993, the walls came down and there was a stronger sense of team. "The linemen didn't just hang out with linemen. Everyone hangs out together," Dawkins said. "That improves our chemistry on the field. When we get into the huddle, we know we can count on each other."

As the season unwound, Dawkins said that sense of security increased: "We got a few bugs out each week and our confidence level grew each week. By the end of the season, our confidence was where it needed to be to make us a Rose Bowl team."

Walking off the field after the game, Alvarez and Tepper exchanged a quick and cold handshake at midfield and went their separate ways.

Tokyo Roses

Even Cory Raymer was bowled over by the scene.

The Badgers' plainspoken lineman, who has a bit of a party reputation, found himself sober aboard a train filled with drunks. Not just one or two lushes, mind you. Hundreds of them, half in the bag, passed out on subway seats.

We're not in Fond du Lac anymore, Toto.

Instead, Raymer was returning late at night to Tokyo's Miyako Hotel, the Badgers' team headquarters for the game against Michigan State, the contest that would determine whether Wisconsin would win a Rose Bowl berth.

Raymer had spent the evening at the home of a Tokyo host, enjoying Japanese food and getting more familiar with the cultures and customs of Japan. Now he ran into one more custom, drinking to excess.

"That was the drunkest I've seen anyone in my life. There wasn't just one person, there were 300 or 400. They all must live at the end of the subway line, so when they get on they can sleep until it closes down, because they weren't moving for anything," said Raymer.

The 290-pound center likes a party, riding his motorcycle through rural Wisconsin, hunting, and grabbing a gyros for a midnight snack. He's a Wisconsin kid through and through. But there was nothing like this back home.

Other Badgers players formed groups and fanned out across Tokyo with their UW alumni hosts, eating at private homes and restaurants.

Split end Lee DeRamus found the experience particularly satisfying. DeRamus joined outside linebacker Bryan Jurewicz and defensive lineman Al Gay for dinner at a Tokyo home. Unbeknown to DeRamus, the Japanese custom of wiping one's hands with a towel is a signal to the host that a guest has had enough to eat. So the food kept coming and DeRamus, the polite guest, kept eating and eating. "I was real full," he said.

As he watched out the subway window for Meguro Station, just blocks from the hotel, Raymer was part of college football history. The Coca-Cola Bowl, now in its eighteenth year, was the only NCAA football game played outside the United States and this was the Badgers' first foreign trip.

The trappings were plenty odd. The Badgers—plus band, cheerleaders, and hundreds of fans—had trekked 6,000 miles to the Pacific Rim to participate in a game that would determine whether they would return to the Rose Bowl for the first time in thirty-one years.

The stakes were clear by the time the Badgers boarded their flight for Tokyo. Win, and they would tie with Ohio State for the conference championship and gain the Rose Bowl berth. A tie-breaker eliminating the team that last represented the conference in the Rose Bowl would dump Ohio State from contention. Lose, and Wisconsin would be the Big Ten's third-place representative in the Holiday Bowl in San Diego on December 30.

The Citrus Bowl, designed to accommodate the Big Ten's second-place team, was out of the question for the Badgers. To end up there, Wisconsin would have needed to tie Michigan State in Japan. Believing that to be a long shot, the Citrus Bowl's selection committee met in Orlando the day before the Badgers left for Tokyo and chose Penn State as the Big Ten representative.

The Tokyo junket took two years to plan and negotiate. The process was labored and criticized in Madison from the outset. Wisconsin was approached by the promoter, Tokyo's TelePlanning International, in 1991. The proposal required the Badgers to relinquish their October 2, 1993, home game against the Spartans in exchange for the December 4 date in Tokyo.

Financially the deal, first discussed after the Badgers finished 1-10 in Alvarez's inaugural year, looked sound. The contract that was hammered out gave the UW $400,000 and expenses for a traveling party of 145. At a time when the UW's football gate receipts had not yet taken off, that figure looked enticing.

Michigan State Coach George Perles had been approached by the promoters earlier about playing in Japan, but flatly refused to surrender a home game. When Perles heard of Wisconsin's willingness to sacrifice a home game, a move criticized by sportswriters nationally after the consequences of the game became clear, he agreed to the shift.

Not everyone at home was happy about Wisconsin's foreign football trek. From the outset, local businesses complained that losing a home football date would hit them in the pocketbook. And with each passing victory, the prospect of playing Michigan State in Tokyo looked more like a boondoggle. The stakes in Japan were suddenly higher than anyone could have imagined two years earlier when the deal was negotiated.

Angry fan Bob Hunt wrote in a letter to *The Capital Times* just days before the team left that the decision was appalling: "What happened to the pride in this great University of Wisconsin? What happened to the ethics of playing before truly home fans? How can UW alumni and fans honestly sing 'Varsity' at this sideshow? The UW has sold its integrity."

Richter was even getting heat from state legislators at the last moment. State Senate Majority Leader Michael Ellis, a Republican from Neenah, wrote a letter less than a month before the game lambasting the idea: "It would be an absolute shame, in my view, for the Badgers to have to face their final, most crucial game far away from home when they could have played in Madison."

Richter responded that if he had the decision to make over again, chances are the Badgers would have stayed home. "It is fair to say that had we been able to predict the success of this football team, we may not have reached the same conclusion," he wrote. "However, we have committed to make the trip and will honor that commitment."

Richter contended the trip would be a solid cultural and educational experience for players. "Hopefully, the Badgers will win the game and realize all of the other positive aspects of this opportunity," he added.

Michigan State officials also questioned the trip, in hindsight.

Alvarez, however, saw some benefits to the trip. The switch gave the Badgers an extra bye week during the season, which allowed them to heal following a punishing game at Indiana. The Far East trip also gave Alvarez a carrot to hold out during recruiting, something more to induce top prep players to come to Wisconsin. And it extended the Badgers' season, giving them additional practice time.

Perhaps the added practice time was the biggest issue. One of the major benefits college coaches see in going to a postseason bowl game is that they can extend their practices, almost giving them the equivalent of another spring practice in the process. That rich-get-richer cycle was one Alvarez desperately wanted to buy into from the time he set foot on the UW campus.

The Japan game allowed the Badgers to extend practices into December, and during the bye weeks Alvarez's staff emphasized working with younger players. They got a head start on spring drills by polishing their rough edges in the fall and giving them more repetitions than they would ordinarily receive.

Although Wisconsin agreed in principle to the contract with TPI, numerous small issues needed to be worked out and a final contract was not signed until the summer before the game. Relations between the school and Japanese officials were sometimes strained and hindered by cultural barriers and varying expectations.

One of the more bizarre demands from TPI was that the UW Marching Band and cheerleaders practice for five hours a day. For the Japanese, the game was as much an entertainment event as a football game. Crowds came to see the whole package and were especially interested in the music and cheerleaders.

That off-beat request on practice time was flatly rejected. After all, even the football players were only practicing two hours a day.

Meanwhile, the trip was stirring up trouble for Wisconsin politicians as well. Gov. Tommy G. Thompson had engineered a Far East trade mission that coincided with the Tokyo game. An early itinerary indicated game day as a "free day in Tokyo." Suddenly, the Republican governor was at the center of a controversy about his appearing to be attending the game at taxpayers' cost.

Aides quickly filled up his schedule to offset the controversy and the day of the game Thompson had scheduled a news conference and meetings with several business people and lunch with a member of the Japanese parliament.

The brouhaha also caused some legislators to drop out of the trip in a controversy that was played out daily in the news sections of every paper in the state.

Alvarez didn't go into the Japan experience blindly. Even before the magnitude of the game was known, he demanded the trip be highly organized. To be successful, he knew that extraordinary care needed to be taken in planning the trip and preparing his players. That meticulous care was a key factor in how the Badgers performed both in practice and the day of the game.

The 1992 Coca-Cola Bowl between Big Eight rivals Nebraska and Kansas State was scouted by Alvarez's Administrative Assistant John Chadima and Associate Athletic Director Joel Maturi. They made careful notes on what to avoid and what the team could do to make the trip smoother.

And, as an assistant to Texas Tech's Spike Dykes in the Japan Bowl a year earlier, Alvarez took careful note of the possible pitfalls of a foreign trip, especially jet lag and the cultural nuances.

Jet lag, the physical malaise that results from disruption of an individual's pattern of sleep and wakefulness, can sap highly trained athletes of their strength and can cause headaches, diarrhea, and nausea. It's not an affliction to be taken lightly several days before your biggest game in three decades.

The Badgers faced a sixteen-hour flight on a chartered Japan Air Lines Boeing 747 from Chicago, with a stop in Vancouver. When they arrived in Japan, they were fifteen hours ahead of Wisconsin time, contributing to the upset.

Working with Dr. Steven Weiler at the UW Sleep Disorders Clinic, the Badgers hatched an elaborate plan to defeat jet lag. The program was aimed at shifting players' body clocks ahead ninety minutes a day in the six days before the Badgers left for Tokyo. It accomplished that by regulating their exposure to light and by changing their sleep patterns.

Players were instructed to wear sunglasses at predetermined times during the day and expose themselves to light during part of the night to help adjust their sleep rhythms. Whether they were in class or on the street, players were told to wear shades.

"It's kind of strange," said defensive tackle Mike Thompson. "But Coach Alvarez has a plan and we're supposed to follow it."

Practice times in Madison also were set back, so by the Sunday before their Tuesday departure, practice began at 11 p.m. and players were staying up until 5 a.m.

Dehydration was another problem countered by Badger Trainer Dennis Helwig. Long flights in enclosed cabins with recirculating air can quickly dry out a body's water reserves and worsen the effects of jet lag. Players were issued two-liter bottles of water as they entered the plane and were asked to drink water every fifteen or twenty minutes.

Meanwhile, players were urged to stay away from caffeine, which could foul up efforts to change their sleep habits. Their diets didn't need to change, since jet lag is best combated with carbohydrates, something they were already accustomed to eating.

Those planning the excursion faced another headache: how to seat the players. The teams were traveling on the same plane, a tricky problem never encountered in other circumstances. Chadima and Michigan State officials agreed on a seating plan that players said worked well: coaches and administrators sat in first-class and business-class sections on the main level. Wisconsin players were seated in coach on an upper floor and Michigan State players sat in the coach cabin on the main floor.

There weren't any incidents, but plenty of sizing up was being done as players occasionally eyed each other during the flight. At the airport, Brent Moss assessed the Michigan State players as they arrived. Before boarding the plane, he leaned over to Alvarez and confessed that these players were some of the biggest he'd ever seen.

The Badgers went into the junket with the built-in advantage of not having played the previous week. The Spartans, however, had suffered a humiliating defeat at home to Penn State just two days earlier. Michigan State had led by 20 points in the third quarter, but the Nittany Lions made a furious second-half comeback that left Perles's team gutted.

"Some of the guys from Michigan State said they had a real hard time adjusting the first few days, because they had played Penn State and were drained from that. Plus, they didn't have the preparation time we had," said Scott Nelson.

"They went from a big emotional game that they lost straight onto a plane where you sit for sixteen hours while you're sore and tired," he added. "I don't think there would have been any problems if we had sat with them, because they were already locked into the Liberty Bowl and it didn't matter if they won or lost."

Arriving at Narita International Airport, about sixty miles from central Tokyo, the Badgers grabbed their bags at about 10:30 p.m. and were whisked through customs with clocklike efficiency. The team boarded a pair of buses bound for the Miyako Hotel, about a mile west of Tokyo Bay.

A few miles from Narita, the Badgers encountered one of the only glitches during their stay in the Far East. The one thing they couldn't orchestrate was Japanese road construction, which is reserved for nighttime.

The Badgers quickly found that the always-snarled Tokyo traffic grinds into a desperate gridlock when crews decide to rip up Expressway number 7.

The longer the team sat in traffic, the worse it got. The players were told not to sleep until they arrived at the hotel as part of the plan to combat jet lag. The wait grew to one hour, then two. Some players amused themselves by watching a Japanese taxi driver relieve himself roadside. That, however, was about the extent of their amusement.

"The bus ride was the worst," said Darrell Bevell. "I have never seen so many ornery guys in my life. You did not want to say one word to anybody. You were scared to open your mouth because someone might knock you out."

Finally, a haggard-looking Badgers team arrived at the hotel at about 1:30 a.m. and headed straight for the comfort of Japanese sheets.

To help assure a seamless trip, Alvarez contacted former University of Iowa lineman Joe Levelis, who was living in Osaka. Levelis, fluent in Japanese, agreed to serve as the team's liaison.

The previous summer, Alvarez had invited Levelis, who coaches a Japanese corporate football team for a retailer, to visit the four NFL training camps held in Wisconsin.

"It's college football on a miniature scale," said Levelis, whose biggest players were about six feet two inches and 220 pounds. "But it's good football and most of the guys know more about the NFL than many spectators in the U.S."

Chadima had led Levelis and twenty-two of his Japanese players from the Mycal Bears on a July tour of the Green Bay Packers, Chicago Bears, New Orleans Saints, and Kansas City Chiefs, the so-called Cheese League, training camps.

One player, running back Mitsuo Sugita, said Japanese sports fans have an expanding appetite for American football. "The Japanese like football more and more and it's really catching on," he said. "People are becoming more interested in what's happening in the United States in football and they are also more interested in football here."

In Japan, Levelis worked with hotel personnel to assure the Wisconsin players had what they needed and met with the team to give them pointers on life in Japan. Levelis explained Tokyo's highly developed subway system and the integrity of the Japanese people.

"One of the first things he told us was, if there's something missing from your room, look first at those with you, not the Japanese," said Raymer.

There were other rules: don't count your change in front of service people, don't blow your nose in public, and always carry a matchbook with the hotel's name and address written in Japanese in case you're lost.

The teams practiced at Jingu Stadium, the home of the Yakult Swallows professional baseball team. The outfield was marked for football with white adhesive tape and Wisconsin's two practices there were held in sixty-five-degree weather under sunny skies.

The Badgers' first practice in Japan was a groggy one. Although they had gotten about six hours of sleep after their arrival, the players were still shaking off remnants of jet lag and the soreness that comes with being jammed in a small airplane seat for sixteen hours. Raymer was relieved to be able to practice again, though he said his first encounter with noseguard Lamark Shackerford shook him to his foundations. "I think every bone in my back cracked at least ten different times," Raymer said.

Although wide receiver J.C. Dawkins said the lengthy trip allowed players to rest their legs, most complained of stiff muscles and joints. The practice was sluggish and players admitted to being a half-step slow. "We had to clean up the rough edges," said Dawkins. "We didn't want a whole lot of free time. We were there for one main goal."

Tokyo's air quality posed problems for Badgers players, especially on that first day of practice. "It seemed like it was different air. It probably had to do with the smog, but it was real hard to breathe. But once we adapted to that after a couple days, we were OK," said Nelson.

Bevell said the jet-lag precautions helped the Badgers bounce back quickly: "We were a little sluggish, but practice felt great.

Perles, on the other hand, had taken few measures to stave off the effects of jet lag. "You can try to do anything you want to change your system as far as sleep and the hours, but you can't do it. So you let nature take over," he said. "It's no problem. That's part of our program. You play with the cards that are dealt. Once we kick off, we won't know if we're in Tokyo or East Lansing or Madison."

Other Badgers players agreed with Bevell that the jet-lag precautions worked. Although it often takes several days to acclimate to the time changes, most felt they were on Japan time by their second day.

"It helped for the first couple of days we were there. We got a good night's sleep and got up at 7 o'clock the next morning. We were excited to be there and knew what we were playing for. We were just flat-out fired up to be there," Nelson said.

The Badgers probably did not require any additional incentive as the game approached, since the stakes were already high enough. But during a banquet for the two teams at the elegant New Otani Hotel just two days before the game, Perles provided some more.

He is known for his rambling, sometimes charming, discourses. At the pregame press conference, a Japanese reporter asked him how Michigan State came to use Spartans as their nickname. What followed was classic Perles.

"The Spartans are a takeoff on the Roman Spartans. The Greeks, excuse me," said Perles. "There was a horse that went along with it. It was a big horse out of wood and a lot of soldiers got on it and it was a gift. They opened the gate and brought it in and the horse won. It's an old horse story."

Even the interpreter threw up his hands at that. So much for the charming side.

Perles fired up Wisconsin players with a remark at the banquet that insinuated that Michigan State did not much care about the game's outcome.

Bevell said the statement struck him as odd, even if the Spartans did have a Liberty Bowl bid sewn up. Others simply resented it and used it as an incentive on the field.

"Coach Perles got up there and said, 'I'll tell you one thing, I don't give a damn about this game.' He said this in a roomful of people. I took that as a personal challenge," said Carlos Fowler. "When people run their mouths and say disrespectful things that's a slap in the face. If you're any type of competitor, if you're any type of man, you won't let anybody say anything like that to you."

Perles's spiel also roused Panos, who could not believe what he was hearing. He wondered how Perles could motivate his players with an attitude like this.

"You don't play football like that, you don't prepare for teams like that—it got me mad," said Panos. "Who was he to say this game didn't mean anything? His speech was a motivator."

Meanwhile, the Spartans faced another disadvantage coming into the game. Michigan State had been unable to have any full-contact drills between Saturday's loss to Penn State and Wednesday's practice in Japan. Sunday was the Spartans' off-day and on Monday the uniforms had to be shipped to Chicago to clear customs. Wisconsin, meanwhile, scheduled its departure for Chicago to allow the Badgers to practice Saturday through Monday.

"We're going to find out if this practice is overrated," Perles said. "You hope your fundamentals and things that are basic are working for you. It happens in the NFL. Players play on Sunday, and sometimes come right back on Thursday, so it's nothing that hasn't happened before."

To help reduce the Spartans' game-planning disadvantage, Michigan State worked on Wisconsin for one day in the week before their Penn State loss. And Perles said the Spartans had no agenda other than winning the game. "We're not playing this game for anyone but ourselves. We're not doing anyone else's work for them. We're playing this game for ourself and ourself alone," he insisted.

Despite speculation to the contrary, Perles was steadfast in his belief that the Penn State loss had no bearing on the Wisconsin game. The Spartans, he said, played a physical football game against the Nittany Lions, moved the ball, and stopped Penn State's ground game.

There was no hangover, Perles asserted. "We'll play this game with all kinds of emotions," he pledged.

On the second day of practice the Badgers appeared to have regained their full athletic capacity and players were more upbeat. Through it all, the team appeared loose, relaxed, but clearly focused on the stakes involved in the game at the Tokyo Dome, called the "Big Egg" by locals.

The previous night, as players dined all over Tokyo, Alvarez took his assistants to a topflight Japanese restaurant for some heavy-duty dining of their own. The staff doffed their shoes, sat on the floor, and eagerly anticipated each new course.

"We sat on the floor and ate everything," said Alvarez. "Everything. Everything they put in front of me. My knees were all right, but my butt was a little sore."

Alvarez was quick to point out, however, that Japanese cuisine was not high on his list: "That's it. Now, burgers and fries."

There were concerns before the team arrived about maintaining a consistent diet and being able to offer the same sorts and quantities of food as were available at the training table in Madison.

UW officials exchanged numerous faxes with dining room managers in Japan in the months before the game, hoping to alleviate those concerns. But it wasn't until they arrived that they were able to iron out the final details.

Team nutritionist Dave Ellis said the distance posed a problem in meal planning: "We were sending out menus in English and it was a challenge for them to decipher what we wanted. Once we got there and were able to get into the dining room and show them the buffet format we wanted and how to manipulate the order of the food and tweak the menus, it started to fall in place."

Hotel personnel, eager to accommodate team officials, made unusual runs to specialty shops to find peanut butter and baked goods requested by the Badgers.

Among players, the anxiety was building. In the previous three and one-half weeks, Wisconsin had played only one game that triggered an unprecedented surge of media hype. The wait helped engender a renewed eagerness to take the field.

"As soon as we beat Illinois and I heard that Ohio State lost, I could have played the game that next day," said Raymer.

Shackerford couldn't help but agree. He'd been watching film and preparing to engage with Michigan State's massive offensive line for two weeks. With the game only two days off, he was antsy.

"There's no more trying to get motivated. We have everything laying out in front of us. We just have to get it," Shackerford said, adding that the only advice he had for teammates was, "Just go out and kick some butt."

On Saturday, the Badgers held a forty-minute walk-through at the Tokyo Dome, the only time they would get to practice in the 50,000-seat enclosed stadium before game day. It was a relaxed affair, with players in helmets and sweats, as television crews strung cable and advertising placards were placed behind both benches for the length of the field.

In the stadium concourse, workers were stuffing hundreds of blue nylon duffel bags with the eighteen-dollar game programs and white golf shirts embroidered with the Coca-Cola Bowl emblem to give to major Japanese financial backers and dignitaries on game day.

Alvarez sized up the stadium, which is reminiscent of the Hubert H. Humphrey Metrodome in Minneapolis, and was wary of the turf. The artificial surface was worn and rippled along base paths in front of the Badgers' bench.

"It's tough turf. I don't like it," Alvarez said. "They'll just have turf burns when they're done."

The accommodations for press-box coaches Brad Childress and McMahon were less than ideal as well. The boxes were low in the stadium, limiting the view. Throughout the game, they would rely on television replay monitors from which they could get a better view of line schemes and coverages.

Worse, the booth was next to the Spartans' booth, so coaches had to be careful how loud they spoke. But with the thunderous noise being made in the stadium, that would be only a minor irritation.

Before the game, green-and-white pompons were placed on seats in half of the stadium while red-and-white ones were placed on the other half.

Sunday afternoon, the Tokyo Dome was perhaps the loudest place in all of Japan. It may have been the loudest place in the Far East. The promoters set up microphones and additional speakers to amplify the band music, and when bands weren't playing they piped in recorded rock music, even while the teams were playing.

An irritating announcer with a Top 40 disc-jockey style called the game in English; another announcer called it in Japanese and at high volume. It was like sitting inside a jet engine.

As fans entered the stadium, they were given "Bucky Bandanas," white bandanas imprinted with the Badgers' football helmet on a field of red roses with the words "On Wisconsin" in English and Japanese. Badgers cheerleaders and even the governor handed out 12,000 of the hankies.

And for all they cost, the game programs included a biography of Alvarez complete with color pictures, but misspelled his name throughout, referring to him as "Barry Alvaretz."

ESPN decided to broadcast the game, but leaned on Big Ten officials to delay it for thirty minutes—until 10:30 p.m. Wisconsin time—to allow the network to complete its coverage of the Kansas-DePaul basketball game. The Big Ten dashed that late-night plan, so ESPN was forced to join the game in progress. But many Wisconsin cable systems sought and received permission to pick up an alternative feed of the game so viewers could see the entire contest.

Michigan State came into the game knowing it had to do what no other Wisconsin opponent had done all season, stop the rush. Early in the game the Spartans seemed to be able to contain Wisconsin's flat-footed offense.

Wisconsin scored first, as Rick Schnetzky booted a 35-yard field goal. On their next possession, however, Jim Miller moved the Spartans with pinpoint passing, completing Michigan State's first scoring drive with a 33-yard touchdown pass to receiver Mill Coleman.

Trailing 7–3, the Badgers drove to the Spartans' 5-yard line, but Spartans linebacker Rob Frederickson stopped Moss for a loss of a yard and the Badgers again brought out Schnetzky. This time, however, he shanked a 22-yard attempt on the first play of the second quarter.

That failed drive left the Badgers searching for something to shake them out of their offensive doldrums and regain an attack rhythm. They found it on Michigan State's next drive.

"Our offense was in limbo and it seemed like neither team wanted to take charge and go after it," said Nelson.

With the Spartans driving at the Wisconsin 43-yard line, Miller backpedaled, looking for tight end Byron Allen. Miller found him on a crossing pattern, but botched the throw and was intercepted by Nelson at the Wisconsin 26. Nelson weaved between Spartans players for a 34-yard return and jolted the Badgers' offense back to life.

"I was just in the middle of the field and they dragged the tight end across the middle. Miller's a right-handed quarterback, so when he's rolling left it's hard to throw across his body and he threw it behind the receiver and it hit me in the numbers. It wasn't like I made any great read. I just broke on it," Nelson said.

In his first game as a starter since cracking three ribs against Ohio State, Nelson made a point: he was back and ready to play. The play was central to the game, giving Wisconsin new vigor.

"After the interception, it seemed like our offense just went down and scored. It jump started us and things started to steamroll from there," Nelson added.

The turnover opened the door to a 7-play drive that ended when Terrell Fletcher ran wide to the left to pick up a 1-yard touchdown to put Wisconsin ahead 10–7. Wisconsin's defense held Michigan State to a 4-down series and a punt on its next possession.

A 24-yard punt return by Keith Jackson simply added to the snowball effect success was having on the Badgers. On the next play, Fletcher ran left for 40 yards, shedding a tackle by defensive back Myron Bell and outrunning strong safety Aldi Taylor for the touchdown that put Wisconsin up 17-7.

Fletcher tipped his helmet to the offensive line. "They just stood on their blocks while I jittered around in the backfield," he said. "After that, it was all daylight."

Michigan State was forced to punt on its next series, but downed Chris Salani's punt at the Wisconsin 1-yard line. Emboldened by their success, the Badgers resumed a jackhammer attack on Michigan State's defense.

After a 5-yard run by Mark Montgomery, the Badgers decided to gamble. From the booth, Childress called a long pass and Alvarez agreed. On the next play, Bevell connected with DeRamus on the left side for 41 yards to establish decent field position.

"I just had to beat my man, and I told Bevell in the huddle that all he had to do was throw it up. I knew I'd find a way to get it," said DeRamus.

Coaches on the sidelines had encouraged DeRamus, since he was close to beating Wisconsin's all-time receiving record held by Al Toon, the former New York Jets star.

"They told me, 'You need one more catch. Go out there and get it,' and they gave it to me," said DeRamus, whose 5 catches for 96 yards in the game gave him 54 catches and 920 yards for the season, putting him ahead of Toon.

The record was even more impressive in that football was far removed from DeRamus's mind growing up in New Jersey. He was a lanky basketball and track star in his sophomore season at Edgewood Regional High School in Atco, New Jersey. For him, the youngest of four DeRamus boys, playing pro basketball was the ideal.

Although he enjoyed playing an occasional impromptu game of tackle football with friends, DeRamus never participated in midget league football or attended football camps. Instead, he spent his time honing his dunking. He remains the school's leading basketball scorer.

"I always played street ball, growing up as a kid. I was always Lynn Swann," said DeRamus. "But I was never serious about it because hoop was my favorite sport. I wanted to be a professional basketball player. In my freshman year, I wanted to concentrate on basketball, and I started on the varsity hoop team as a freshman."

DeRamus went to high school football games as a spectator, to watch close friends Michael London and Keith Jackson play. Today, all three are wide receivers on the Wisconsin team, with DeRamus coming to Wisconsin with London in 1991 and Jackson coming to Madison via the junior college route in 1993.

Between his sophomore and junior years, London and Jackson convinced

DeRamus to try out for the football team. DeRamus agreed and found himself in line with other Edgewood athletes waiting to pick up their gear before the first practice.

"When I first went to pick out my equipment, I picked up one of those helmets the defensive ends wear with the bar in the middle. I took arm pads, every kind of pad they had, but Michael and Keith straightened me out and I eventually got the right stuff," said DeRamus.

It was obvious DeRamus had the right stuff to play football. He came with 4.4-second speed in the 40-yard dash and an angular body well-suited to his receiving role.

In his first season playing organized football, DeRamus won all-state honors and the family's mailbox started to bulge with mail from college recruiters all over the nation. His interest in pursuing basketball on the college level also started to wane.

"I was killing DBs in my senior year, and I decided, I'm going to have to go with football," said DeRamus, who averaged 31.9 yards a catch as a prep senior.

"I swear I got a letter from every college in the country. Miami used to come and see me, come to my track meets, but I always wanted to play in the Big Ten. I never even heard of Wisconsin," he said.

DeRamus heard of Wisconsin's interest through a friend of his brother's, former University of Iowa defensive end Leroy Smith.

"Leroy said, 'Coach Wyatt's a cool guy. Listen to him,'" DeRamus said.

DeRamus said the recruitment was not pumped full of the hyperbole some other programs were using. It seemed to him to be more honest and straight-forward, more aimed at rejuvenating a tired program.

"Coach Alvarez was straight-up, down to earth, not the kind of guy to sell you a whole bunch of nonsense," said DeRamus.

While visiting DeRamus's Sicklerville, New Jersey, home, Alvarez picked up on DeRamus's family nickname, "Babe," a moniker which has followed him to Wisconsin. The nickname started as "Baby Lee," since his father is Lee Sr.

"My mom was saying, 'Babe, this, and Babe, that.' Coach Alvarez started laughing and said, 'That's what I'm calling you from now on,'" DeRamus said with a laugh.

DeRamus made an immediate and lasting impact on UW football, and started rewriting record books as a freshman. Against Eastern Michigan, his 89-yard touchdown pass reception was the longest ever by a UW player. De-Ramus was unaware of the feat until he returned to the bench and spoke with Receivers Coach Jay Norvell.

"I didn't even know I broke it. Then Coach Norvell came over and said, 'See what you can do if you listen in practice?' I looked up and it was flashing across the scoreboard that I just broke the record," he said.

During his first season, cornerback Troy Vincent (who was a first-round draft pick of the Miami Dolphins in 1992) schooled DeRamus relentlessly on pass routes and how to beat the secondary. After practice and in the locker room, Vincent would hook up with DeRamus and discuss technique. DeRamus soaked it up like a sponge.

"If it wasn't for him beating me up and keeping me after practice, I don't know where I'd be today," DeRamus said.

DeRamus went on to lead the Big Ten with a 16.2-yards-per-catch average and as a junior challenged all of Wisconsin's pass-catching marks.

DeRamus's play in 1993 also made him the first Badger since David Charles in 1978 to lead the team in receiving three years in a row.

"I'm one of those guys who sets goals constantly," said DeRamus. "The records are nice, as long as I reach my goals. That's the top priority."

As he entered his senior season, DeRamus had 1,974 receiving yards and 119 catches and needed only 130 yards and 13 catches to set records in both categories.

DeRamus knows it's a cliché. Still, he insists the team's attitude was crucial to Wisconsin's success in 1993. "We took it one game at a time. We focused in on that one game every week. That was a mentality we all picked up. There was the twenty-four-hour rule; we celebrated a victory for twenty-four hours, then put it behind us. Everyone abided by it. We were all business come Sunday."

Seven plays after DeRamus's catch, the Badgers completed a 99-yard drive as Moss ran right for 3 yards and a touchdown that put Wisconsin ahead 24–7 at halftime.

Bevell was unaffected by the noise throughout the game, insisting that Minneapolis' Metrodome was still the loudest stadium he's played in. But he conceded the circumstances of the game were a bit weird. "They were screaming when you were in the huddle and quiet when you were on the line, but I don't think it had an effect on me," he said.

After the half, Wisconsin continued its domination. Although the Spartans added a pair of field goals by Bill Stoyanovich and a 2-yard touchdown run by tailback Duane Goulbourne, the Badgers did not lose the offensive rhythm sparked by Nelson's interception.

Wisconsin, however, continued its offensive assault, as Schnetzky connected on a 27-yard field goal and DeRamus caught a 7-yard touchdown strike from Bevell to give Wisconsin a 34–17 lead with 11 minutes left in the game.

Stoyanovich's second field goal, a 33-yarder with 8:15 left in the fourth quarter, trimmed Wisconsin's lead to 34–20. Predictably, it also set up a Michigan State on-side kick, which was recovered by Spartan Myron Bell at the Spartans' 49.

The field goal and recovered on-side kick allowed Michigan State to recapture the momentum it had lost earlier in the game. But Wisconsin's defense snuffed out the Spartans' hopes on the next play. As Miller passed for Coleman at the Wisconsin 8-yard line cornerback Kenny Gales slashed in front of the receiver to make the interception.

"That interception pretty much iced the ball game," said Alvarez.

Wisconsin continued to rush with ease as the game wound down. On its next series, Moss chunked a 26-yard gain, followed by a 33-yard run through the right side by Fletcher. The 92-yard drive ended as Moss plunged up the middle for a 1-yard touchdown with 3:47 to play, to give Wisconsin a 41–20 lead.

As the clock accounted for the game's final seconds, there was an outpouring of emotion unlike any other of the Alvarez era. Alvarez bear-hugged Richter and went on to throw his arm around fullback Montgomery. Linebacker Sylas Pratt clenched a rose between his teeth as he shared an embrace with Panos.

For his part, Panos was low-key. He sustained a concussion late in the game when he was hit in the helmet by the knee of a Michigan State player. He refused to come out of the game.

"I had to keep playing. I couldn't ask for time out in the biggest game of my life. No way," said Panos. "I was really out of it at the end of the game."

The closeness of the moment impressed Bevell. Unlike Madison, where players needed to wade through crowds of friends, autograph seekers, and other hangers-on, the crowds at the Tokyo Dome dispersed.

"As much as I wanted to be in Madison celebrating, it was really a good experience to be over in Tokyo because you got to be there with the team, the coaches, and a few of the people that mattered," Bevell said.

"We stayed out there for forty minutes hugging each other and soaking it in," he added. "You could find Lee DeRamus or Terrell Fletcher if you wanted to. They weren't lost in the crowd."

Nelson darted through the crowd to blow off the steam of five years of grinding work. "It was relief," he said. "You hugged every person you ran into, whether it's a media guy or a band member or a cheerleader. I couldn't believe what we just did. There was a sense of disbelief. Then they handed out those hats and we put the hats on and it was probably the proudest feeling I'll ever have."

The hats were manufactured in anticipation of a victory and bore the Wisconsin flying "W" emblazoned with a rose and the words "Rose Bowl." Big Ten Commissioner James Delany handed Alvarez three dozen red roses, purchased at a Tokyo florist earlier in the day for the handsome sum of $320. The band played "Varsity," then the "Bud Song" as players danced the polka at midfield.

Governor Thompson was allowed onto the field and Wisconsin fans leaned over railings and beseeched him to have the guards allow them onto the field. Though Thompson tried to convince a security guard, his clout apparently ended at the state line.

Alvarez, nursing a cold, showed no ill effects as he met with Wisconsin reporters in a tunnel behind one of the stadium's dugouts. Soon, though, Japanese officials herded Alvarez into an interview room where an interpreter translated his responses. American reporters, working on extended deadlines, did their best to ask rapid-fire questions that prevented the interpreter from translating Alvarez's answers.

After showering and absorbing the congratulations of the many parents who traveled to Tokyo, players returned to the hotel and stowed their gear. Many boarded the hotel shuttle for Meguro Station, and took a subway to Roppongi, Tokyo's renowned nightlife district. Fowler hung out one of the windows of the bus, waving his arms and calling "Konnichiwa," the Japanese word for hello, and "Rose Bowl!" There was no curfew and players planned to take full advantage of that rare benefit to check out the plentiful nightclubs.

While they cruised Roppongi's night spots, groups of Wisconsin players regularly encountered Spartans players. The mood, however, generally was festive on both sides.

"The game was over and we were going to have fun, so we spent time with those guys. Most of them said, 'Hey, you guys are the best and we wish you the best,'" Nelson said.

During the course of the night, Nelson met Miller, the Spartans' quarterback, in a bar. They joked about Nelson's interception and both generally expressed relief that the game was history.

"Miller said, 'I'm glad this thing is over; now we can go home.' That's basically the way it was by the end of the week for everyone: Let's get out of here."

In Madison, fans poured from State Street bars to celebrate the victory. In a hallway at the Tokyo Dome, Defensive Coordinator Dan McCarney was wondering what it was like back home. "I wish I was in Madison tonight," he said. "I imagine they're having a lot of fun. I hope my house is still standing when I get back."

Cindy Alvarez, who stayed behind in Madison because she endured the trip to Tokyo just a year earlier, went downtown with a friend to check out the revelry. One of the first sights she saw was their teenaged son, Chad, strolling down the street with some buddies, smoking a fat cigar.

Aimee Jansen, the student rescued from the crowd surge by walk-on Mike Brin, was among those on State Street that night. But her lingering fear of crowds convinced her to leave. As she made her way out of the throng, she spotted Brin, who had not made the trip to Tokyo. "I just panicked. I had to get out of there," she said.

On Monday, the Badgers did not leave Narita until late afternoon. To pass the time after their 8:30 a.m. checkout, the Badgers—some light on sleep after their celebrations the previous night—toured an open-air fish market and visited shrines and temples in the Asakusa area.

When it came time to board JAL flight 7008, players were eager to end the ordeal. On the return flight, players shared good-natured stories and the Spartans were generally congratulatory to the Badgers, wishing them luck in their Rose Bowl encounter with UCLA.

The Badgers and Spartans flew into Chicago's O'Hare International Airport. From there, the Badgers bused back to Madison. Along the way, people waved and honked their horns and a man and a young boy in a pickup truck at the state line erected a sign congratulating the Badgers.

As the buses passed, the man got in the truck and the pair followed the Badgers to their welcome home rally in Madison. Arriving in the city, the Badgers picked up a police escort to the stadium, where several thousand fans waited to welcome the victors.

The week after the Michigan State game, telephones in the football office were constantly busy. It seemed like every alumnus from Superior to Kenosha was calling to offer congratulations. The office was packed with perhaps twenty dozen roses and the place was beginning to smell like a funeral home.

The weirdest call of the week, though, was taken by receptionist Shannon Marsh. It was from a woman who assumed the coaches would be awash in roses upon their arrival from the Far East.

The caller wanted to know if she could have the roses when they were dead. Seems she wanted to use the petals from the congratulatory blooms to make potpourri air freshener.

In time, the scent of roses would overpower the entire state.

"It's Going to Be a Great Ride"

The recorded message on the answering machine at Alvarez's house was one of the first things to change after the victory in Tokyo.

Instead of the standard, "We're not available, but please leave your message," Cindy changed it to "We don't have any tickets for the Rose Bowl, but if you'd like to leave a message. . . ."

The fever had taken hold.

Travel agencies were furiously booking charter flights, students were standing in long lines for game tickets, and personnel at the Dane County Regional Airport were mapping battle plans for the airport's busiest day in history as dozens of charter flights were scheduled.

Almost immediately after the Tokyo game, Alvarez had a representative in Madison obtain a season's worth of videotapes from UCLA. In turn, Wisconsin provided the Bruins with their season's games.

Wisconsin's video experts, led by Jim Roberts, worked in their $500,000 computerized video control room at the opposite end of the hall from Alvarez's office meticulously breaking down the UCLA tapes so tendencies could be determined and coverage schemes devised.

As that process went on, shortly after the Badgers' arrival from Tokyo, Alvarez, Richter, and other UW officials turned around and headed for Pasadena to scout practice facilities and plan for the New Year's Day game.

The Rose Bowl was not exactly a seat of honor for the Big Ten, which had lost nineteen of the last twenty-four games to its Pac-10 opponents. There were numerous theories, but Wisconsin Wide Receivers Coach Jay Norvell believed it had to do with stepping outside the routine.

Norvell, son of UW Athletic Board member and 1963 Rose Bowl player Merritt Norvell, played for Iowa in the 1982 and 1986 Rose Bowls. The Hawkeyes lost both games, to Washington 28–0 and to UCLA 45–28.

"The whole trip and environment is out of your realm," he said. "Midwest schools are going from snow and ice to fairly nice weather, and usually it's a home game for the West Coast. You're an outsider."

Norvell said Big Ten teams that lost in Pasadena usually were shaken out of their typical game plans early and failed to return to their strengths.

"When I was at Iowa, we got out of the things we did well so early in those games that we could never get back in," he said. "The most important thing is to stay in our game and play with emotion. But emotion's got to be a controlled thing."

Returning from Tokyo, Badgers players were buoyed by the football mania that swept the state. The Rose Bowl hype was in full swing, and for a group of players who had lived through the bad time, this was a treasured time.

"I was driving by a gas station and a guy was selling T-shirts and you want to stop and say, 'I play on the team; let's see what you've got here.' You feel so proud about what we've done this year," said Scott Nelson.

The buildup did not surprise strong safety Reggie Holt, who came to Wisconsin in Morton's last year. After a wrenching switch from quarterback to defensive back, Holt many times had found himself on the brink of quitting the team.

Alvarez convinced him to stay, and Holt prospered as a safety. "People in Wisconsin deserve the fun and the bowl game," said Holt. "I'm surprised there wasn't a riot."

The practices in Madison leading up to the Rose Bowl were intense and players were well-drilled by coaches on what to tell the media, especially about UCLA. The party line was this: UCLA has gobs of team speed, enough to make your head spin. Woe is me, what an uphill climb for the pluggers from the Midwest!

In the weeks before the game, it became the mantra of players and coaches who hoped it would be written enough nationally that the Bruins would start to believe their own press clippings. Even when reporters did not ask, Badgers players proffered observations about how incredibly athletic this UCLA bunch was.

Behind the scenes, Wisconsin players and coaches knew from day one that they could whip this bunch, that UCLA was not the powerhouse they were touting to the media.

Bevell admitted later there was a massive propaganda campaign at work in the weeks before the game. "They tell us what to say sometimes and we try to make it believable, whether we believe it or not," he said. "It's true. They were very fast, they were very athletic. But by no means did we think we were going to lose."

Perhaps the Badgers' biggest victory during the off weeks before the Rose Bowl was the decision by Brent Moss to remain at the university for his final year of eligibility and bypass the NFL draft. The decision was made in Alvarez's office on December 16, as Moss and his father, Henry, met with Alvarez.

In a conference call with several NFL personnel experts, Moss was urged to stay in school to improve his pro prospects for 1995. Among those on the line were Green Bay Packers General Manager Ron Wolf, Ken Herock of the Atlanta Falcons, Dick Steinberg of the New York Jets, San Diego Chargers General Manager Bobby Beathard, and San Francisco Scouting Director Vinny Cerrato.

After the season, Moss never looked back on his decision to stay at Wisconsin, especially given the advice of the NFL officials who said his leaving school would be premature.

"No. I wasn't ready. Staying one more year and helping the team out, that was my main concern," he said.

Moss made his decision on the same day he was awarded the *Chicago Tribune*'s Silver Football Award, presented each year to the Big Ten's most valuable player. It was the first time a Wisconsin player won the award since Ron Vander Kelen earned the honor thirty-one years earlier.

It had been a long, sometimes turbulent, trip from high school to Big Ten stardom for Moss. It is eminently unfair to ask eighteen-year-olds to handle life capably, much less under a microscope. Yet, top college athletes, propelled into the public eye because of their prodigious achievements on the football field, are subjected to the burdens of greatness far before they are ready.

For Brent Moss, the attention was sometimes a painful load, as he worked to make the grades needed for him to set foot on the turf at Camp Randall Stadium.

Athletes sometimes use hardship and pain as fuel for their on-field performance. Moss is a case in point. He used the 1993 season to vault to prominence as one of the nation's most prolific rushers. Yet, as he rewrote record after record, lurking in the background was his urge to prove people wrong; a satisfaction in making the doubters believe; a chip placed on his shoulder not by Moss, but by others.

Moss's career at Wisconsin has always had a darker side. As a freshman, he was not allowed to compete or receive an athletic scholarship because he did not meet NCAA academic standards. His working-class parents, Henry and Elaine, worked extra shifts to keep him in classes at Madison, something for which Moss is grateful.

His grades, of course, became an instant topic of publicity and speculation.

The state's top prep football player, one of the bright lights of Alvarez's new Badger reign, was ineligible to play and people were talking.

More distressing, however, were the people who were talking to Moss. In a dorm room he shared with receiver J.C. Dawkins, a high school teammate, crank callers used his plight to taunt him and inflict wounds that linger today.

"Hey Brent, what's two plus two?" they would ask.

Moss never forgot the jeering calls in the middle of the night. In fact, the voices echoed through his 1993 season, driving him to become the best rusher in the Big Ten and the most successful in Badgers history.

Moss is no Pollyanna. In fact, his outlook tends to be grim and pessimistic. But it is a well-thought-out approach to life and has helped him cope both with adversity and with stardom.

"People want to see you fail and all of the success we had last year didn't change that," said Moss. "Just because I did something good doesn't put me out of that category. They wanted me to fail from the get-go."

"I always think of the worst before I think of the best. If you think of the worst, anything from there will be better."

Not even rushing for a school-record 1,637 yards, averaging 5.2 yards a carry and scoring 16 touchdowns changed Moss's thinking. He set the school's season rushing record in the Illinois game, breaking Billy Marek's 1,281 yards set eighteen years earlier.

Moss, however, is stand-offish about success and always trying to ward off failure.

"I don't think about failure. If it happens, it happens and it's something I'll have to deal with. The best way I can do it is stay out there and try to be successful," said Moss.

The 1993 season also has failed to change him personally, he insists.

"I'm still the same person inside. I still feel the same way about playing football. Those are things I did in the past. That was last year. This is the year I have to shine," said Moss.

But there were other challenges to encounter before Moss made it to his season of glory. Moss and high school girlfriend Stacy Johnson became parents in March 1992, near the end of Moss's sophomore year.

At times, the strain of domestic life, football, and a college education was a challenge, but Moss and Johnson stayed together. Again, Moss is grateful.

"She has helped me out in tough times where I didn't want to play some-times, or didn't want to go to school. She always set me straight, 'You have to do this and you have to do that.' She helped to bring some responsibility to my life," he said. "I thank her for that."

At first, Cyrus was a well-kept secret. But as the 1993 season rolled on, Moss spoke more freely about his son and his love for him.

"I worry a lot about my boy. I feel better talking about it now. I'm not real comfortable talking about my personal life, because what if something happens that's bad? People are going to run me down," said Moss.

Since they were eleven years old, Moss and Dawkins have played football together. They first played football on a youth league team coached by Dawkins' father, and they later played together at Racine's Washington Park High School.

As a high school senior, Dawkins caught 15 passes, an amazing 12 for touchdowns. He credits Moss's running abilities for drawing defenses and leaving him open to catch passes.

That's one reason it was fitting that Dawkins was the first to tell Moss during January 1993 that Moss's lost year of eligibility had been restored.

The NCAA passed rules that corrected inequities in college entrance test scoring that restored the year Moss lost because his test scores fell a fraction of a point off the mark.

Dawkins, on campus to host a recruit during the Christmas break, was told of the news by Alvarez and immediately called Moss's family.

"It felt good to break the news," said Dawkins.

Moss said the news came as a relief, since he was under a good deal of pressure to make the most out of what he believed would be his final year in college.

After the 1993 season, pressure has taken on a new meaning for Moss.

"I don't put any pressure on myself. I have confidence in myself. And whatever happens, I'm man enough to take responsibility for it," said Moss. "I don't think there's pressure, but I kind of like being under pressure anyway."

From the outset, Alvarez liked Moss's hard-bitten attitude, both on and off the football field. The head coach quickly tabbed Moss with the nickname "The Alleycat." In a university-produced preview of the 1994 Badgers football team, Alvarez is quoted as saying he gave Moss the name "because of his ferocity in the heat of battle."

To be more specific, however, Alvarez gave Moss the name after he returned to campus following a weekend in Racine that resulted in Moss picking up a shiner in a late-night altercation.

Alvarez said he admires Moss's tenacity, especially through his early academic troubles when "Prop 48 became his middle name."

That persistence was something Moss's father instilled in his son. Moss recalled trying to walk out on his high school track team as a sophomore.

"I tried to quit track when I was in high school. I was on my way to sectionals and I quit because I got into it with my coach," said Moss. "Dad literally grabbed me and told me, 'You're not going to quit. I didn't raise any quitters.'"

The next day, he returned to the team.

Moss's career at Wisconsin has been full of ups and downs. In his first season, he was hobbled by ankle injuries and rushed for just 219 yards.

In 1992, coaches tried to convert him to a fullback, an experiment that Moss was not wild about and which ultimately failed. Moss went back to tailback and managed to gain 739 yards to become Wisconsin's leading rusher and the seventh-rank back in the Big Ten.

"It's been worth it, but it's been a long climb," said Moss.

As Moss walked out of the locker room at the Rose Bowl and headed up the tunnel to a waiting bus, he possessed a streak of 11 straight games in which he rushed for 100 yards or more. The streak surpassed the former UW record of 7 games put together first by 1952 Heisman Trophy winner Alan Ameche and later by Larry Emery.

Before spring conditioning began in 1994, Moss would be named the Big Ten's MVP and selected by the Touchdown Club of Columbus, Ohio, as the nation's running back of the year. His honors are all safely ensconced in a newly purchased curio cabinet in his parents' home.

"I'll probably just let them sit there. My mom is the type who really worries about me. I know my father does, too, but he won't show it; he's kind of laid back. Kind of like me," Moss said.

"It's kind of cool to be able to give them these trophies, because I felt pretty bad in my freshman and sophomore years. I was going through things I thought I'd never get out of. I thought I'd always be in trouble."

Moss entered 1994 as a senior, the nation's top returning rusher and with the same hunger to prove people wrong. The bottom line was: he wanted to make fans appreciate his true potential as an athlete.

And as a man.

Fresh from two days off of practice to celebrate the holiday, Wisconsin players boarded a chartered jet the afternoon of Christmas Day, bound for Los Angeles International Airport. Almost everywhere they went, they encountered enthusiastic fans. As they boarded buses for the airport outside of the McClain Facility, eleven-year-old Eric Grahn of Janesville held up a sign that said "Good Luck, Guys!" bearing a map of the state and three red roses.

Arriving three and one-half hours later at LAX's Gate 35, the Badgers were greeted by about seventy-five well-wishers, including Wisconsinite Gary Bliss of Brodhead, who took a more opportunistic approach with a sign saying "Welcome Badgers!!! Need Two Tickets." The gambit didn't work but Bliss, decked out in a Wisconsin T-Shirt, did get Bevell to pose with him for a snapshot.

Alvarez and his wife were greeted by Tournament of Roses officials who presented them with a bouquet of roses and attached embroidered rose lapel stickers to their clothes. The team boarded buses at the airport and were escorted to the team headquarters at the Doubletree Hotel in downtown Pasadena, about forty minutes away.

Throughout the week, the Badgers received what amounted to a phony, but most effective, police escort. The motorcycle escorts, not on-duty police officers, were hired through a private firm and guided the team effortlessly through Los Angeles's pre-earthquake freeway traffic.

With their Harley-Davidsons dressed out to look like police motorcycles, they were a luxury all week. They blocked traffic at freeway entrances, created openings for lane changes, and used loud horns to gain the attention of uncooperative motorists. Most times there were only three motorcycles, but the way they darted in and out of traffic, it seemed more like ten. It was the only way to travel in Los Angeles.

Vendors had set up shop in the Doubletree Hotel lobby, selling everything from sweatshirts to lapel pins. Wisconsin fans, players' families, and UW Athletic Department officials swarmed around the vendors' tables.

After arriving, the Badgers' itinerary included the two words that may be the most sacrosanct in all of college football: "no curfew." But even that promise was a two-edged sword.

Cory Raymer, who had spent much of his holiday downtime in Fond du Lac partying, wasn't in the mood for checking out California night spots. A night in the whirlpool and a warm bed were all he required. And besides, the lack of a curfew was buffered by the 7:15 a.m. wake-up call Sunday and Monday.

Alvarez, who savored the bowl hoopla, was not about to deprive his players of the pre-Rose Bowl traditions. "I've seen coaches who beat the kids up and they're difficult to motivate and bitter about going to a bowl game the next year. They need to get involved with all the activities, then focus in on the game," he said.

And coaches did not want preparation for the Rose Bowl to vary far from the routine players were accustomed to at home.

That, Alvarez felt, was a key to the season: never vary. Even on the Tokyo trip, he worked to keep schedules close to what players were used to in Madison. Since he never required bed checks in Madison on Saturday, Sunday, and Monday, he did not post a bedtime in Pasadena, either.

The team's list of goals, an internal document which the Badgers don't speak about during the season, ended with: "win a January 1 bowl game."

The idea of winning the bowl game was central to that goal. Alvarez and five assistants—Dan McCarney, Bernie Wyatt, Kevin Cosgrove, Bill Callahan, and Brad Childress—had coached in the Rose Bowl and none had won. Another, Receivers Coach Jay Norvell, played in a losing Rose Bowl.

Uniformly the coaches traced their lack of success in the games to faulty goals. At Illinois, where Childress, Callahan, and Cosgrove coached, the goal was to get to a bowl game.

The Badgers' first day of practice in California was overcast and temperatures were in the mid-60s. Everywhere they went, people were apologizing for the cold weather, which seemed like a luxury compared to Wisconsin's sub-zero chill.

Things went smoothly, except for the fact that some players had left their practice jerseys in Madison. Bevell, for instance, wore number 6 instead of number 11. Alvarez, who closed practice to the media, said there was no sinister intent to conceal the players' identities. By Tuesday, the correct practice jerseys had arrived.

After the Badgers' first day of practice in California, they boarded buses and headed for Universal Studios and a complimentary tour.

While the Badgers slept at the Doubletree that night, they were joined by an outsider who was treated to a rude awakening the next morning. A man sneaked into the Badgers' snack room at the hotel—a room stocked with lean-meat sandwiches, fruits, and isotonic drinks—and fell asleep.

He was given a rude rise-and-shine Tuesday morning by McCarney and John Palermo, who discovered the man asleep on a sofa in the room. Beside him was a plate with banana peels, apple cores, and other remnants of his marauding midnight snack. "At first I thought he was a homeless guy," said McCarney. "But he was wearing a $300 leather coat and had a pager."

Alvarez almost chose Occidental College, just ten minutes from the team hotel, as the site for the Badgers' practices. Iowa had used Occidental for practices in 1982, and he liked the convenience of the junior college.

After visiting there, however, Alvarez opted instead for more distant Citrus Community College, whose grass field was in better shape.

Citrus Community College is about twenty minutes east of Pasadena, just off Interstate 210 in Glendora, at the base of the San Gabriel Mountains. The bleachers in the stadium are surrounded by earthen berms covered with low-lying vines.

The field is ringed by a chain link fence, and another fence restricts access to the stadium. For the first three days of practice, reporters were permitted to sidle up to the chain link fence. But starting Wednesday, a UW police officer along for the trip denied access to the stadium as the mood became more businesslike.

In early December, just after returning from Tokyo, Alvarez and Richter were in Pasadena to scout potential practice sites and make arrangements for the Rose Bowl trip. While sitting in the lounge at the Doubletree Hotel, they spotted Los Angeles Dodgers Manager Tommy Lasorda, who was there for an unrelated speaking engagement.

Alvarez flagged down Lasorda, who was with Henry Dyer, basketball coach at Cal State-Los Angeles. Alvarez and Richter introduced themselves. Several minutes into the conversation, Richter realized the bearded Dyer was a former teammate on the Washington Redskins.

After chatting for a while, Alvarez asked Lasorda to speak to the Badgers during the week of practice leading up to the Rose Bowl.

On Tuesday, Lasorda agreed to take advantage of an uncluttered and sunny morning just before he left for New Year's in Las Vegas, to drive out to Glendora to speak to the team. Before the Badgers huddled up, Lasorda and Richter traded barbs.

Lasorda, a former major league pitcher, challenged Richter, a former UW baseball player, to a duel at Chicago's Wrigley Field. "He has about as much chance of hitting me as a one-legged man has in an ass-kicking contest," Lasorda said. "If Pat hits me, I will immediately walk in the clubhouse, I will get a rope, I will tie one end around my neck, and tie one end around a rafter, and jump."

Richter's quick reply: "Well, the rafters at Wrigley Field are awfully low."

And while Richter was wary of Lasorda's hanging curve ball, he seemed game for the matchup.

Lasorda had given twenty pregame talks to football teams during his career and kept meticulous records on their game-day performance. He was exceedingly proud of his 18–2 record. His only two losses came after talks to the Air Force team before its games against Notre Dame and San Diego State.

Alvarez signaled his players to take a break in practice and huddle around Lasorda at midfield. Then, the sixty-three-year-old baseball legend took center stage:

"I've spoken to twenty college football teams and I'm 18-2. So I think that there isn't any doubt in my mind that Wisconsin is going to win the Rose Bowl. And if I were a betting man, which I'm not . . . a lot of other managers do, but I don't, I would say it's Wisconsin all the way.

"I managed in four World Series and I know what it's like when you come to a game of this magnitude. All it means is that you have worked so very, very hard and have put all the things that your coaches have worked with you on together and have had a tremendous season. This is the game that's going to make the season complete.

"The only way you're going to win this game is, you've got to continue what you did in Tokyo and what you did the rest of the games in order to be successful. Winning is so very, very important when the active competition begins.

"To tell you how bad I want to win, I can remember a few years back when we were playing in Cincinnati and I left that morning and went to church. And who came in and sat right next to me, but the manager of the Cincinnati Reds, Johnnie McNamara. I knew why he was at church and he knew why I was there. At the conclusion of the Mass, he and I walked down the center aisle together, and as we approached the front door, he said to me, 'Wait for me outside, Tommy, I'll be right out.' I watched him and he went over to the side of the church and knelt down and lit a candle. Instead of me going out the front door, I went over to the other side of the church and I walked in front of the altar and when he left, I went over and blew that candle out.

"He was not lighting that candle for a dead relative. And all through the game I kept yelling, 'Hey Mac, it ain't going to work buddy! I blew it out!' We clobbered them that day 13-2."

Lasorda concluded his remarks by pointing out the importance of the game not only to the team, but to its followers:

"Winning is so very important in our lives. But remember one thing: you came a long way. You don't just represent the university now. You represent your conference. You're representing your entire state. There's probably going to be 100,000 people there to watch you play football. And I guarantee you one thing: you put it all together, all the hard work, you envision what it's going to be like when you're carrying Coach Barry Alvarez off the field on New Year's Day. Good luck and God bless you all."

In the days after the talk, Lasorda took heat from California fans who felt that he had betrayed the home team, even though the Bruins had not invited him. But what the hell? His record was about to improve 19-2.

Phil Dobbs stood in the end zone beaming with pride as he watched the Badgers' sun-drenched workout. Dobbs had a special stake in the Wisconsin program, one that was fundamental to the UW's success all season. He had coached Moss and Dawkins at Racine's Washington Park High School and guided them along the convoluted recruiting trail that finally led both athletes to Alvarez.

As a high school senior, Moss, the state's top prep player, sloughed off Wisconsin because of Don Morton and his veer offense. Moss and Dobbs knew Moss was better suited to an I-formation offense that would make full use of his battering-ram style of running.

Although Moss nearly committed to George Perles at Michigan State, Alvarez won him over. Dawkins was snatched out of the grasp of Purdue. Dobbs also was won over.

"They have worked a miracle in four years," said Dobbs. "And it's so heartening to see Brent play such a big role in that miracle after all he's been through."

Celebrities checked in and out of practice all week. Olympic track star Suzy Hamilton, a UW graduate, stopped by to pick up a Badgers football helmet she had ordered earlier as a Christmas gift for her husband, Mark. And Chuck Long, the former Iowa quarterback, stopped in to greet Alvarez.

A veteran of nine previous bowl games, Alvarez was a man in his element.

For the three previous years, Alvarez was a wretch at Christmas. After you become accustomed to going to bowl games, he discovered, sitting home watching bowls on television is torture. And when he broke down and went to the 1991 Rose Bowl game, it was worse.

"They were the worst three Christmases of my life," Alvarez said, standing in the lobby of Lawry's restaurant in Beverly Hills waiting for his team to be seated for the annual Beef Bowl dinner.

Lawry's, renowned for its prime rib, has sponsored the pre-Rose Bowl dinner for thirty-eight years. As players are seated, servers move from table to table with carts of food, slicing off twelve-ounce cuts of meat and serving whipped potatoes and vegetables.

It was another odd landscape as Raymer dined next to eighteen-year-old Tournament of Roses Queen Erica Beth Brynes and her court. As she picked at her meal, Raymer pounded down his food and soaked in the refined ambience.

Bevell also was called upon to help serve the meal. He donned a chef's hat and carved some prime rib for Alvarez. Later, he grabbed a video recorder and wandered around the room saving the moment on tape. He became especially animated when he spotted the media table and dashed over to record sportswriters who were scarfing down the meal.

Parodying reporters' constant laments to him, Bevell thoroughly enjoyed himself, zooming in and out with the video recorder. "Just one more question! Just going to take up a little more of your time! Hey, whatcha eating there?"

By midweek, Alvarez noticed signs that his team was becoming more single-minded about football. Tuesday's practice was marked by hard hitting and Alvarez took the pads off on Wednesday to avoid injuries and bring players back down to earth. "I want them to save it for Saturday," he said.

Fullback Mark Montgomery said there was a sense that the Badgers were ready to hit their season's peak performance in the days before the Rose Bowl. "Our coaches told us all year, 'Make sure that the last game of the year is the one you peak at,'" he said.

And players also were riding high on the support they had seen throughout the Los Angeles area for the Badgers, and not just from the ever-present Wisconsin fans.

"At Universal Studios and Disneyland, it was surprising how many people from California are saying, 'Hey, we want you to beat UCLA,'" said Montgomery.

But there were two sides to that coin. Raymer, who ran into one guy with a baseball cap that said "UCLA Sucks," also met some Bruins backers while walking around Universal Studios.

"People would come up and say, 'UCLA is going to kick your butt' and that's the tough part because a couple of them were women and you kind of cringe at that," he said.

In previous seasons, players tended to tighten up before big games. But there was never a sign of that during preparations for Wisconsin's final six games. Players were loose, confident, and focused. Throughout the season that focus almost never varied.

"Our guys have been focused all year," said Alvarez. "We had guys pull out people they thought were dead after the Michigan game and came around the next week and were focused. You travel halfway around the world and they stayed focused."

Some Badgers were fighting the flu or sinus infections, but no one was sick enough to miss practice and the illnesses abated by week's end.

Throughout the week, the hometown team was worried about the health of Bruins quarterback Wayne Cook, who missed more than two days of practice at Spaulding Field in Westwood with the flu. When he returned to practice, Cook's sore throat prevented him from calling signals.

For a Bruin, Rick Neuheisel had mighty fond memories of Camp Randall Stadium. The UCLA wide receivers coach, a former Bruins quarterback, threw his first touchdown pass in a game in Madison twelve years earlier.

On September 18, 1982, just a week after Wisconsin's monumental victory over top-ranked Michigan, the Bruins came into Camp Randall. The Bruins took control of the game early, with Tom Ramsey as the starting quarterback. That opened the door for Neuheisel, Ramsey's backup, who was born in Madison.

"There was a real fever, the fans were so supportive of the team," said Neuheisel. "In the locker room at halftime, we listened to that Budweiser song and the locker room was literally shaking because they were going so crazy. There was stuff falling from the ceiling. We thought we better make a run for it."

This from a team that practices near the San Andreas Fault.

Neuheisel that afternoon connected with receiver Mike Sherrard for the first of 15 career touchdown passes as the Bruins defeated Wisconsin 51–26.

Despite all the hype about the 1994 Rose Bowl being a clash between the brute force of the Big Ten and the finesse and speed of the Pac-10, Neuheisel played down the teams' differences.

"People like to make it sound like the Big Ten doesn't have any speed, and I don't think that's true," he said. "Athletes are on the national scope and everybody's got good players. The fact that they're from Wisconsin and we're from California doesn't make any difference. It's a nationwide recruiting scene."

UCLA Coach Terry Donahue came into the game with an 8–2–1 record in postseason appearances and he was one of two coaches nationally to win eight straight bowl games between the 1982 and 1991 seasons.

Preseason predictions in 1993 had pegged the Bruins for a sixth- to eighth-place finish in the conference. That made the Bruins' Pac-10 championship especially sweet for Donahue, who was given up for lost after the Bruins opened with a thud by losing their first two games.

"Fans were very, very critical," said Donahue, who managed to placate them by finishing 8–3 and seizing the conference championship. "I don't monitor the talk shows, but people tell me I'm not a hot topic."

Donahue's approach to bowl games changed drastically after he led the Bruins to the 1976 Liberty Bowl and UCLA was thumped 36–6 by Alabama. Donahue had a relaxed approach to bowl game preparation then, but he was disabused of that attitude by a storm of criticism.

"I kind of thought at that time that bowls should be a total reward and you shouldn't really care about who won and who didn't," he said. "After Alabama clocked us and wiped us out, I came back to town and got ripped. I would say that I began to realize people were serious about bowl games."

One of the challenges for Donahue was keeping players' attention in the weeks before the Rose Bowl. Because the game was across the metro area at the Bruins' home field, Donahue tried to schedule events such as a dinner at a Beverly Hills ribs restaurant to make the experience special. "You have to keep players from getting bored so they don't feel like practices are mundane and are punishment," he said.

Another traditional stop was Anaheim's Disneyland. Players from both teams were feted in a brief celebration in front of the train station on Disneyland's Main Street. Amid Disney's slick pageantry, players eyed one another, coldly analyzing one another.

Then they went their own ways, free to view the Disney attractions and enjoy the rides. As they did, Alvarez had lunch with his wife along Main Street, still reveling in the moment: "I just love this stuff."

Since their victory over Michigan State, the Badgers seemed driven by their underdog status. Even though the Badgers possessed a better record and ranking than UCLA, oddsmakers installed Wisconsin as a 7-point underdog. Players took that to heart, egged on by a coaching staff who viewed Wisconsin's status as a motivator.

"People have found reasons why we were going to lose all year and reasons why we weren't any good," Alvarez said. "We thrive on that. It really doesn't make any difference when you take the field whether you are the underdog or not. I get a kick out of everybody who says they know who's going to win. Most haven't even seen us play."

Alvarez was most tickled by a Los Angeles pundit who predicted the Bruins would steamroll Wisconsin by nearly three touchdowns. "Somebody had us at minus twenty," he said. "We'll remind players of that. I just hope they're not right."

Inside linebacker Eric Unverzagt had a message for the doubters: "Obviously, they have no respect for us. Maybe they think this is a fluke year. Maybe they think we'll be good for one year and then be back down again. I'll tell you this: Wisconsin football is not about running around blocks."

At midweek many of the charters started to leave from Madison, jammed with people who were ready to party in the finest Wisconsin tradition. Mendota Gridiron Club Associate Director Wayne Esser said one charter flight attendant told him, "We ran out of beer over Nebraska, and flushed over Utah."

In the makeshift football office in a room at the Doubletree Hotel, receptionists answered an unexpected avalanche of telephone calls from Wisconsin alumni up and down the West Coast. Where is the UW Marching Band playing? When is Pat Richter going to appear at the alumni reception? Where is Donna Shalala staying in Los Angeles? And, of course number one on the hit parade, how can I get tickets?

Ah yes, tickets. The forty-six-dollar ducats were going for up to $500 apiece as the demand engendered by bowl-deprived UW fans rocketed. That widespread demand was the breeding ground for disappointment and outrage for up to 2,000 Badgers fans who wound up without tickets.

Some learned the bad news from charter operators before they left for California, but many others found out once they were airborne or after they had reached Los Angeles. The snafu stirred a hornet's nest of trouble that is still roiling through Congress and the courts.

The problem was that some charter operators did not have firm commitments from ticket brokers before offering transportation and ticket plans. When the price of tickets soared, the brokers sold them elsewhere to snare a quick buck. That left many small, reputable travel agencies in Wisconsin scrambling to find tickets to appease their customers. And the cost of those tickets was enough to put some agencies in financial peril.

For the first time since President Clinton made a joking reference to Shalala's Badgers at a cabinet meeting before the Michigan game, Wisconsin football was again a hot topic at the highest levels of the U.S. government.

U.S. Rep. Scott Klug (R-Wisconsin) started receiving calls from irate fans who were in California but deprived of Rose Bowl tickets. He immediately called for investigations by Atty. Gen. Janet Reno and the Federal Trade Commission. Then, he introduced legislation called the "Badger Fan Protection Act," to guard against similar incidents.

A rule already on the books inside the Department of Transportation required charter operators offering tours to the Super Bowl to have game tickets in hand or under written contract before advertising tours. It did not, however, carry over to other events.

The rule had worked and by January 27, federal Transportation Secretary Frederico Pena proposed expanding the rule to cover other special events, such as college bowl games, the NCAA Final Four, and the Olympics.

"Although a vast majority of tour operators follow the rules, we will not tolerate personal fouls committed against sports fans," Pena said. "The rule we are proposing will prevent the problems suffered by Wisconsin Badger fans from being repeated in the future."

Klug said the rule change turns up the heat on ticket brokers who sold out Wisconsin fans at the Rose Bowl. "Its focus is on the charter operators, but by raising the ante for them, we raise the legal stakes for ticket brokers who broke the hearts of countless Badger fans and broke the bank accounts of Wisconsin travel agents, who had to buy thousands of tickets on the street for an average of $500," he said.

While Klug and the Wisconsin congressional delegation worked to stop future abuse, state Atty. Gen. James E. Doyle began a sweeping investigation of the hundreds of complaints received by his office to determine if criminal charges could be brought.

All the political grandstanding, however, couldn't do much for fans who made it to Pasadena but could not wrangle tickets to the game. The Mendota Gridiron Club was scouring the metropolitan area for tickets and Esser, a distinguished-looking gray-haired man, was wheeling and dealing to get tickets into the hands of as many Wisconsin partisans as possible. People came to see him as the godfather of Rose Bowl tickets. The city of Pasadena opened its downtown Civic Center to fans interested in gathering to watch the game on television and the UCLA Bruins boosters also invited Wisconsin fans into their tent on the Rose Bowl grounds to watch the game unfold.

The morning before the Tournament of Roses Parade, parade mavens start taking up positions along curbs on Colorado Boulevard. As the day progresses, the crowds thicken and people start arguing over footlong strips of pavement.

By nightfall, it's something of a snakepit with a party edge. Lawn chairs, sleeping bags, coolers, and makeshift kitchens line the cramped sidewalks in anticipation of the New Year's Day extravaganza.

Red-clad Wisconsin fans were everywhere. UCLA boosters cruising the boulevard berated the Badgers fans, often in a good-humored manner. One convertible filled with young men with blue face paint drove past a group of Badgers fans and mooed loudly while shooting long plastic strands of Super String at the group.

You get the feeling that maybe this is a one-night exchange: people with homes are living on the street and the homeless have a roof over their heads.

Of course, it wasn't true. But even those without a home took notice of the Badgers fans. In a park across from Pasadena City Hall the day after the game a homeless man talked about Wisconsin's fans. "How many of them are there? Man, they're everywhere. The people around here sure like how you people from Wisconsin spend money. They're hoping you come back every year," he said. "I bet you are, too."

There was no bitterness among players about their newfound celebrity among a growing horde of Badgers fans. Sure, many in the army of fans had not been there to support the team in the lean times. This was hardly the time to nitpick about having developed, at long last, a following.

"People are more than welcome to get on the bandwagon," said Panos. "It's going to be a great ride."

Before walking on the lush turf of the Rose Bowl for the first time since 1984, when he was an assistant at the University of Illinois, Wisconsin Offensive Coordinator Brad Childress knew this was a moment to be embraced. To get to the Rose Bowl, he said that sometimes you need more than a great football team. Sometimes, you need a little luck.

"I was a twenty-seven-year-old at the time and you have the sense of being invincible. You don't think it's going to be ten years before you go back again. Heck, Wisconsin hasn't been there for more than thirty years," he said. "You have to make sure you enjoy it. Wins are special and sometimes, as football coaches, you win one and get to enjoy it from the time you walk from the press box to the locker room to your car."

Then, he offered what may have been the most pungent advice of what by now was a storied season: "Take time to enjoy what's happened here, because there are no guarantees."

15

Snow Angels on the Rose

W̲elcome to Barry's house.

As he walked on the manicured grass field in the brilliant sunshine during pregame warmups at the Rose Bowl, Alvarez watched the stands fill up. As the minutes passed, it was increasingly evident that the Badgers would have a major, stunning crowd advantage for the eightieth Rose Bowl game.

Red was everywhere in the Rose Bowl, which is hugged by the San Gabriel Mountains at the floor of a gorge called Arroyo Seco.

The Badgers' faithful, who traveled 2,000 miles to see the game, vastly outnumbered those of the Bruins, whose serene Westwood campus was only twenty-five miles away. Although many Wisconsinites were shut out because of the ticket scandal, far more than expected made it into the stadium.

Even though the Rose Bowl is the home of UCLA football, Wisconsin fans were dropping into their seats by the thousands until it appeared that there were sixty thousand to seventy thousand Badgers fans among the 101,237 in the stands. It was evident that UCLA ticket holders had decided en masse to convert their tickets into tuition money.

Only about a third of the stadium was occupied by blue-and-gold-clad Bruins fans. After the Bruins' return from the 0–2 dead early in the season, this was the best UCLA could muster. It was the first, though not necessarily the greatest, embarrassment UCLA would suffer on this seventy-five-degree Saturday afternoon.

"Doesn't Camp Randall look lovely today?" a confidently beaming Alvarez asked players as they stretched.

Before the game, Alvarez sold Badgers players on the idea of this being a home game. During Alvarez's visit to Pasadena after the Japan trip, he was given the choice of locker rooms at the Rose Bowl. It was a no-brainer: Alvarez booted UCLA out of the home locker room, forcing the Bruins to dress in the visitors locker room at their own stadium.

That meant Wisconsin also would wear its home uniforms, red jerseys with white pants, and the Bruins would wear their white road uniforms. Anything to gain an advantage.

Even players felt at home as they dressed for the game, enjoying their pregame rituals. "I like to get to the locker room, get all my stuff, and go to the bathroom throne and do all my thinking there," said Carlos Fowler. "If I'm in someone else's locker room, I'm going to feel like it's not just right. At the Rose Bowl, it felt fine."

In keeping with Alvarez's credo of never changing schedules, he ordered the team moved to an undisclosed location in Los Angeles following a brief walk-through and team picture-taking session at the Rose Bowl Friday afternoon.

He reasoned that since the team stayed in a Madison hotel on Friday nights before home games, the Badgers needed to abandon their headquarters at the Doubletree for a night to keep up the tradition. Besides, the team needed to escape the noisy party atmosphere that grew daily at the hotel and was sure to be at a crescendo on New Year's Eve. Since Los Angeles was crawling with Badgers fans, Alvarez kept the location a deep secret, not even telling members of his extended family.

After visiting the Rose Bowl, the Badgers departed for the luxurious Hotel Intercontinental in Los Angeles's downtown financial district. They slept in peace, with lights out an hour before the New Year arrived on the West Coast.

The next day, buses got the team to the stadium twenty minutes earlier than usual. Alvarez wanted players to don their pants and jerseys and walk into the stadium to get a feel for the atmosphere before the bulk of the crowd arrived. That, he reasoned, would cut down on the jitters just before kickoff.

As Scott Nelson walked around the field, he spotted a friend from Sun Prairie leaning on the fence and went over to chat with him. "He was all fired up, and seeing a familiar face helped bring me back down to earth. I was so jacked up, seeing him made me feel a little more comfortable," said Nelson.

In the pregame meeting, Alvarez also repeated Wisconsin's simple game plan: run the ball and don't give up big plays on defense. And then, he said it again for the umpteenth time: just get a little better than the last game, and the Badgers would be fine.

Flowery speeches are not Alvarez's forte. He was direct, to the point, sometimes profane. But during his talk, a wave of emotion cascaded through the room. After a week of Hollywood fanfare, reality had arrived.

"When he talked to us, everyone was crying. You couldn't help it and started to feel a little weak. But this was what it was all about," said Nelson, who walked out of the locker room prepared to play his final game in the cardinal and white.

Not once during all of Wisconsin's preparations for the Rose Bowl did Alvarez bring up the 1962 Badgers team and their trip to Pasadena. The past had become an ugly stepsister to the brighter here and now.

"My team doesn't have anything to do with the 1962 team. If I went back to all the traditions and all the records, we wouldn't be here," said Alvarez. "That's all we read about at the beginning of the season: how many times we hadn't won on grass, how many times we hadn't won on the road. The list goes on and on. We tried to build our own standards this year."

There was trouble brewing, even several days earlier at the Happiest Place on Earth. As UCLA and Wisconsin players roamed Disneyland in Anaheim days before the game, there were sidelong glances and disparaging remarks tossed back and forth between players.

Even before the game started, the Bruins' dam burst. Trash talking was rampant during pregame drills, coming largely from the UCLA side of the field. Although Wisconsin players expected trash talking, the verbal fusillade during the pregame was pushing the envelope.

Lee DeRamus, not one to blush at the profanity that accompanies college football, seemed surprised the yipping started that soon. "They talked constantly," he said. "That's the first time I've seen it start that early. They were calling us rookies and cheeseheads and saying we were overrated."

One of the loudest mouths on the field, UW players said, was that of Bruins defensive back Marvin Goodwin. That really stuck in Bill Callahan's craw.

"He really let his behind show," Fowler said of Goodwin. "He was in there telling us, 'You think you know what physical football is? We'll show you what physical football is!' Coach Callahan was really hyped. After warmups, he was yelling, 'They can't talk trash to us! Get out there and get after them!'"

For his part, Fowler liked it when teams ran at the mouth. "It got to a point where when a team started saying things like that to us, it was like an omen. I looked forward to teams talking trash because we knew then we had their number," he said.

He may have had something there. Days earlier, psychologist Patricia A. Barth told the *Houston Chronicle* that the sort of trash talking that has become commonplace in college athletics is counterproductive. "It seems self-defeating, because it always riles the other team up," she said. "One of the defenses against envy is devaluation. Rather than let oneself know that this is an enviable sort of opponent, he puts the opponent down to protect himself from 'the gnawing tooth of envy.'"

Whatever the psychological reasons, the yammering went on as the game got under way. The Bruins' defense seemed to be more heavily involved than its offense, and Wisconsin's offense was more than happy to throw it back in their faces.

"It was ridiculous," said Joe Panos. "They were saying they'd teach us what smash-mouth football was all about. I'm not going to talk until somebody starts in on me, but I figured, let's let our pads do the talking."

All season long, various Badgers players and units had proven the skeptics wrong. First, there was Darrell Bevell and his unexpected improvement, then the offensive line proved its dominance. With the season now in its twelfth game, the inside linebackers also had proved their mettle in an efficient, workmanlike manner.

Yusef Burgess made a quiet contribution to the Badgers throughout the year. He shied away from publicity, but as a senior he clearly enjoyed his only season as a starter.

Coming into the season, questions about Wisconsin's defense tended to coalesce around the inside linebackers. Burgess and Eric Unverzagt had never started at the position and expectations were high that they could make an immediate impact.

Alvarez's defensive scheme leans heavily on inside linebackers. The purpose of the defensive line is to clear a path for those linebackers and a drop in performance there would be hard to conceal.

Burgess labored in obscurity for three seasons after being recruited out of Clinton High School in the Bronx during Alvarez's first year. All told, he had 28 solo tackles—and only 6 in 1992—entering the 1993 season.

The first years took an emotional toll on Burgess, who came to question his own abilities. "It was pretty rough," he said. "But it's like the real world. You've got somebody ahead of you who's got the experience. My boss wasn't going to put me in there because I'm crying about how much time I want to play. I had to wait my turn. I had to prove a lot to myself and to this team."

Burgess took a studious approach to earning and retaining his starting role, spending hours analyzing game film and devising ways to attack various schemes.

"I watched and tried to recognize situations and get sharper," the 230-pounder said. "At this level, size is not really the issue. It's more mental and being prepared for the game."

In the process of justifying his starting role, Burgess said he found emotional support from other players who realized the pressure both he and Unverzagt were facing. "My teammates believed I could do it. I fed off of those guys," said Burgess.

As the season progressed, Burgess found it was helpful to build his play on the foundation of high expectations instead of being intimidated by the burden the expectations imposed. "In a situation where people are looking at me wondering if I can do the job, it was a big motivator," he said. "Anytime someone tells you that you can't do something, you leave that in the back of your mind and let it drive you."

It drove Burgess to become the team's leading tackler, an integral part of the defense with a work ethic that was held up by coaches as a model for other players.

Burgess started every game and finished the season with 100 tackles, including 10 for losses and 2 quarterback sacks. In addition, he caused 7 fumbles and recovered 2 others. "It's important for us to go out there and be as physical as we possibly can to create turnovers and keep our offense on the field," said Burgess. "We want to finish the game just as strong as we start it."

The whirlwind turnaround the Badgers experienced was as much a surprise to Burgess as anyone. "I would have predicted at the seminary that we would have been successful. But the magnitude of our success, I don't think anyone could have put a finger on it. Week by week, we focused on the job at hand and went in confident," he said.

At the Rose Bowl, Burgess was an indispensible cog in the Badgers' defensive machinery. The kid whose abilities were doubted at the start of the season quickly became a defensive hero in Wisconsin's biggest game in three decades.

Meanwhile, Unverzagt also showed promise. His career at UW had been troubled, but he bore the problems well and with grace. As a freshman, Unverzagt was pressed into service as a long snapper well before he was ready.

Although he had limited experience with long snapping in high school, it clearly was not his calling. All season, walk-on punter Sam Veit played shortstop, fielding one-hoppers or leaping to make the grab on Unverzagt's snaps.

Following games, Unverzagt never dodged reporters, always answered honestly about his shortcomings on special teams, and coaches came to respect him for his effort.

But his career was again sidetracked as a sophomore when injury forced him to take a redshirt year. In his third year with the program, Unverzagt said he wanted to shed his negative past.

"I'm trying to establish myself as a linebacker instead of a special teams flop," said Unverzagt, who had 75 tackles, 8 for loss, and broke up 2 passes in his 1993 season.

Unverzagt's recruiting visit came a week after the Badgers narrowly lost to Michigan State in Alvarez's first season. "I was out with some buddies and when they said Wisconsin lost to Michigan State 14–9, I said, 'Really!?' At first I didn't believe that they came that close," said Unverzagt.

During that visit, he spent considerable time with Burgess, a fellow New Yorker. "Yusef was a big influence," said Unverzagt. "He wasn't my host, but since he was from New York, we talked a lot. He said he knew Wisconsin was going to do something. He said we could play with every team except Michigan."

With both players, Inside Linebackers Coach Kevin Cosgrove used their inexperience as starters as a motivational tool.

"We didn't want our kids coming into the season thinking they'd be a weakness of the defense," said Cosgrove. "The other thing was leadership. I always thought that linebackers are the leaders of the defense. And I told them that if they don't lead, nobody leads."

As they stood on the sidelines waiting for the coin toss at the Rose Bowl, both Burgess and Unverzagt felt ready to lead.

One of the Badgers' few setbacks during the day came after Tournament of Roses grand marshal and "Star Trek" icon William Shatner conducted the coin toss—the silver coin, three inches across, came up UCLA.

UCLA Coach Terry Donahue decided to defer until the second half, allowing the Badgers to open up on offense. Although Wisconsin's first drive stalled at the UCLA 46, the Badgers showed an early ability to balance their offense. Brent Moss carried 7 times during the 11-play series and gained 14 yards and Bevell completed 2 of 3 passes.

The Wisconsin punt coverage team pinned UCLA deep in its own territory on the punt, which was downed at the Bruins' 3-yard line. Wayne Cook showed his ability to move the team against the Badgers' defense. But the chip on the Bruins' shoulder would hold them back all day.

During that first drive, Cook connected on a 25-yard pass to J.J. Stokes, who was driven out of bounds by Kenny Gales at the Wisconsin 46. But Stokes took exception to Gales's style of tackling and whacked him in the head, drawing a 15-yard personal foul. It was 1 of the 3 penalties that would cost UCLA 40 yards in the first period.

The Bruins managed to continue the drive and came away with a 27-yard field goal by Bjorn Merten to take a 3–0 lead.

The Badgers' response was to drive 78 yards in 10 plays, helped by a pass-interference call on Bruins defensive back Teddy Lawrence, who leaned on J.C. Dawkins in the end zone.

Four plays later, the offensive line blew the Bruins off the line and Moss went over left tackle for a 3-yard stand-up touchdown with 11 seconds left in the first quarter.

Turnovers would swing the game the Badgers' way in the second quarter, as Jeff Messenger picked off a Cook pass. The interception, however, did Wisconsin little good as Bevell came back two plays later and was picked off by Goodwin.

But the Bruins' trouble with turnovers was far from over. On the resulting series, Cook's shotgun pass to Stokes was fumbled and Lamark Shackerford recovered at the UCLA 32.

"Stokes stopped his trash talking after he made that fumble," Nelson said.

From there, the Badgers drove to the Bruins' 1-yard line, where Moss showed he was more accustomed to running on turf than on grass. On first and goal, he slipped for no gain as he ran left. The next play was a rerun. Finally, on third and goal, Moss took Bevell's handoff and stretched straight ahead for the touchdown on a delayed call by the officials. The Badgers took a 14–3 lead into the home locker room at halftime.

A half of play and a halftime to reflect did not take the edge off of the Bruins' trash-talking attitude. If anything, there was a renewed vigor in their verbal assaults.

All of the animosity blossomed into an on-field rumble between the teams on Wisconsin's first possession of the third quarter. After UCLA's Carl Greenwood and Nkosi Littleton stopped Moss for a loss of 1 on a crucial fourth down and 1 at the Bruins' 9-yard line, tempers flared.

In a flurry of action, Mark Montgomery tried to pull a UCLA linebacker off of Moss as a fight took hold between the teams. As DeRamus was trying to pull players apart, he claims to have been accosted by Goodwin. Those two locked up and wrestled their way to the UCLA sidelines near the end zone.

Goodwin said he was reacting to someone hitting him in the back when he turned on DeRamus. "We got into a little tussle and the next thing I know, I'm ejected from the game," he said.

Also ejected were Bruins free safety Donovan Gallatin, DeRamus, and Montgomery, who was playing his last game as a Badger.

One of the ironies of the fight was that DeRamus and Goodwin used to play against each other in high school basketball games. Goodwin, who played at Woodrow Wilson High School in Camden, New Jersey, shrugged off the connection during some pregame interviews, something that irritated DeRamus.

"To me, I was kind of happy to be playing against him. He was an old homeboy and I wanted to go out and play against him and show my stuff," said DeRamus. "His comment was: 'That was back then. I don't remember him.'

"I guess he never did like me, because I used to dunk on him in basketball," said a smiling DeRamus.

At first, being ejected from the game was a crushing blow. DeRamus failed to make a catch in the game, something that had happened only once in his previous 34 games.

"That's the part that really hurt. You get kicked out of the biggest game in your career, of course you have second thoughts. I look at it this way: if it wasn't for me making certain plays at certain times, maybe we wouldn't have been in the Rose Bowl," DeRamus said.

That approach to the situation did not sink in right away, though. As an international television audience looked on, DeRamus and Montgomery—two of the team's most upbeat players, with omnipresent and infectious smiles—headed for the bench, downcast.

"Me and Mark were over there crying. Then, we figured, 'Yo, we've got to pick these people up!' After a few minutes, we jumped up and started hollering, 'Let's go! Let's go!'" DeRamus said.

Donahue, while not condoning the brawl, claimed the fight may have been the product of the Bruins' defensive players' frustration at being held by the Badgers, who were not getting called for the violations.

Throughout the game, Bevell said there were some chippy incidents involving UCLA players that rankled him.

"I lost my head a couple of times because I was so mad," he said. "I got cut down in the fight. I'm running over to break it up and a guy jumps off the pile and tries to blow my knee out, then runs to the sidelines and hides."

And that was not the only case of questionable behavior by Bruins players during the game, Bevell said. "One of the plays was dead and I went down to get the ball and a guy jumps on me and is stepping on me as he's getting up. You don't have to do things like that," he said. "They were doing a lot of cheap things."

Incidents similar to the Rose Bowl brawl brought uncharacteristically swift rules changes from the NCAA Rules Committee, which met at the end of January. The new rules set forth a rigid code of conduct with significant penalties assessed to the brawlers.

Under the new rules, players or coaches who leave the bench to fight or who join a fight that spills into the bench area will be ejected and suspended for the subsequent game. And players fighting during the game will not only draw a suspension for the remainder of the half, but for the next half, even if that half is in the next game. And officials will take the field an hour before kickoff to assure there are not any skirmishes during pregame preparations.

The Bruins began the fourth quarter by narrowing Wisconsin's lead to 14–10 as running back Milliner ran for a 6-yard touchdown on the third play of the quarter.

But the Bruins, who entered the game with the best turnover margin in the nation, played uncharacteristically fast and loose with the football for the entire game. The opportunities were there, but the turnovers kept killing them.

Perhaps the most crucial turnover was committed by running back Ricky Davis, who swept around the right end for a gain of 12 on the Bruins' next possession but fumbled. Wisconsin's Mike Thompson recovered the ball.

The turnover set up Wisconsin's third and final touchdown drive, one that would end improbably 5 plays later. With the Badgers at the 8-yard line, Bevell scrambled out of trouble, then wove his way along the left side for a touchdown with 10:53 left.

Bevell was notoriously, almost hilariously, slow afoot. His running plays seemed to take forever to develop and seldom resulted in much of a gain. His slowness was an open joke in the locker room and on the field. This time, however, Bevell picked up his blockers, and added a juke that helped spring him for the score.

There was Bevell, arms raised in triumph, scooting through the end zone . . . laughing.

The play—on which Bevell threw a pair of touchdown passes against Illinois—was designed to go to the right, either to tight end Mike Roan running down the hash marks or to fullback Jeff Wirth along the sideline.

Both receivers were well covered and Bevell felt the pressure from the Bruins' pass rush.

"I looked to the right side and I felt the guy coming around me with [Mike] Verstegen. I saw the hole open up, so I took off," said Bevell. "One of their guys leaped around and grabbed me, but I got away."

Responding to the rush, Bevell ran left. "I thought, 'Run straight.' I always run sideways and don't get any yards," he said.

A split-second later, Bevell saw Dawkins out of the corner of his eye and tried to cut off of his block.

"There was a guy there and somehow I made him fall down. I don't know what I did. Everyone says it was the best move they ever saw," said Bevell. "I could not believe it. I was laughing, the players were laughing at me, a television guy walks by and he's laughing at me. I went to the phone and Coach Childress was laughing at me.

"It was the most amazing play. It was so much fun."

After Bevell slashed into the end zone, Cory Raymer lumbered up to a Bruins defensive back and blurted, "I can't believe you let *our* quarterback score a *touchdown*!"

Then Raymer ran up to Bevell, laughing. "How the hell did you do that?!" Raymer asked him.

Meanwhile, Panos was hurting. He twisted his left knee with about 11 minutes left in the game, but as he did in Tokyo, he refused to come out.

"Coach Callahan asked me along the sidelines if I needed to come out," Panos said. "I told him this old dog could go for another 11 minutes. There was nothing keeping me out of the game unless there was bone sticking out of my leg."

Also in pain was Fowler, who had broken his left wrist late in the third quarter. He also refused to come out of the lineup, and finished the game against offensive lineman Vaughn Parker, one of the toughest competitors in the Pac-10.

"We knew they were going to throw and we needed to keep up the pressure on Cook. No way was I coming out," Fowler said.

The Bruins' next possession was stalled when split end Kevin Jordan fumbled after a pass reception and Nelson recovered. Although the Badgers were not able to score on the ensuing series they ran precious time off the clock in their bid to hang onto the game.

But the Bruins made up for lost time on their next drive, a 15-play series that included 14 pass attempts and ended when receiver Mike Nguyen caught a 5-yard Cook touchdown pass in the right center of the end zone.

Donahue ordered a 2-point conversion attempt, but Cook's pass to Jordan was incomplete in the end zone and Wisconsin clung to a 21–16 lead with 3:38 to play.

Wisconsin tried to keep the ball on the ground and chew up some clock during a drive in which the Bruins were forced to expend all of their timeouts. A defensive stand by UCLA ended when Moss was stopped for no gain by Littleton and Tony Bennett on third and 1 at the Wisconsin 44.

Using the timeouts was necessary to give UCLA another chance, but as the Bruins took possession with 1:43 left, the onus was on Cook to use the time wisely. The Bruins managed to do that, finally driving to the Badgers' 18-yard line after Stokes caught an 18-yard strike over the middle.

That is when things started to go haywire for UCLA.

On the next play, Cook made an inexplicable mistake which may well have cost the Bruins the game. With 15 seconds to play, the UCLA quarterback was forced to scramble on first down. Instead of throwing the ball away to stop the clock, he ran for a 3-yard gain to the Wisconsin 15, where he was tackled by Thompson.

Cook's gaffe allowed the clock to continue running.

"When he ran the ball, I didn't even look at the clock," said Nelson. "I was looking at the coaches and they were about to make the call and the crowd was starting to count down. It was really the first time I'd heard the crowd all day. I looked away from the coaches and to the scoreboard and it said 3 seconds and they still hadn't put the ball down. There was no way they were going to get the play off."

As Cook waved madly to get his Bruins lined up, time expired for the boys from Westwood.

"Watching Darrell Bevell run into the end zone was the second greatest run I've ever seen in my life," Alvarez said. "The best was when we started cheering that 3-yard run by Wayne Cook."

DeRamus said while those final seconds were nerve-wracking, there was also an almost contradictory sense of confidence along Wisconsin's sideline.

"At one point in the game, there was a feeling like we were destined to win this game. There was no way we were going to lose."

Alvarez was immediately taken in a bear hug by Jim Hueber along the sidelines, as Wisconsin won its first Rose Bowl.

The sights on the playing field were like snapshots from a dream. There, at midfield, a victory dance featuring Jamel Brown, Theo Carney, Henry Searcy, and Royce Roberson all wearing the quickly distributed Rose Bowl champion caps was well under way.

Moments later there was Mike Brin, hero of the crowd surge incident after the Michigan game, lying on his back on the painted red rose in the center of the field.

Brin came to Pasadena with the first group of Badgers players, but he did not play a snap in the game. Didn't expect to. His elation, though, was no less than any of the starters. "When the crowd started to count down—4, 3, 2, 1— I ran toward the student section. I was almost crying," said Brin. "Then, thinking back on what the weather was like in Wisconsin, I went out to the 50-yard line and started to make snow angels on the rose."

From the field, Nelson motioned to the stands. Rev. Michael Burke helped Nelson's girlfriend, Becky Kliefoth, get onto the field after the game to join him for the postgame pandemonium. "I was talking with three reporters and I wanted to celebrate with the guys," said Nelson. "Then, I saw her out of the corner of my eye and I had to gather myself again."

There, on the 40-yard line, Nelson got down on one knee and proposed marriage. He then produced an engagement ring which Burke had held for him during the game to seal the deal. Becky tearfully agreed.

"It was a scary moment, but it turned out pretty good," said Nelson. "It was fun to have her be part of it and share it with her, too. I never did get a chance to run around on the field with the guys, but I've got it on tape and can remember every play of the game."

Panos, at Alvarez's urging, accepted the Rose Bowl trophy and held it high over his head to the glee of fans in the stands. Soon Moss was announced as the game's MVP, and accepted a delicate trophy made of sheets of glass. The award seemed somehow out of place in the hands of a man who lives for surviving shattering impact.

After the game, Moss gave his trophy to his parents, Henry and Elaine.

Dan McCarney recalled how people snickered after the coaching staff ordered the words "The Road to the Rose Bowl Begins Here" painted in cardinal and white above the door leading from the McClain Facility to the stadium years earlier.

No one was laughing now. At least not at the Badgers.

At the 45-yard line, Donna Shalala watched the fairy tale play out. Like most, the outcome left her somewhat bewildered. "I was so numb," she said. "Barry had trained me not to expect it for a couple more years. You don't get your dreams all the time. This was like a dream come true. And I'm a grown-up.

"I knew we had put everything in place. But for it to all come together? That's doesn't happen very often."

Sara Woboril sat in the Rose Bowl stands soaking it all in. Trampled at

Camp Randall Stadium following the Michigan game, she wasn't about to miss this moment.

As the jagged outline of the mountains retreated behind the drapery of darkness, Woboril thought back on the years of Wisconsin football frustration. And she remembered the stadium horror barely two months earlier. At this intoxicating moment, the good outweighed the bad.

"After all I went through, I thought that Wisconsin better make it to Pasadena," she said. "It was amazing. As I sat in the Rose Bowl, I remembered coming to Camp Randall a few years ago and chanting 'Rose Bowl! Rose Bowl!' every time they scored a touchdown or made a first down. It was all a big joke. Football was a joke."

As flashbulbs sparkled amid the throng of Wisconsin fans at the Rose Bowl in the darkness and chill of the early evening, jacked-up players danced the polka as the UW Marching Band held forth with the Fifth Quarter. The Bud song rang crisply across Arroyo Seco: "When you say Wisconsin, you've said it all!"

Woboril sat astonished, much like Alvarez had in his Tokyo hotel suite only a few weeks earlier.

"We're here! We won the Rose Bowl! Where do we go from here?"

16

That Rosy Glow

In the weeks after the Rose Bowl victory, it became evident that the story of Alvarez's revival of the Wisconsin football tradition could be seen on several levels.

Ultimately, it may have had less to do with football than with rebuilding a sense of community.

That was the underlying theme from the day Alvarez arrived on campus. Coaches needed to repair relations with high schools, players with one another, and the university with fans and boosters.

As the Badgers charged victorious out of the bright lights and down the tunnel at the Rose Bowl, there was a swelling of spirit that swept across the state. That curious, communal construction of self-esteem absent in the Dairy State for nearly a generation was complete.

While the Badgers' victory dances were lit with the glitter of popping flashbulbs in the Rose Bowl, the character of the celebrations back in Wisconsin varied widely from home to home and tavern to tavern from Madison to Mondovi, from Prairie du Chien to Land O' Lakes.

Back in suburban Madison, Tom and Mary Ellen Mitchell turned off the television after the Rose Bowl. Along with sons Daniel and Matthew, they built a six-foot-high "W" with strings of red Christmas lights. As the family stepped back in the red glow to admire their work, their lives were changed in a small but meaningful way they are not likely to forget. As season-ticket holders, they had watched the team wallow in failure for years. The new year was barely nineteen hours old as a sense of pride overcame them.

At the same time, down on State Street, an estimated 12,000 people made a beery surge into the pedestrian mall to create their own raucous memories from atop bus stops and in the branches of trees.

All of them, witnesses to sports history, shared an unadorned, unjaded pride. It was unlike that of boastful University of Michigan fans, who had grown bored, over time, of going to the Rose Bowl. Wisconsin's victory gave football fans a treasured memory unlike any other since the legendary 1967 Ice Bowl game between the Green Bay Packers and Dallas Cowboys. The Badgers' season of seasons was one to be treasured.

In California, Alvarez relished the next day, reading the newspaper accounts of Wisconsin's triumph. Throughout the week, the Los Angeles media had a heyday picturing Wisconsin fans as hayseeds and cheeseheads. Now, he could sit back with *The Los Angeles Times* and enjoy the moment.

"I read the articles about how the rubes snookered those people out there," he said. "I kind of enjoyed that."

The day after the victory, Badger players had a choice of going to a Los Angeles Raiders game or taking a jaunt to Hugh Hefner's Playboy mansion. Some stayed until Monday and left on side trips of their own. One group took a side trip to Las Vegas before returning to the chill of Wisconsin.

As they went their separate ways, Alvarez knew he had built more than a 10–1–1 record and national respect.

"This is a team that believed in themselves," he said. "They believed in the plan that we gave them. Regardless of the doubters, regardless of whether we were underdogs or favorites, regardless of what people said or what they had to overcome. They believed in one another."

That showed in the accomplishments of the season. Wisconsin was nationally ranked for fourteen straight weeks in 1993. In the thirty years leading up to the Rose Bowl season, the Badgers had been ranked for a total of ten weeks.

Wisconsin had achieved a school record ten victories and placed eight players among first-team all-Big Ten selections. The Badgers won four road games, equaling a 1974 mark, and crowds at Camp Randall Stadium had improved 80.9 percent since Alvarez's arrival in Madison.

Days after the victory, UW Police Chief Riseling had the Rose Bowl emblem and "1994 Rose Bowl Champs" painted on the sides of campus squad cars.

Only one thing seemed to raise the hackles of the blissful Wisconsin fans, both in Pasadena and in America's Dairyland, on New Year's Day 1994. And they talked about it for weeks afterward. The source of their anger wasn't poor play-calling or bad calls by officials.

It was something that cut to the heart.

It was mispronunciation.

In this case, it was the way ABC television analyst Bob Griese mangled the pronunciation of the state's name, referring to it constantly as "WES-consin." In state homes, taverns, and even for those with miniature televisions at the Rose Bowl, Griese was persona non grata.

At a welcome-home rally for the Badgers at Camp Randall Stadium on January 3, the traditional Budweiser-song cheer of "When you say Wisconsin, you've said it all!" was changed to "When you say WES-consin, you've said it wrong!"

The football team traveled to Milwaukee days after returning from Pasadena to accept congratulations from Vice President Al Gore, who filled in for President Clinton for the visit the day after Clinton's mother died.

Even Gore went out of his way to play to the anger of Wisconsin fans, jokingly referring to the state where his mother went to law school as "WES-consin."

The furor even spilled over into the halls of the state capitol, as state Rep. Marlin Schneider wrote an angry, attention-getting letter to ABC Sports chastising Griese, the former Purdue and Miami Dolphins quarterback.

The letter, written two days after the Rose Bowl, points out that there are only six words in the New College Edition of the American Heritage Dictionary that begin with "WES," and WES-consin is not among them.

"Over the years, I have listened painfully to national newscasters mispronounce Oconomowoc, Manitowoc, Eau Claire and Prairie du Chien and have not loudly complained. But when you don't even know that we are WISconsin and not WESconsin then enough is enough," Schneider wrote. "I know that out in California and on the East Coast, we are just a bunch of beer and brats cheeseheads without the refinements of chablis and croissants, nevertheless we do take pride in our state and resent having it butchered by the American Broadcasting Co."

His tirade continued: "How do you think it would go over if you pronounced 'California' as 'Colorfornia' or 'Los Angeles' as 'Los Angels?' Then why can't we get a break from you national hot shots who make fun of the lack of geography training by high school and college students who can't tell Miami of Florida from Miami of Ohio?"

Dennis Lewin, senior vice president of ABC Sports, wrote back ten days later with an apology: "Unfortunately, Mr. Griese has a problem pronouncing the word. In fact, during the telecast, ABC Sports personnel pointed out to him this mispronunciation, but (despite being a Midwesterner from Indiana and a graduate of Purdue) he was unable to correct his speech pattern.

"We recognize why the people in the great State of Wisconsin are sensitive, but hope you understand how difficult it is to change a lifelong speech pattern. We will continue to remind him."

The Rose Bowl ticket fiasco also continued to enrage Wisconsinites who were cheated out of a chance to see the history-making game months after the contest. By late April of 1994, Wisconsin Atty. Gen. James Doyle filed lawsuits against three tour operators for alleged violations of the state's deceptive advertising laws. The suits sought restitution for customers as well as civil penalties for the firms.

In all, Doyle's office received 803 formal complaints against sixty firms involved. By the time the lawsuits were filed, Doyle reported that nearly $250,000 had been returned to state residents in refunds.

But the ultimate outrage was yet to come. It set the stage for another contest between the Badgers and Bruins, this one played out in a courtroom.

On April 21, *The Los Angeles Times* reported that UCLA in early December sold 4,000 Rose Bowl tickets to Angelo M. Mazzone III, a California businessman who formerly served as an associate athletic director at the school.

Mazzone paid the forty-six-dollar face value of the tickets, and gave UCLA a $100,000 donation to boot, the *Times* reported. The next day, Dane County Circuit Judge Angela Bartell allowed Madison lawyer James Olson to include UCLA as defendants in a class-action lawsuit on behalf of as many as 1,000 fans who did not receive tickets.

Meanwhile, UCLA Athletic Director Peter Dalis defended the move, telling the *Los Angeles Daily News* that UCLA could not have anticipated the ticket demand when the tickets, primarily in the end zone, were sold to Mazzone on December 2.

Doyle seized the moment to dash off a letter to UCLA Chancellor Charles E. Young, asking that the university surrender to the Wisconsin Justice Department any donations it received for selling blocks of tickets.

"These funds should be used to provide restitution to those remaining Wisconsin consumers who suffered losses as a result of Rose Bowl ticket problems," Doyle wrote.

"The excess tickets your institution had in its possession and knew would not be used by UCLA fans could have helped to ease the problems which Wisconsin consumers experienced. I am very disappointed that UCLA gave priority to donors instead of offering its unused tickets to University of Wisconsin fans. Clearly, your institution has benefited at the expense of Wisconsin consumers."

Commercial interests swooped in to capitalize on the Rose Bowl victory. Everything from T-shirts to watches to commemorative coins to jewelry swamped stores across Wisconsin and consumers carted it off by the armload.

In the sixty days after the Rose Bowl one screen-printing operation sold more than $1 million worth of T-shirts on the wholesale market, while dozens of other licensees also reported heavy sales.

The Athletic Department sold highlight videos and the U.S. Postal Service offered commemorative envelopes imprinted with the flying "W" and bearing a rose stamp and a special cancellation.

Hoping to snare some publicity in the days before the Rose Bowl, a jock manufacturer sent reporters complimentary athletic supporters like those that would be presented to the players in Pasadena. The supporters bore the words: "ROSE BOWL-1994-WISCONSIN."

The flying "W" seemed to be everywhere in the weeks and months after the Rose Bowl. Richter, in Lillehammer, Norway, to watch his son, Barry, compete with the U.S. Olympic hockey team in February, kept bumping into people wearing Wisconsin garb.

As Greenfield's gold medal speedskater Dan Jansen competed in Norway, CBS cameras showed his relatives, one in a Wisconsin Rose Bowl sweatshirt, cheering from the stands. And when Jansen returned home, Alvarez appeared at a rally and parade to present him a Wisconsin cap to replace the Carolina Panthers cap he wore in interviews shown globally after he won the gold in the 1,000 meters.

Alvarez, just back from a postseason Hawaiian vacation, said he ran into Wisconsin stuff everywhere. "The paraphernalia is all over the place, just like Michigan and Notre Dame," he said.

And football's booster base, so eroded in the Don Morton years, had regained unprecedented vigor. The Mendota Gridiron Club during Alvarez's tenure, and at his urging, had expanded.

When Alvarez took the job, the club had only a Madison chapter and a depleted branch that was teetering near extinction in populous southeastern Wisconsin. In ensuing years, it expanded to Wausau, La Crosse, Oshkosh, and Chicago.

The wider base and the Badgers' unprecedented success had the money pouring in from donors across the nation.

According to Mendota Associate Director Wayne Esser, the Badgers' success and Alvarez's unflagging efforts to help rebuild the booster club resulted in the group garnering a record $660,000 in 1993.

That compares with a base of about $220,000 during the Morton years and the previous all-time high of about $400,000 during the Dave McClain years. Esser said Alvarez's attention to fundraising and to donors played a major role in reversing the club's fortunes.

"He spoke to anybody, anywhere," Esser said of Alvarez, recounting the countless dinner speeches and golf outings. "Barry and his staff have been tireless in getting football back on its feet."

People were clearly carried away by Rose Bowl euphoria. In the town of Blooming Grove just outside Madison, the town board approved renaming Gay Avenue in honor of Alvarez. Residents there had complained that they didn't want to live on a two-block-long dead-end street with a name—taken from an old-line farming family—associated with homosexuals.

The *Wisconsin State Journal* in Madison attacked the move as "clear evidence that when prejudice is set loose, anyone can be a victim." The newspaper said discarding history in favor of naming a street after a coach who had one great season was a "recipe for regret" cooked up in the heat of the moment.

"And what of Alvarez, whose success last year was indeed a marvel? If his team flops next year, will the stigma of defeat prompt a re-naming of the street?" the newspaper asked in an editorial.

Despite the furor, the red-and-white street sign went up in mid-March.

And Rev. Burke, who held Nelson's engagement ring for him during the Rose Bowl, also became enmeshed in controversy. Burke came under fire for traveling with the Badgers, something he had done for eighteen years. Ann Gaylor, of the Madison-based Freedom From Religion Foundation, attacked Burke's travels with the Wisconsin team. She questioned whether a publicly funded institution should be so closely affiliated with a priest. Richter countered that Burke's expenses were paid by the Mendota Gridiron Club, not the UW.

But a resulting university probe found that the source of the funds was not clearly outlined and said that Burke should fund his own travels in the future. The review also determined that Burke had led team prayers before and after games. What had been a long-standing, friendly relationship between Burke and the Badgers had mushroomed into a constitutional question of church-state separation while players watched in amazement.

"He is just a friend. He's not pushing any religion. The whole thing really makes me mad," said Scott Nelson.

In the future, UW lawyer Casey Nagy said that players will determine for themselves whether prayers will be on the team's pre- and postgame schedules. That will avoid any implication that coaches are requiring the prayers. "If the players choose to supplement the established routine and invite the participation of Burke or any other person, that will be their prerogative," Nagy said.

At the team's postseason banquet, Richter lampooned the issue, mentioning that he often saw Burke "at Camp Randall Cathedral, er, I mean Stadium," to the laughter of many of the 2,000 people in the heavily pro-Burke crowd.

On the UW campus, it was a case of supply-side athletics. A rising tide began to lift all boats. Football's success and the rising popularity of an improved basketball program fed into the momentum for a new basketball arena, to replace the sixty-four-year-old Fieldhouse.

All the glory, it was hoped, would fuel a drive for a new 15,000-seat facility to replace the venerable but uncomfortable and outdated sandstone barn whose time had passed it by. By February, the UW Board of Regents approved a $250,000 study that could launch the $50 million to $60 million project.

This project was spoken of as a pie-in-the-sky venture, something impossible to consider before 1989. The department's budgets were a laughingstock in the state capitol and at the ticket office. Wise budgeting and a turnaround in football revenues helped the department embark on an ambitious plan to change the landscape of UW athletics.

Among the other side effects was an increase in ticket prices from twenty dollars a game for season-ticket holders to twenty-two dollars in fifteen sections of the stadium as the department worked to build a $559,000 reserve into its latest budget and add two women's sports to help meet gender equity targets.

And officials were projecting the average home game would draw 72,000 fans, a number that would have been unimaginable only four years earlier as college football attendance nationally was on the decline.

After years of persistent deficits, the department had regained its fiscal health and was beginning to make an unprecedented investment in the future. And it was exploiting the newfound popularity of college football at the UW.

What happened in Pasadena had a carryover impact on the general interest in sports in Wisconsin. That's a side benefit the Milwaukee-based Wisconsin Sports Authority is eager to exploit.

The authority was begun in 1990 to promote and attract amateur and professional sports events to the state as an economic development tool. Every time a Wisconsin sport gains the national attention the Badgers did in 1993, it makes the agency's job easier.

"It instilled a can-do attitude as far as sports is concerned," said authority Vice Chairman Joseph Chrnelich, a former Badgers basketball player. "There was a feeling that anything could be accomplished. It helped raise the awareness of Wisconsin sports. You can't put a price tag on that kind of exposure."

Following the Rose Bowl, Joe Panos weighed participating in three all-star games that had extended invitations, the East-West Shrine game, the Senior Bowl, and the Hula Bowl.

Alvarez advised him to stay away from all three because of the chances that Panos might aggravate the knee injury he sustained in the closing minutes of the Rose Bowl. Panos, however, bucked that advice and went to the Senior Bowl.

"Like an idiot, I went and I never should have," said Panos, who was drawn to the game in Birmingham, Alabama, partly because of the rapt attention it draws from pro scouts.

During the first day of workouts, another player fell on Panos's injured knee and Panos withdrew from competition. The knee healed nicely, but as the off-season wore on, he became increasingly itchy about his future in the pros.

During March, he was worked out by NFL scouts every two or three days. They poked, prodded, and found every conceivable measure to ascertain Panos's potential value come draft day in April.

In early March, Panos was given an extensive evaluation by Washington Redskins Offensive Line Coach Jim Hanifan, who projected him as a guard. Hanifan put him through a rigorous battery of tests, including a series of drills to test his balance. "A couple of the things I needed to see, he showed," said Hanifan, who cited Panos's power and explosion off the ball as major positives.

All the attention, though, had only put Panos on edge: "I literally can't sleep at night waiting for the draft. It seems like every week is a month. It's getting tiresome."

On April 25, 1994, both Panos and Montgomery were taken in the NFL draft by the Philadelphia Eagles. Panos went in the third round as the seventy-seventh pick overall and Montgomery lingered into the seventh, and final, round.

Just after 9:30 a.m. on that Monday, Panos received a phone call at his parents' home in Brookfield from Philadelphia Coach Rich Kotite informing him of the Eagles' selection. It was just another chapter in Panos's storybook career.

"Four, five, six years ago, I just wanted to play. I wanted to be on the Badgers' team. Now, all of a sudden, I've got this," Panos said. "It was a dream of mine to get a chance to play in the league and it came true.

"It's tough leaving Wisconsin, not just the school but the state. I'll always be a Badger. We went through a lot together, going from 1–10 to Rose Bowl champs. Life goes on and now it's time to take the next step."

Montgomery, meanwhile, was chosen as the 206th player in the draft. Before the draft began, Montgomery had decided that he would likely end his football career and go on to a career in law enforcement if he was not drafted. Montgomery said he had little desire to pursue the free-agent route through the NFL.

"As the rounds went by, I was more and more nervous," said Montgomery, who along with Panos was a member of the Senior Bowl team coached by Kotite's staff. "Finally, when Philadelphia called, it was a shock. I couldn't believe it."

Alvarez's exposure, meanwhile, left him awash in fan mail and gifts of all sorts in the weeks following the Rose Bowl victory. One woman sent a composite photograph with his face looming over the Rose Bowl; another sent a mirror with the image of Bucky Badger frosted into the surface.

Perhaps the most notable of all was a masterful work of taxidermy from Bob and Pat Meeker. Alvarez received a stuffed badger with a kicking tee at its feet that allowed the ball to be supported by the beast's paw. In addition, he received all the paperwork needed for him to possess the stuffed creature.

There seemed to be no end of it. A printer called the university to get the names of all the coaches' wives so he could print complimentary stationery for them. And a Madison electrical firm was distributing 1994 football schedule cards with January 1, 1995, designated as the Badgers' return to a bowl game.

And if you believe in the power of the computer, Badgers' fans had even greater reason to smile. The Badgers finished the season ranked sixth in the Associated Press media poll and fifth in the CNN/*USA Today* coaches poll. But one ingenious writer, Jimmy Burch of the *Fort Worth Star-Telegram,* transcended the polls after the season ended.

Burch, using software developed by Nashville, Tennessee computer programmer Lance Haffner, went to some lengths to set up a computer-based Division I playoff using eight bowl-eligible teams seeded on their final national ranking. Wisconsin was assigned the low seed in the tournament.

The games were played at neutral sites under dome-like conditions and the computer used the teams' offensive and defensive tendencies to determine winners. In addition, Burch used what he called the "Cheesehead Clause," which required the Badgers to defeat opponents twice and eliminate the chance of a fluke victory by Wisconsin.

In Burch's first round, Wisconsin defeated Nebraska 23–14 and turned around and edged the Cornhuskers 28–27. Next on the docket was Notre Dame and the Badgers defeated the Fighting Irish 22–15 and 35–14. In the second game, Bevell completed an amazing 13 of 14 passes.

Finally, the Badgers faced Florida State. In the first game, the Badgers defeated the Seminoles 36–30 as Fletcher scored two touchdowns and Montgomery, Moss, and Carl McCullough each added a touchdown.

The rematch ended with the Badgers defeating the Seminoles 17–7 to capture the newspaper's mythical national championship.

Amid all the euphoria there was one concern however: keeping Alvarez at Wisconsin. It had been a concern of Richter's since Alvarez first set foot in Madison.

Aside from his success as a field coach, Alvarez was drawing national attention as a recruiter. His 1993 class was ranked second in the Big Ten and tenth nationally by recruiting guru Tom Lemming. It was Wisconsin's best ranking ever, and gave struggling schools another strong incentive to eye Alvarez.

After Alvarez's second season, his contract was extended for three years; it was again extended after the 1992 season. While there was never a strong run made at Alvarez by another program, Richter was anxious.

Alvarez's contract, which ran through 1998, failed to provide Richter enough assurance that he could hold on to the man who made this rebirth possible. Having watched as the Badgers' program was battered by the disruptive transitions of the 1980s, Richter was in no mood for change.

"We want to put our stamp on this, and we've only begun," he said. "I've told Barry, and he believes it, that this could be as good a college job as there is in the country. Why did Joe Paterno stay at Penn State? Why did Bo Schembechler stay at Michigan? More and more, it becomes the environment you work in and the challenge."

By the time the Badgers achieved a 6–0 record after the Purdue game, Richter knew that Alvarez's stock was soaring nationally and he began to consider an unprecedented long-term agreement that he hoped would keep Alvarez at Wisconsin for the length of his coaching career.

There were persistent rumors, always denied by Alvarez, that he would leave Wisconsin if and when Tom Osborne stepped down at Nebraska or Lou Holtz walked away from the head coaching job at Notre Dame. And he flatly denies any interest in bolting to the National Football League.

Nonetheless, Richter and Alvarez began talking about a contract, and the talks were friendly and cooperative. Ultimately, they relieved Richter's fears that Alvarez would pack his bags and go.

While talking with reporters at Disneyland during the week before the Rose Bowl, Alvarez revealed that he and Richter had spoken informally about a long-term deal, one that seemed within striking distance for the university. Progress on a long-term deal was doubtlessly helped along as Alvarez garnered postseason awards.

In addition to being named the Big Ten's coach of the year, Alvarez became the first Wisconsin coach to be named national coach of the year by Kodak, the Bobby Dodd Foundation, and *College and Pro Football Newsweekly.*

On January 19, just eighteen days after the Badgers' Rose Bowl victory, the UW Athletic Board agreed in principle to a fifteen-year contract that would keep Alvarez at Wisconsin until he is sixty-two. "No contract is unbreakable, but we want to provide some strong reasons for staying at Wisconsin," said Richter.

The agreement includes annuities that mature in five-year increments and could be worth more than $1 million in donated money over the length of the contract. To earn the money, all Alvarez must do is stay at the UW. That, in addition to his base salary of $122,400 and full use of broadcast revenues, will make him a rich man if he stays.

"Since I took this job in 1990, I have always said that I am happy at this institution and confident that I can accomplish all of my coaching goals here," Alvarez said. "This contract represents a commitment from the university to both me and my program. I appreciate the confidence in me that the university has shown by making this arrangement, and my final acceptance of the contract cements my commitment to the UW."

The deal was strategically timed during the recruiting rush before the February date for signing national letters of intent. Richter acknowledged that he hoped high school prospects took note of the university's commitment to Alvarez.

"It sends a signal to recruits everywhere that Barry Alvarez will be the coach of the University of Wisconsin for a long time," said Richter. "He wishes to build on the solid foundation that he has already established at the UW, and we are excited about that desire."

It also afforded some comfort to Richter in the face of the periodic speculation about Alvarez's future. It allowed him to slough off reports like the one from ESPN's Chris Mortenson that Alvarez would be among the coaches considered when the NFL expansion Carolina Panthers named a head coach.

The deal done, Alvarez returned to recruiting.

Several days later, linebacker Brandon Williams, one of the top prep players in New York state, committed to play for Wisconsin, citing the agreement and the stability afforded at Wisconsin.

Despite his agreement on the terms of a fifteen-year, incentive-laden contract, rumors continued to swirl around Alvarez and his future. Lou Holtz's momentary flirtation with the Jacksonville Jaguars' head coaching job in February stopped hearts in Madison, where fans feared Alvarez would bolt to South Bend if Holtz left.

Alvarez, however, denied all the reports and said he preferred to stay at Wisconsin. "We've gone through a lot of work here and I'm kind of selfish. I'd hate to turn this over to anyone else right now," Alvarez said, again denying any interest in leaving for the pro ranks. "I've never been interested in pro football and I doubt that I ever will be."

Shalala watched from afar, and with considerable pride, as the Wisconsin sports turnabout was accomplished. Even in the corridors of the U.S. capitol, she was recognized as much for her ties to the renaissance as for her position of power. "You walk down the halls of Congress and people yell, 'Go Badgers!' It's really amazing," said Shalala.

She hopes the renewal of sports at the UW will be recognized nationally as a textbook case of a university's chief executive integrating the academic and athletic missions of a university.

"I hope it is a model, but it really does take paying attention," she said while attending Wisconsin's regular-season basketball finale at Indiana University's Assembly Hall in Bloomington. "It's not just appointing an athletic director and walking away. It's more than that. It's making sure the resources are there, making sure that you do it the right way and have high ethics.

"It's not easy to do it clean."

During the basketball season, President Clinton told Shalala he was pulling for the Badgers to make it to the National Collegiate Athletic Association basketball tournament. An Arkansas Razorbacks fan, Clinton periodically checked on the fortunes of Shalala's Badgers.

"He asks me all the time how the Badgers are doing," Shalala said. "He said to me, 'I hope you get into the NCAA tournament so we can go to the Final Four together.'"

Just a day after the Indiana game, the Wisconsin basketball team under second-year head coach Stu Jackson was invited to the National Collegiate Athletic Association tournament for the first time since 1947, another historic breakthrough by a coach hired during Shalala's tenure.

A thirty-one-year Rose Bowl drought and a forty-seven-year absence from the basketball tournament had been broken in the short space of three months, erasing the gloom that shrouded Badgers sport history. Now there was a clean slate for both revenue sports. Football was selling season tickets at record levels and basketball was selling out the Fieldhouse.

"That's a responsibility we have now is not to let it slip," said Richter, who was six years old the last time the Badgers went to the basketball tournament. "Now we have a change in mentality. People we have here now, Stu [Jackson] and Barry and others, are shooting higher."

Because of the program's success in 1993, Alvarez realized one of the toughest challenges he and his players will face in 1994 is staying on top. "That's a roadblock for us to negotiate this fall," said Alvarez. "My goal is to prepare this team to be the best it can be."

Wisconsin's Rose Bowl triumph established a dramatic new hierarchy in the Big Ten, and a new political order as well. Alvarez expects the UW to be the focus of backstage criticism from other coaches jealous of the Badgers' quick rise to prominence.

That theory makes some sense. What Alvarez accomplished at Wisconsin is bound to raise eyebrows among college presidents who look at their own football programs and ask: "Why can't we do that?" That turns up the heat on coaches of poor-performing programs and increases the sniping and jealousy.

Still, Alvarez seems unconcerned about his new status in the conference. He insists what's been achieved at Wisconsin is the result of hard work, a good staff, and solid recruiting—not because of cheating and cutting corners.

"If they say we cheated to get kids, who could they mean? Joe Panos? Lamark Shackerford? Nobody wanted those kids. They came here and worked and made something of themselves in a program they believed in," Alvarez said.

Recruiting took on a distinctively different flavor after the Badgers' 1993 season. Wisconsin's coaches found that the Badgers were a bigger, more inviting target for competing schools. Opposing schools were hitting harder at Wisconsin than ever before, one of the downsides of a successful season. Badgers coaches were battling negative recruiting at every turn, as they had for years, only now they were a bigger target.

"They took us a little more seriously now," said Alvarez, sloughing off the rough treatment by his peers. "I don't really care. I just want to keep winning football games."

In some cases, players were scared off by Wisconsin's improved depth, the result of years of solid recruiting. Providence, Rhode Island, tailback Buddy Rogers, for instance, decided to attend up-and-coming Maryland instead of Wisconsin. Although he labored over the decision for weeks, his choice came down to playing time.

That was an attribute Wisconsin coaches were able to sell widely in the past. Now, however, it was a tougher sell at most positions.

"If somebody's trying to duck competition, you don't want him anyway," Alvarez reasoned.

UCLA's Terry Donahue recalled running into the same sort of problems after the Bruins played in a spate of bowl games in the mid-1980s. "It works every which way," he said. "When we were going to so many bowl games, we'd lose a few kids because they didn't think they could play here."

One thing Alvarez found out on the recruiting trail was that the Rose Bowl gave the Badgers another wedge to convince top players to come to Madison. He was no Pollyanna, however, and knew that one postseason appearance was no cure-all in recruiting's cutthroat arena.

"One bowl game doesn't lock things up. It adds one more thing to the package to sell," he said after signing thirteen players who were rated by analyst Tom Lemming as the fifth-best class in the Big Ten.

That was a marked dropoff from the previous year, when Wisconsin recruited its best class ever and was rated tenth nationally. But it was only half the size of the previous year's class and it filled Wisconsin's positional needs well.

The Badgers decided against recruiting offensive linemen in this class, which eliminated many in-state athletes. The only Wisconsin players signed by Alvarez were player of the year Aaron Stecker, a running back from Ashwaubenon, and wide receiver Donald Hayes of Madison East.

That decision probably contributed to the Badgers' lower ranking in 1994, since it forced Wisconsin to go farther from home to attract prospects. "The farther you go, the lower your batting average," said Alvarez. "Just because you went to one bowl game and won? There's a lot of other teams that won those. Some [players] are going to fall in love with this place, some won't."

The 1994 recruiting season was marked with disadvantages for the Badgers. The extended season crimped coaches' recruiting schedules and no basketball games were scheduled during the available recruiting weekends. The basketball games are a traditional favorite form of entertainment among recruits.

And the Rose Bowl hype provided its own legion of distractions for the staff. "I had more calls on my machine from people wanting Rose Bowl tickets than kids wanting to commit to go to school here," said Rob Ianello.

Ianello's future at Wisconsin, however, was imperiled at the NCAA convention in 1993 when college presidents voted to abolish recruiting coordinators and shift those duties to head coaches and their nine-member staffs. The reasoning boiled down to cost-cutting, but the decision was hotly criticized throughout college football coaching ranks.

"The college presidents are silly," said Lemming, the recruiting guru. "They're always trying to pry into college football and pound their chests. This is a thing to save $45,000 for each job and it's going to cost them double that for recruiting. It's spreading the responsibility to a lot more people, they'll have to hire a lot more clerical people. They have no idea what recruiting coordinators do or are, most of them."

The decision, Lemming said, also would diminish the coaching pool as many programs rushed to make recruiting coordinators assistant coaches.

"They see ten positions and they ignored the fact that the tenth one is the second most important one to the head coach," said Lemming. "If you don't have the talent, you're not going to win."

But the action stuck and that put Ianello in a sticky position after the 1993 season. None of Wisconsin's assistant coaches left after the Rose Bowl, assuring stability in the program. That equilibrium, however, pushed Ianello out of a job.

Although UW officials considered making him director of football operations, the NCAA rules would have prevented him from performing 70 percent of his existing recruiting role. Ianello, who had turned down better-paying offers from Illinois, Maryland, Tennessee, and Arizona State to stay with Alvarez over the last four years, found himself on the brink of unemployment as the 1994 recruiting season wound down.

When University of Arizona Head Coach Dick Tomey called just before the February 2 signing date, Ianello was eager to accept his offer as an assistant coach. In that position, Ianello basically would serve as recruiting coordinator, as a staff opening allowed Tomey to restructure the Wildcats' staff.

"It was something I needed to do career-wise," said Ianello. "The NCAA would have really restricted what I do. Maybe I would have been able to do 30 percent of what I did. The opportunity to do what I wanted to do for a top-quality program was too good to pass up. Barry's got a good staff. They needed to stay and I'm glad they did stay."

For Ianello, it seemed to be the perfect time to move on. "It's the right time to leave a place, after you go to the Rose Bowl and accomplish what we did. A year ago, I didn't have the same feeling. There was a lot of unfinished business a year ago, a lot of things you work hard to establish just weren't done yet," he said.

Lemming questioned the wisdom of the NCAA rule, saying it would only jack up administrative costs in the long run and overburden assistant coaches. Moreover, the rule would weigh heavily on Wisconsin, which didn't have the luxury of keeping Ianello as an assistant. The burden could become even greater in recruiting for the next calls, since academic standards are higher, making it a tougher year in which to find qualified players.

"For a young guy, his skills on the phone were nationally known," he said. "That's what he did best. The NCAA said he couldn't do it anymore. I don't envy their position right now. Barry's got his hands full."

But Ianello's duties will fall to Bernie Wyatt, a seasoned pro, and Alvarez expects there will be no dropoff in production.

Defensive concerns loomed large for Alvarez as spring drills began. Carlos Fowler and Lamark Shackerford were missing from the line and he shifted outside linebacker Bryan Jurewicz to left tackle and looked at junior Jason Maniecki at noseguard. Sophomore Tarek Saleh took over at outside linebacker.

Jeff Messenger moved to free safety to cover for Scott Nelson's absence and senior Jamel Brown took over at strong safety. The inside linebacker spot vacated by Yusef Burgess was being contested by sophomores Pete Monty and Pete Diatelevi.

"We must replace some very experienced players on defense," said Alvarez. "There is talent waiting to step in, but you're always cautious when experience is lacking."

Wisconsin's football program was finally on solid ground, high ground. During the team's banquet, Richter reached into a pocket and retrieved the Notre Dame bowl game medal that Alvarez had given him four years earlier in his Miami hotel room.

"We haven't waited as long as I thought, quite frankly," Richter said. With that, he handed the medal back to Alvarez.

In the days after the Rose Bowl, Fowler underwent surgery on his fractured wrist and had a cast applied. As a physician worked on the cast, Fowler signed autographs with his right hand for fans working at UW Hospital. "It's a good thing it was my left hand that was broken and not my right," he said.

It was an injury Fowler, who signed a free agent contract with the Denver Broncos in April, will remember for a long time. As luck would have it, the stitches were arrayed in a strikingly appropriate shape.

"I'm marked for life with a 'W' on my wrist," said a smiling Fowler.

"But, hey, that's just fine."

Appendix

Big Ten Standings

Wisconsin	9-1-1	6-1-1
Ohio State	9-1-1	6-1-1
Penn State	9-2-0	6-2-0
Indiana	8-3-0	5-3-0
Michigan	7-4-0	5-3-0
Illinois	5-6-0	5-3-0
Mich. St.	6-5-0	4-4-0
Iowa	6-5-0	3-5-0
Minnesota	4-7-0	3-5-0
N'western	2-9-0	0-8-0
Purdue	1-10-0	0-8-0

Big Ten Leaders

Rushing
Brent Moss, Wis.   134.5

Pass Efficiency
Darrell Bevell, Wis.   161.1

Receiving
Omar Douglas, Minn.   88.0

Total Offense
Len Williams, NU   212.3

Scoring
Tyrone Wheatley, MI   8.0

All-purpose Yardage
Tyrone Wheatley, MI   155.9

Kick Scoring
Craig Fayak, PSU   7.2

Punting
Jim DiGuilio, IU   43.2

Punt Returns
L. Gissendaner, NU   13.9

Kickoff Returns
S. Hammonds, PSU   26.5

1993 GAME SUMMARIES

UW 35, Nevada 17

WolfPack	0	3	0	14	—	17
Badgers	14	0	14	7	—	35

Team stats	Nev	UW
First downs	23	22
Rushing yards	35-123	48-172
Passes	33-47-4	19-27-1
Passing yards	308	263
Total offense	82-431	75-435
Punts–avg	4-36.0	3-38.7
Fumbles–lost	1-0	0-0
Penalties–yards	6-68	4-34
Possession time	27:49	32:11

Individual leaders
Rushing—Nev: Crishon 20-93, Holmes 10-29; W: Moss 19-74, Fletcher 18-62
Passing—Nev: Vargas 33-47-4-308; W: Bevell 19-27-1-263
Receiving—Nev: Reeves 12-142, Stephens 8-90; W: Dawkins 3-85, Montgomery 4-52

UW 24, SMU 16

Badgers	0	0	10	14	—	24
Mustangs	3	10	3	0	—	16

Team stats	UW	SMU
First downs	23	18
Rushing yards	52-244	29-141
Passes	18-26-1	19-37-2
Passing yards	198	233
Total offense	78-442	66-374
Punts–avg	5-42.0	6-43.0
Fumbles–lost	1-1	2-1
Penalties–yards	3-35	6-57
Possession time	36:02	23:58

Individual leaders
Rushing—W: Moss 27-181, Fletcher 18-71; SMU: Shepard 12-77, Flanigan 13-55
Passing—W: Bevell 18-26-1-198; SMU: Flanigan 15-27-2-192, Eldred 4-10-0-41
Receiving—W: DeRamus 7-112, Roan 5-48; SMU: Berry 9-115, Whitmore 3-45

UW 28, Iowa State 7

Cyclones	0	0	0	7	—	7
Badgers	14	7	7	0	—	28

Team stats	ISU	UW
First downs	11	25
Rushing yards	39-137	48-252
Passes	9-15-1	15-21-0
Passing yards	88	196
Total offense	54-225	69-448
Punts–avg	6-35.5	2-38.5
Fumbles–lost	2-0	2-2
Penalties–yards	8-53	6-53
Possession time	27:33	32:27

Individual leaders
Rushing—ISU: Doxzon 13-59, Knott 5-33; W: Fletcher 19-124, Moss 21-105
Passing—ISU: Utter 6-9-1-47, Doxzon 3-6-0-41; W: Bevell 15-21-0-196
Receiving—ISU: Branch 2-36, Hughes 2-18; W: DeRamus 6-88, Roan 3-38

UW 27, Indiana 15

Badgers	13	7	0	7	—	27
Hoosiers	2	0	13	0	—	15

Team stats	UW	IU
First downs	20	15
Rushing yards	56-354	35-101
Passes	5-15-2	15-30-0
Passing yards	123	186
Total offense	71-477	65-287
Punts–avg	5-38.2	9-40.4
Fumbles–lost	2-1	2-2
Penalties–yards	3-33	5-22
Possession time	32:30	27:30

Individual leaders
Rushing—W: Moss 32-198, Fletcher 10-99; IU: Chaney 12-61, Glover 10-34

Passing—W: Bevell 5-15-2-123; IU: Paci 15-30-0-186
Receiving—W: DeRamus 3-116; IU: Lewis 6-102, Baety 5-47

UW 53, Northwestern 14

Wildcats	0	14	0	0	—	14
Badgers	7	20	19	7	—	53

Team stats	NU	UW
First downs	20	28
Rushing yards	35-77	55-315
Passes	21-31-3	18-19-0
Passing yards	256	218
Total offense	66-333	74-533
Punts–avg	3-40.3	0-0.0
Fumbles–lost	1-0	3-2
Penalties–yards	8-51	4-35
Possession time	29:15	30:45

Individual leaders
Rushing—N: Robinson 13-36, Wright 6-23; W: Moss 15-125, Fletcher 22-106
Passing—N: Williams 19-26-2-221, Schnur 2-5-1-35; W: Bevell 17-18-0-207
Receiving—N: Gissendaner 9-98, Senters 3-55, Morris 4-42; W: Dawkins 7-80, DeRamus 2-44

UW 42, Purdue 28

Badgers	7	14	14	7	—	42
Boilers	0	0	7	21	—	28

Team stats	UW	PU
First downs	29	20
Rushing yards	61-201	35-143
Passes	18-26-0	16-24-1
Passing yards	256	239
Total offense	87-457	59-382
Punts–avg	3-34.0	4-39.8
Fumbles–lost	2-0	1-1
Penalties–yards	5-37	4-25
Possession time	38:58	21:02

Individual leaders
Rushing—W: Moss 29-139, Fletcher 14-40; P: Alstott 12-87, Rogers 13-55
Passing—W: Bevell 15-20-0-204, Macias 3-6-0-52; P: Trefzger 14-19-0-218, Pike 2-5-1-21

Receiving—W: DeRamus 3-50, Montgomery 3-46, Dawkins 3-36; P: 4-54, Rogers 3-45, Ross 3-40

Minnesota 28, UW 21

Badgers	0	0	14	7	—	21
Gophers	7	14	0	7	—	28

Team stats	UW	UM
First downs	36	16
Rushing yards	42-182	35-118
Passes	31-48-5	17-30-4
Passing yards	423	267
Total offense	90-605	65-385
Punts–avg	3-29.3	6-32.5
Fumbles–lost	1-1	1-1
Penalties–yards	7-42	8-58
Possession time	34:15	25:45

Individual leaders
Rushing—W: Moss 27-130, Fletcher 8-43; M: Darkins 17-83, Carter 14-39
Passing—W: Bevell 31-48-5-423; M: Eckers 17-30-4-267
Receiving—W: DeRamus 9-156, Dawkins 9-131; M: Early 3-98, Douglas 5-51

UW 13, Michigan 10

Wolverines	0	3	7	0	—	10
Badgers	3	10	0	0	—	13

Team stats	UM	UW
First downs	20	24
Rushing yards	32-111	48-225
Passes	21-31-2	15-22-0
Passing yards	248	118
Total offense	63-359	70-343
Punts–avg	2-52.0	4-37.0
Fumbles–lost	1-1	0-0
Penalties–yards	6-59	2-13
Possession time	26:53	33:07

Individual leaders
Rushing—M: Davis 16-69, Powers 7-34; W: Moss 26-128, Fletcher 9-78
Passing—M: Collins 21-31-2-248; W: Bevell 15-22-0-118
Receiving—M: Toomer 6-112, Smith 5-56; W: DeRamus 3-32, Dawkins 4-27

UW 14, Ohio State 14

Buckeyes	7	0	0	7	—	14
Badgers	0	7	7	0	—	14

Team stats	OSU	UW
First downs	21	17
Rushing yards	34-128	48-227
Passes	17-33-3	11-18-1
Passing yards	290	105
Total offense	67-418	66-332
Punts–avg	5-34.2	6-37.8
Fumbles–lost	1-0	2-2
Penalties–yards	8-54	2-10
Possession time	27:31	32:29

Individual leaders
Rushing—OSU: Harris 19-99, Bẏnotè 8-41; W: Moss 25-129, Fletcher 12-58
Passing—OSU: Hoying 12-22-2-177, Powers 5-11-1-113; W: Bevell 11-18-1-105
Receiving—OSU: Galloway 6-150, Sanders 4-62; W: DeRamus 4-55

UW 35, Illinois 10

Badgers	7	14	7	7	—	35
Illini	0	3	7	0	—	10

Team stats	UW	UI
First downs	26	13
Rushing yards	54-301	25-106
Passes	17-22-0	12-27-0
Passing yards	222	121
Total offense	76-523	52-227
Punts–avg	3-23.0	5-44.2
Fumbles–lost	0-0	1-0
Penalties–yards	3-13	0-0
Possession time	37:46	22:14

Individual leaders
Rushing—W: Fletcher 18-139, Moss 27-124; I: Platt 10-74, Douthard 11-32
Passing—W: Bevell 17-22-0-222; I: Johnson 12-27-0-121
Receiving—W: DeRamus 8-125, Roan 4-65; I: Douthard 4-47

UW 41, Michigan State 20

Spartans	7	0	3	10	—	20
Badgers	3	21	3	14	—	41

Team stats	MSU	UW
First downs	21	27
Rushing yards	37-166	45-286
Passes	19-25-2	14-19-0
Passing yards	216	235
Total offense	62-382	64-521
Punts–avg	3-45.3	0-0
Fumbles–lost	0-0	1-0
Penalties–yards	6-59	2-27
Possession time	31:16	28:44

Individual leaders
Rushing—MSU: Goulbourne 16-90; W: Moss 28-147, Fletcher 10-112
Passing—MSU: Miller 19-25-2-216; W: Bevell 14-19-0-235
Receiving—MSU: Coleman 4-86, S. Greene 5-64; W: DeRamus 5-96, Roan 4-52

UW 21, UCLA 16

UCLA	3	0	0	13	—	16
Wisconsin	7	7	-	7	—	21

Team stats	UCLA	UW
First downs	31	21
Rushing yards	40-212	46-250
Passes	28-43-1	10-20-1
Passing yards	288	96
Total offense	83-288	66-346
Punts–avg	2-35	6-38
Fumbles–lost	5-5	2-0
Penalties–yards	9-95	12-89
Possession time	29:03	30:57

Individual leaders
Rushing—UCLA: Davis 13-88, Hicks 8-67, Washington 4-39, Millner 3-12, Cook 11-11, team 1- (minus 5). W: Moss 36-158, Fletcher 7-64, Bevell 1-21, Montgomery 2-7.
Passing—UCLA: Cook 28-43-1-288; W: Bevell 10-20-1-96
Receiving—UCLA: Stokes 14-176, Allen 4-32, Jordan 3-34, Washington 3-8, Nguyen 2-26, Adams 1-7, Davis 1-5; W: Dawkins 4-33, Fletcher 2-29, London 2-20, Jackson 1-9, Moss 1-5

1993 WISCONSIN FOOTBALL STATISTICS

TEAM STATISTICS	WISCONSIN	OPP
Total First Downs	298	229
First Downs – Rushing	158	95
First Downs – Passing	121	123
First Downs – Penalty	19	11
Rushing Att – Yds	603-3009	411-1563
Rushing Yards per Game	250.8	130.3
Pass Comp – Att – Int	191-283-11	227-373-23
Passing Yards	2453	2740
Passing Yards per Game	204.4	228.3
Punting Number – Yds – Avg	40-1457-36.4	55-2154-39.2
Fumbles – Lost	18-9	18-11
Penalties – Yards	53-421	74-601
Sacks by – Yds Lost	25-139	9-49
Third Down Conversions	88-151	66-149
Third Down Conversion Pct.	.583	.443
Fourth Down Conversions	3-8	7-16
Fourth Down Conversion Pct.	.375	.438
Avg. Time of Possession	33:34	26:26

SCORING BY QUARTERS	1st	2nd	3rd	4th	TOT	AVG
WISCONSIN	75	107	95	77	354	29.5
Opponent	29	47	40	79	195	16.3

RUSHING	G	ATT	GAIN	LOSS	NET	AVG	PG	TD	LP
Moss, Brent	12	312	1672	35	1637	5.2	136.4	16	56
Fletcher, Terrell	12	165	1020	24	996	6.0	83.0	9	57
Montgomery, Mark	12	50	231	1	230	4.6	19.2	1	24
McCullough, Carl	9	31	164	2	162	5.2	18.0	1	41
DeRamus, Lee	12	2	19	0	19	9.5	1.6	0	18
Johnson, Ron	11	3	4	0	4	1.3	0.4	0	3
Burns, Jason	2	2	4	2	2	1.0	1.0	0	4
Bevell, Darrell	12	35	67	70	-3	-0.1	-0.3	2	21
Macias, Jay	4	2	0	6	-6	-3.0	-1.5	0	0
Team	3	1	0	32	-32	-32.0	-10.7	0	0
WISCONSIN	12	603	3181	172	3009	5.0	250.8	29	57
Opponents	12	411	1818	255	1563	3.8	130.3	10	

PASSING	G	ATT	CMP	INT	PCT	YDS	YDS/G	RTNG	TD	LP
Macias, Jay	4	7	4	0	.571	63	15.8	179.9	1	22
Bevell, Darrell	12	276	187	11	.678	2390	199.2	155.2	19	49
WISCONSIN	12	283	191	11	.675	2453	204.4	155.8	20	49
Opponent	12	373	227	23	.609	2740	228.3	120.8	12	

TOTAL OFFENSE	G	PLAY	RUSH	PASS	TOTAL	AVG
Bevell, Darrell	12	311	-3	2390	2387	198.9
Moss, Brent	12	312	1637	0	1637	136.4
Fletcher, Terrell	12	165	996	0	996	83.0
Montgomery, Mark	12	50	230	0	230	19.2
McCullough, Carl	9	31	162	0	162	18.0
Macias, Jay	4	9	-6	63	57	14.3
DeRamus, Lee	12	2	19	0	19	1.6
Burns, Jason	2	2	2	0	2	1.0
Johnson, Ron	11	3	4	0	4	0.4
Team	3	1	-32	0	-32	-10.7
WISCONSIN	12	886	3009	2453	5462	455.2
Opponent	12	784	1563	2740	4303	358.6

RECEIVING	G	REC	YDS	AVG	YDS/G	C/G	TD	LP
DeRamus, Lee	12	54	920	17.0	76.7	4.5	6	42
Dawkins, J.C.	12	36	512	14.2	42.7	3.0	4	49
Roan, Mike	12	34	396	11.7	33.0	2.8	3	30
Montgomery, Mark	12	27	226	8.4	18.8	2.3	1	24
Fletcher, Terrell	12	13	131	10.1	10.9	1.1	1	25
Nyquist, Matt	10	10	80	8.0	8.0	1.0	4	14
Moss, Brent	12	5	24	4.8	2.0	0.4	0	7
Jackson, Keith	12	4	67	16.8	5.6	0.3	1	30
London, Michael	11	3	39	13.0	3.5	0.3	0	19
Wirth, Jeff	12	2	6	3.0	0.5	0.2	0	3
Zullo, Vince	12	1	22	22.0	1.8	0.1	0	22
Brunston, Jevon	9	1	16	16.0	1.8	0.1	0	16
Burns, Jason	2	1	14	14.0	7.0	0.5	0	14
WISCONSIN	12	191	2453	12.8	204.4	15.9	20	49
Opponent	12	227	2740	12.1	228.3	18.9	12	

| SCORING | TD | PAT | | DXP | SAF | FG | PTS |
		XP	2PT				
Moss, Brent	16	0-0	0-0	0-0	0	0-0	96
Fletcher, Terrell	10	0-0	0-0	0-0	0	0-0	60
DeRamus, Lee	6	0-0	0-0	0-0	0	0-0	36
Hall, John	0	28-31	0-0	0-0	0	1-6	31
Schnetzky, Rick	0	17-17	0-0	0-0	0	4-7	29
Nyquist, Matt	4	0-0	0-0	0-0	0	0-0	24
Dawkins, J.C.	4	0-0	0-0	0-0	0	0-0	18
Roan, Mike	3	0-0	0-0	0-0	0	0-0	18
Montgomery, Mark	2	0-0	0-0	0-0	0	0-0	12
Bevell, Darrell	2	0-0	0-1	0-0	0	0-0	12
Jackson, Keith	1	0-0	0-0	0-0	0	0-0	6
McCullough, Carl	1	0-0	0-0	0-0	0	0-0	6
WISCONSIN	49	45-48	0-1	0-2	0	5-13	354
Opponents	24	20-21	1-3	1-1	0	9-12	195

PUNTING	G	NO	YDS	AVG	LP	BLK
Veit, Sam	10	39	1457	37.4	53	0
Team	3	1	0	0.0	1	1
WISCONSIN	12	40	1457	36.4	53	1
Opponents	12	55	2154	39.2		1

PUNT RETURNS	G	NO	YDS	AVG	TD	LP
Jackson, Keith	12	3	33	11.0	0	24
Nelson, Scott	12	8	70	8.8	0	13
Brunston, Jevon	9	8	56	7.0	0	20
WISCONSIN	12	19	159	8.4	0	24
Opponents	12	16	92	5.8	0	

KICKOFF RETURNS	G	NO	YDS	AVG	TD	LP
Fletcher, Terrell	12	3	76	25.3	0	29
Jackson, Keith	12	23	457	19.9	0	36
McCullough, Carl	9	2	34	17.0	0	19
Nyquist, Matt	10	1	13	13.0	0	13
WISCONSIN	12	29	580	20.0	0	36
Opponent	12	40	599	15.0	0	

INTERCEPTIONS	G	NO	YDS	AVG	TD	LP
Messenger, Jeff	12	7	41	5.9	0	21
Nelson, Scott	12	5	120	24.0	0	44
Gales, Kenny	12	4	28	7.0	0	15
Brady, Donny	12	3	11	3.7	0	11
Unverzagt, Eric	11	1	11	11.0	0	11
Burgess, Yusef	12	1	3	3.0	0	3
Holt, Reggie	12	1	0	0.0	0	0
Brown, Jamel	12	1	0	0.0	0	0
WISCONSIN	12	23	214	9.3	0	44
Opponents	12	11	98	8.9	1	

MISCELLANEOUS YARDS (Blocked FGs and Fumbles Advanced)

PLAYER	G	ATT	YDS	AVG	PG	TD
Shackerford, Lamark	12	1	17	17.0	1.4	0
Wirth, Jeff	12	1	5	5.0	0.4	0
WISCONSIN	12	2	22	11.0	1.8	0
Opponents	12	0	0	0.0	0.0	1

DEFENSIVE LEADERS

	GP	SOLO	AST	TOT	TFL-YDS	SCK-YDS	PBU	FC	FR
Burgess, Yusef	12	63	37	100	10-22	2-12	1	7	2
Holt, Reggie	12	56	31	87	3-10	0-0	0	0	0
Unverzagt, Eric	11	51	24	75	8-21	2-9	2	0	0
Shackerford, Lamark	12	45	15	60	6-24	2-12	1	0	2
Gales, Kenny	12	49	8	57	1-1	0-0	5	0	2
Hein, Chris	12	35	18	53	5-10	1-1	2	0	0
Nelson, Scott	12	41	11	52	0-0	0-0	3	1	3
Fowler, Carlos	12	25	24	49	7-26	3-17	1	2	0
Thompson, Mike	12	26	21	47	13-89	10-83	3	0	2
Messenger, Jeff	12	36	10	46	2-4	0-0	6	1	0
Brady, Donny	12	28	10	38	1-3	0-0	5	0	0
Brown, Jamel	12	22	12	34	0-0	0-0	0	0	0
Jurewicz, Bryan	12	18	8	26	5-19	1-7	0	0	0
Pratt, Sylas	9	17	9	26	0-0	0-0	0	0	0
Cascadden, Chad	12	13	4	17	3-9	1-7	1	0	0
Saleh, Tarek	10	7	4	11	0-0	0-0	0	0	0
Wirth, Jeff	12	5	4	9	0-0	0-0	0	0	0
Lurtsema, Rob	11	4	3	7	1-4	1-4	0	1	0
Yocum, Chad	5	3	4	7	1-3	1-3	0	0	0
Diatelevi, Pete	12	4	3	7	0-0	0-0	0	0	1
Maniecki, Jason	10	5	1	6	2-3	1-2	0	0	0
Carney, Theo	12	6	0	6	0-0	0-0	0	0	0
Zullo, Vince	12	5	0	5	0-0	0-0	0	0	0
Monty, Pete	12	2	3	5	0-0	0-0	0	0	0
Weems, Cyrill	9	4	1	5	0-0	0-0	0	0	0
Johnson, Ron	11	1	3	4	0-0	0-0	0	0	0
Orlando, Todd	3	3	0	3	0-0	0-0	0	0	0
Searcy, Henry	11	3	0	3	0-0	0-0	0	0	0
Carter, Daryl	11	1	2	3	0-0	0-0	0	0	0
DeRamus, Lee	12	3	0	3	0-0	0-0	0	0	0
Dawkins, J.C.	12	3	0	3	0-0	0-0	0	0	0
Rafko, Nick	10	2	0	2	0-0	0-0	0	0	0
Roan, Mike	12	2	0	2	0-0	0-0	0	0	0
Krueger, Lee	12	1	1	2	0-0	0-0	0	0	0
Montgomery, Mark	12	1	1	2	0-0	0-0	0	0	0
Spiller, Rod	5	1	0	1	0-0	0-0	0	0	0
Panos, Joe	12	1	0	1	0-0	0-0	0	0	0
Schneck, Dan	1	1	0	1	0-0	0-0	0	0	0
Hall, John	12	1	0	1	0-0	0-0	0	0	0
Bevell, Darrell	12	1	0	1	0-0	0-0	0	0	0

HONORS & AWARDS

Academic all-Big Ten
Jason Maniecki
Matt Nyquist
Joe Rudolph
Sam Veit

CoSIDA Academic all-District IV
Matt Nyquist

AP All-American
Brent Moss (2nd team)
Joe Panos (2nd team)
Lamark Shackerford (3rd team)

UPI All-American
Brent Moss (2nd team)
Lamark Shackerford (2nd team)
Darrell Bevell (honorable mention)
Lee DeRamus (honorable mention)
Joe Panos (honorable mention)
Cory Raymer (honorable mention)

***Football News* All-American**
Brent Moss (3rd team)
Joe Panos (3rd team)

***Football News* Freshman All-American**
Bryan Jurewicz (3rd team)

***College & Pro Newsweekly*
All-American**
Brent Moss (2nd team)

***Chicago Tribune* Silver Football**
(Big Ten Most Valuable Player)
Brent Moss

College Running Back of the Year
(Columbus Touchdown Club)
Brent Moss

**Bobby Dodd National Coach
of the Year**
Barry Alvarez

***College & Pro Newsweekly* Coach
of the Year**
Barry Alvarez

**Dave McClain Big Ten Coach
of the Year**
Barry Alvarez

All-Big Ten (media)
Darrell Bevell (1st team)
Yusef Burgess (2nd team)
Lee DeRamus (2nd team)
Reggie Holt (2nd team)
Jeff Messenger (1st team)

Brent Moss (1st team)
Joe Panos (1st team)
Cory Raymer (1st team)
Michael Roan (1st team)
Joe Rudolph (1st team)
Lamark Shackerford (1st team)
Mike Thompson (honorable mention)
Mike Verstegen (honorable mention)

All-Big Ten (coaches)
Darrell Bevell (1st team)
Yusef Burgess (honorable mention)
Lee DeRamus (2nd team)
Reggie Holt (honorable mention)
Jeff Messenger (2nd team)
Brent Moss (1st team)
Joe Panos (1st team)
Cory Raymer (1st team)
Michael Roan (honorable mention)
Joe Rudolph (2nd team)
Lamark Shackerford (1st team)
Mike Thompson (honorable mention)

Big Ten Offensive Player of the Year
Brent Moss

Hula Bowl
Lamark Shackerford

East-West Shrine Bowl
Joe Panos

Senior Bowl
Mark Montgomery
Joe Panos

Rose Bowl Most Valuable Player
Brent Moss

**Athlon's Defensive Player of
the Week**
Mike Thompson vs. Northwestern
(10/9)

Big Ten Offensive Player of the Week
Brent Moss vs. Indiana (9/25)

Big Ten Defensive Player of the Week
Jeff Messenger vs. Nevada (9/4)

***Chicago Tribune* Player of the Week**
Darrell Bevell vs. Nevada (9/4)

ESPN Player of the Game
Lamark Shackerford vs. Indiana (9/25)
Darrell Bevell vs. Purdue (10/16)

ABC Player of the Game
Michael Roan vs. Illinois (11/20)